D1364402

MotoGP
Season Review 2006

Published in November 2006

A catalogue record for this book is available from the British Library

ISBN 1 84425 344 9

Library of Congress catalog card no. 2006924152

Haynes Publishing, Sparkford, Yeovil,
Somerset BA22 7JJ, UK
Tel: +44 (0) 1963 442030
Fax: +44 (0) 1963 440001
E-mail: sales@haynes.co.uk
Website: www.haynes.co.uk

Haynes North America, Inc.,
861 Lawrence Drive, Newbury Park,
California 91320, USA

Printed and bound by J.H.Haynes & Co Ltd,
Sparkford, Yeovil, Somerset BA22 7JJ, UK

Managing Editor Louise McIntyre
Design Lee Parsons, Richard Parsons
Sub-editor Kay Edge
Special Sales & Advertising Manager
David Dew (david@motocom.co.uk)
Photography Front cover, race action and portraits by Andrew Northcott/AJRN Sports Photography – except portraits of Kenny Roberts (p7) and Loris Capirossi (p20) and p154 by Mark Wernham; sequence on p195 by Martin Lauricella/Cellopix; technical details by Neil Spalding

Author's acknowledgements

Thanks to:

Eva Jirsenska, Nick Harris and Phaedra Haramis (Dorna); Mike and Irene Trimby (IRTA); my colleagues at British and International Eurosport; Dr Martin Raines, Andrew Northcott, Mark Wernham, Neil Spalding, Barry and Andrea Coleman, Eddie Laycock, Yoko Togashi, Patrick Bodden (Motorcyclist Magazine), David Dew, Peter Clifford, and all the team members and racers who have taken the time and trouble to explain to me what was really going on.

Particular thanks must go to Kenny Roberts Snr for writing so many words for the foreword without resorting to one expletive.

CONTENTS
MotoGP 2006

MotoGP
Season Review 2006
Julian Ryder

ALPINESTARS. NICKY.
ONE GOAL. ONE VISION.
+39 0423 5286

FOREWORD
KENNY ROBERTS Snr

No one has ever seen a better season in Grand Prix motorcycle racing than the one we witnessed in 2006. We've witnessed – especially with the closing of an era – something that won't be seen again. There are those who will challenge that statement. But I stand by it and I've seen a few Grands Prix.

What we had in 2006 was the best racing in the world in every respect. No one has ever been treated to such amazing, technologically superior equipment and such an awesome amount of racing talent.

The 990 machines have become the best GP bikes ever – the most powerful, the fastest, the best handling. To arrive at that level of technical excellence required grueling, non-stop technological development all season long. My team alone had to build six different chassis in order to keep up our standing in the championship.

And no single rider dominated the season. Valentino Rossi had a very non-Rossi season, even if he managed to claw his way back from several DNFs and take the grid at the final GP at Valencia with an eight-point championship lead. The rookies were just as impressive, applying relentless pressure to more experienced riders all season long and winding up on the podium on more than one occasion.

MotoGP had all the dramatic moments anyone could hope for... including a couple that were actually shocking – Nicky Hayden having his championship points lead demolished by a team-mate's miscalculation in Portugal and Valentino Rossi throwing away both his bike and a chance for an even bigger piece of GP history at the championship-making race at Valencia. Had it not been for that crash, Rossi would almost certainly have won every championship of the 990 four-stroke era – five in all.

Nicky Hayden rode an intelligent, well-planned race at Valencia, came third, and the record books will show that Hayden is the MotoGP champion of 2006.

No rider is ever handed a GP win, let alone a championship. And none of the riders made things easy for Hayden. Far from it. Nicky worked hard all season long for his championship – week after week, race after race, turn after turn. When his points lead crumbled into a deficit, he didn't mope around; he put his head down, kept working, and went from protecting that points lead (as much a handicap as an asset, really) into full attack mode. And, as Nicky said at the press conference after his championship-winning performance in Valencia, he didn't "just beat the kid down the block!". He certainly didn't.

As an American, naturally, I'm pleased to see an American rider crowned MotoGP champion. It's a world sport and I think it's important for Americans to compete. But, to quote Nicky, again, it's an incredible paddock in Grand Prix racing at the moment. Here are all the best racers from all over the world. They are stars. And they proved that to us all season long. MotoGP bills itself as the best form of racing in the world, and it delivered on that statement in 2006.

Now, things are set to change. Next year we go from the 990cc bikes to the 800s. These bikes will be different. Some will be smaller, their engines will behave differently, and they will handle differently. And, most importantly, the riders will have to adapt to these new machines. Will the bikes be harder to ride? Will smaller riders like Dani Pedrosa have an advantage? Nicky Hayden is still improving; will that continue when he rides an 800? Rossi is almost certainly riding at his best; will that be good enough to win races and championships in the new 800 era that is about to begin?

There are a lot of questions hanging over next year's 800cc bikes. Nobody has the answers. And the 2007 season will likely be exciting. But I'll say it again – we will never again see a season like the one we had in 2006. It was the best ever.

KENNY ROBERTS Snr

WORLD CHAMPION 1978, 1979, 1980

THE SEASON
MAT OXLEY

YOUNG GUNS GO FOR IT

Ex-Superbiker Nicky Hayden won the final 990 MotoGP crown with a bravura end-of-season flourish but the 2006 season will also be remembered for welcoming a new breed of young gun, the fast-evolving technology of the premier class neatly matching their immaculate 250 styles

MotoGP's final 990 season turned out to be the best ever: action-packed, overflowing with drama, with more twists and turns, more cruel twists of fate and whoops of joy than some grown men can handle.

During 2006 Nicky Hayden and Valentino Rossi once again proved themselves to be genius bike racers and, arguably even more importantly, true sportsmen befitting the mould carved out by Rudyard Kipling: 'If you can meet with triumph and disaster and treat those two impostors just the same.... yours is the earth and everything that's in it'.

Both men suffered fortune and misfortune during 2006, luck playing a role in the championship outcome, just as it had the last time the title went down to the wire in 1992, when Mick Doohan was robbed by the ugly consequences of what should have been an innocuous tumble at Assen.

During 2006 the luck swung this way and that. For Rossi, the luck that for so long had swung with him, swung right back in his face. For once the Midas touch eluded MotoGP's golden boy – he got taken out at the first corner of the first race, he endured engine

breakages and tyre failures, he suffered a bone-crunching crash and all manner of chassis woes. 'Something seems to have gone wrong for us,' he grimaced after his M1's smoky demise at Laguna, and he wasn't wrong.

As it turned out, all these trials and tribulations were just another test of his remarkable character. While Rossi wore the look of a condemned man after his M1 blew at Le Mans and then again at Laguna, he mostly grinned through the misfortune, arriving at the final two races relaxed and sniggering, with all the cares of someone going on a long summer holiday. It's said that the longer a rider holds on to a title the less he wants to let it go (witness Doohan and Wayne Rainey, who looked more haunted with each crown they stowed away in their trophy cabinets), but not Rossi. Either he has a miraculous way of compartmentalising his life or he's so assured of his own greatness that he was happy to deal with triumph or disaster, whatever came his way. At least the final, fatal twist to his 2006 campaign was of his own making. 'I was jealous of the mistakes Yamaha made and I wanted to make one too,' he joked at Valencia.

Luck was mostly kinder to Hayden, if only because more of the wrongness was dumped on his main rival, though the good luck deserted the American at the moment he needed it most. Like Rossi, he dealt with misadventure like a true hero, putting HRC's Estoril debacle behind him and going into the final showdown with his head held high and the throttle wide open. It was an awesome display of the powers of self-belief and never-say-die guts and determination. As Eminem raps on nickyhayden.com: 'Look, if you had one shot, or one opportunity to seize everything you ever wanted, one moment, would you capture it or just let it slip?'

Not many people would have bet on Hayden reversing an eight-point deficit at Valencia, if only because this scenario had only panned out once before in 58 years of premier-class racing, when Rainey sneaked ahead of the mangled Doohan at Kyalami in '92. But Hayden didn't blow his one shot, he didn't let it slip, he made it happen, he seized the moment and thrust himself into a position that put Rossi under pressure. It was old-school win-it-or-bin-it, rostrum-or-hospital stuff, the performance of a lifetime and a day that will glow in his memory always. His gutsy Valencia ride should also silence those who doubted that he has the stomach for the fight. 'I was either going to the front or going down,' said Hayden and he meant it. Cometh the hour, cometh the man...

The Kentucky Kid is a deserving recipient of motorcycling's greatest prize and will make an engaging World Champion, just like Rossi before him. And if the concept of karma truly exists, then the crown will sit easy on Hayden's head, for as Rossi says: 'Apart from being a great rider, Nicky's really a nice guy, one who gives his all to finish first on the track, but who doesn't have mean thoughts off of it. That's important'.

Hayden is also a journalist's dream, a charming young 21st century man whose hip-hop lexicon has a gnarly phrase for every occasion. 'I had Rossi but I didn't just step on his throat when I had him down,' he said of the gaping points lead he enjoyed following his runaway Laguna win, then when his points lead was haemorrhaging during those four crucial races at Brno, Sepang, Phillip Island and Motegi: 'We gotta stop the bleedin'.'

Apart from that tricky run from Czecho to Japan, Hayden was a new man in 2006, no longer the rookie who would roll over and die whenever he came under

Below Double 250 World Champ and MotoGP Rookie of the Year Dani Pedrosa consults with mentor Alberto Puig

Opposite top Casey Stoner samples the joys of a photo opportunity in Shanghai along with Makoto Tamada and Andrea Dovizioso

Opposite bottom Coming soon to a MotoGP bike near you? 250 Champ Jorge Lorenzo

fire. He was a bona fide gunslinger, ready to swap paint and hide with anyone. 'During 2005 I'd be in the lead group, just fighting to run that pace and stay there,' he said during the summer. 'Now I feel the pace is more comfortable so I can fight back.' No doubt, the knowledge that he really can be king will make him an even stronger racer in 2007.

While Hayden took a few seasons to get fully up to speed in MotoGP, former 125 and 250 winners Dani Pedrosa and Casey Stoner seemed in more of a hurry, sometimes with crunching consequences. The 20-year-old upstarts abused their MotoGP apprenticeships, treating their elders and so-called betters with total disrespect. Remarkably, Stoner took pole position in only his second premier-class race at Losail and his first podium finish one race later. Pedrosa scored pole and race victory at the next event in China and followed that with his second pole a week later in France. Truly, it seemed like the kids had taken over the classroom.

The achievements of the young Spaniard and Australian immediately enshrined their talents, putting the pair right up there with the greats – Pedrosa the first rider since 1980s legend Freddie Spencer to achieve such success in a rookie premier-class season, Stoner the second youngest pole-sitter after Fast Freddie. And they weren't the only new kids in on the act as 23-year-old ex-Supers star Chris Vermeulen took pole at Istanbul and Laguna.

'I expected it to take two years to get a pole, not two races,' said Stoner. And the kids weren't the only ones stunned by their speed. 'Casey was racing like he's been in this class for ten years,' said Rossi after winning at Losail.

Below Casey Stoner using all the track and more

Bottom It's a family affair: Nicky Hayden embraces dad Earl after winning the title

Stoner's secret? An even earlier start to his career than the multiple world champ: 'I was doing the throttle of a Pee Wee when I was 18 months old, my cousin sitting on the back.' Youth may be wasted on the young, as Irish wit Oscar Wilde once opined, but not always.

Stoner and Pedrosa made their GP debuts in 2001 when they were both just 15. Indeed they're the first of GP racing's 15-year-old 125 racers to make it into the big class, at a stroke reducing the average age of Honda's MotoGP riders from 30 years and one month before the 2005 season to 23 years and five months at the start of 2006. Incredibly, they've each been racing at world level for six seasons now, Pedrosa riding like a vet during 2006 (his Estoril mistake a momentous exception), Stoner less so, the feisty Aussie's refusal to race at anything less than 120 per cent reminiscent of compatriots Doohan and Wayne Gardner during their reckless GP apprenticeships.

Of course, it wasn't enough for the young upstarts to remind us of daring 500 racers of yore, because both had to put up with plenty of paddock know-alls advising them 'you wouldn't have gone so fast so quick on a 500, you know'. There was truth in the jibe but there was also another truth, that Pedrosa and Stoner arrived at a time when a sweeping 250 riding style was better suited to premier-class riding than at any point in almost a quarter of a century. And this was due to advances in bike technology and tyre performance that would have had an effect if we were still racing 500s.

The defining aim of the premier-class engineer is always same – tame the beast. The 500s were already well on the road to user-friendliness in the 1990s when big-bang engines, pump-spec fuel and improving front tyres raised corner speeds and allowed rookie 500 racer Max Biaggi to rattle class-master Mick Doohan in 1998. The Roman's instant success prompted Doohan to suggest that the latest 500s were so easy to ride that even 250 riders could ride them. And no doubt it will be just the same when current 250 firebrands Jorge Lorenzo and Andrea Dovizioso graduate to MotoGP. *Plus ça change...*

The switch to softer four-stroke engines and the whirlwind development of engine-management systems merely accelerated premier-class riding techniques down the 250 road. That's the legacy of the 990s. But the well-behaved power curve of a digitally managed big-bore four-stroke doesn't necessarily make riding any easier, it just means that riders will get on the throttle sooner and harder, while they're still cranked well over and barely past the apex of the corner. Because that's what racers do – when engineers make their motorcycles easier to ride, they don't ease back in the comfort zone, they eat it up, spit it out and ask for more. That was Pedrosa and Stoner in 2006, utilising their hard-over, hard-on-the-gas 250 technique to push the limit a little further. And sometimes too far. They certainly weren't relishing the RCV's easy-riding sweetness while cruising around, enjoying the scenery.

It's the same with tyres. Recent developments in the world of rubber have also encouraged 250 techniques. During 2006 Michelin and Bridgestone produced bigger-footprint rear slicks that offered more edge grip, further focusing the importance on smooth, high-speed cornering, instead of the old-school, pick-it-up-and-fire-it-out technique. This was the same direction in which Michelin had been working since 2001, when they first encountered the outrageously powerful 990s.

Above It was the sponsor's idea...

Below Nicky Hayden lets it all out in parc fermé at Valencia

Fatter front-tyre footprints have also contributed to a neater, wheels-in-line style, allowing riders to brake deeper into corners (which, of course, means they nibble away at the other end of this technological advance, braking later than before). This also requires a much smoother approach to corners. Back in the 1980s 500 riders used to square-off turns, jerking the bike on to its side, then picking it up to minimise the time spent of the edge of the tyres, especially the front. As three-time 500 king Rainey observed: 'The key to my riding style was getting through the front-tyre area really quick, getting the front tyre out of the way so I could get on the throttle and on to the rear tyre. When you brake and flick, it's all front tyre, which is kinda risky.'

Such is the shift to 250 techniques that during 2006 former dirt tracker Hayden worked at brainwashing himself out of the sideways style he learned while getting dizzy on dirt ovals across the USA. Last season Hayden often talked of this personal re-education and there's no doubt that kicking the sideways habit helped him become MotoGP world champ.

That MotoGP riders ride more like 250 riders than ever before is beyond doubt, but whether that's a good thing or not is less sure. If more riders are able to ride their bikes to the limit then that's good for racing. Close-quarter combat – as enjoyed at its best during 2006 at Mugello, Sachsenring and Estoril – is what motorsport is all about. It's also what makes bike racing far superior entertainment to car racing. Hi-tech control systems have one other benefit – one day they'll make road riding safer too.

But there are also mumblings of discontent among fans who like their motorcycle racing just about as far sideways as it will go. Bike race fans who know what they're talking about like to see riders apparently involved in a fight to the bitter end with their motorcycles, wrestling them this way and that, laying black lines into the turns, etching big black smears on the exits, because that way they can see who has the cleverest technique and the biggest balls. However, traction control is making the fine art of throttle control redundant, never mind that riders like Colin Edwards have dedicated much of their lives to this ancient craft. As the sometime Texas Tornado said: 'I've spent my life learning throttle control, but now you just grab a big handful and let the software figure out how much stick the thing can really take.'

Fans also enjoy bikes snapping out of control and twisting sideways on the throttle because it's fun watching someone courting disaster and getting away with it. And thanks to 21st century technology, riders almost certainly

Above Another impressive rookie; Chris Vermeulen consults with his Suzuki team manager Paul Denning

do get away with it. There's no doubt that traction control and electronic engine-braking systems will one day banish these sights from MotoGP as surely as the industrial revolution swept the cart horse and ploughshare from the countryside. It's progress, dude. For good or for bad, you can't stop it. And anyway, Loris Capirossi still manages to communicate the crazed, wobbling madness of what it must be like to ride a MotoGP bike on the giddy edge, never mind that he's got MotoGP's best traction control system at his service.

Progress will continue unabated with the new 800s. Some insiders suggest that the bikes will be even more like 250s, because their smaller engines allow better mass centralisation for more agility and extra corner speed. Others reckon they're currently more like the old 500s – more peaky, more on the edge, but that spikiness will be massaged and manipulated by engineers toiling to tame the beast. So the 800s will continue the evolution of premier-class machinery from blunt hammer to rapier blade. And they almost certainly won't be any slower than the 990s.

Hopefully there'll be more of them than there were 990s in their swansong season. Over the past few years Aprilia, KTM, WCM and Proton KR have fallen by the wayside in MotoGP, suggesting that indie engine manufacturers can't compete with the industry establishment, and leaving the grids looking somewhat bare. Thus F1 and Indycar genius Mario Ilien couldn't have arrived with his first two-wheeler at a better moment. (And wouldn't it be nice if he could get some of his F1 mates to spend some money in MotoGP?) From an engineering point of view the Ilmor crew seems more prepared to accept that bike racing is a very different science from car racing than had previous car-to-bike engineers like Cosworth and King Kenny's F1 boffins. Let's hope that their willingness to adapt will bring results.

The Ilmor won't fill the grid alone but there are other signs that MotoGP is past its leanest years, with both Suzuki and Kawasaki aiming to get more bikes on the grids from 2008. And if the Ilmor doesn't cut it, the world won't end. Team Roberts may have failed miserably with its self-build V5 but it succeeded brilliantly during 2006 with its Honda-powered KR211V. King Kenny Roberts started pushing this angle in the early 1990s: let the major manufacturers build the engines and let MotoGP's cottage industry build the chassis. If Roberts Junior hadn't made that rookie mistake of misreading his pitboard at Estoril, the KR211V might have given King Kenny's team the first hybrid GP win since Rainey won GPs on a ROC-framed YZR500 in 1993. Which just goes to show that MotoGP isn't yet the exclusive reserve of the super-rich factory teams.

MotoGP needs to hold on to that and continue to present itself as something very different from F1 – real racing where skill and genius still count for as much as dollars and yen. If you're in any doubt about that, listen to someone who knows what he's talking about. 'I didn't like the atmosphere in the paddock and the pressure of the media in F1,' said Rossi during June after he'd called off his engagement to Ferrari's F1 team, to sighs of relief from Dorna and groans of pain from his track rivals. 'Also, in F1 the racing is more about the car than the driver, it's an engineer's sport more than a racer's sport.' As usual, the man is not wrong...

1 Jim Redman, RC181. 2 Jim Redman, RC181. 3 Mike Hailwood, RC181. 4 Mike Hailwood, RC181. 5 Mike Hailwood, RC181. 6 Mike Hailwood, RC181. 7 Mike Hailwood, RC181. 8 Mike Hailwood, RC181. 9 Mike Hailwood, RC181. 10 Mike Hailwood, RC181. 11 Freddie Spencer, NS500. 12 Takazumi Katayama, NS500. 13 Freddie Spencer, NS500. 14 Freddie Spencer, NS500.
24 Randy Mamola, NS500. 25 Freddie Spencer, NS500. 26 Randy Mamola, NSR500. 27 Randy Mamola, NS500. 28 Freddie Spencer, NSR500. 29 Freddie Spencer, NSR500. 30 Freddie Spencer, NSR500. 31 Randy Mamola, NS500. 32 Freddie Spencer, NSR500. 33 Freddie Spencer, NSR500. 34 Freddie Spencer, NSR500. 35 Freddie Spencer, NSR500. 36 Wayne Gardner, NSR500. 3
46 Wayne Gardner, NSR500. 47 Wayne Gardner, NSR500. 48 Wayne Gardner, NSR500. 49 Wayne Gardner, NSR500. 50 Wayne Gardner, NSR500. 51 Eddie Lawson, NSR500. 52 Pier-Francesco Chili, NSR500. 53 Eddie Lawson, NSR500. 54 Eddie Lawson, NSR500. 55 Eddie Lawson, NSR500. 56 Wayne Gardner, NSR500. 57 Mick Doohan, NSR500. 58 Wayne Gardner,
68 Wayne Gardner, NSR500. 69 Daryl Beattie, NSR500. 70 Mick Doohan, NSR500. 71 Mick Doohan, NSR500. 72 Mick Doohan, NSR500. 73 Mick Doohan, NSR500. 74 Mick Doohan, NSR500. 75 Mick Doohan, NSR500. 76 Mick Doohan, NSR500. 77 Mick Doohan, NSR500. 78 Mick Doohan, NSR500. 79 Mick Doohan, NSR500. 80 Mick Doohan, NSR500. 81 Mick Dooha
91 Mick Doohan, NSR500. 92 Mick Doohan, NSR500. 93 Mick Doohan, NSR500. 94 Mick Doohan, NSR500. 95 Luca Cadalora, NSR500. 96 Mick Doohan, NSR500. 97 Alex Criville, NSR500. 98 Alex Criville, NSR500. 99 Mick Doohan, NSR500. 100 Carlos Checa, NSR500. 101 Mick Doohan, NSR500. 102 Mick Doohan, NSR500. 103 Mick Doohan, NSR500. 104 Alex Criville, NSR5
114 Mick Doohan, NSR500. 115 Tadayuki Okada, NSR500. 116 Alex Criville, NSR500. 117 Max Biaggi, NSR500. 118 Mick Doohan, NSR500. 119 Alex Criville, NSR500. 120 Mick Doohan, NSR500. 121 Alex Criville, NSR500. 122 Carlos Checa, NSR500. 123 Mick Doohan, NSR500. 124 Mick Doohan, NSR500. 125 Max Biaggi, NSR500.126 Mick Doohan, NSR500. 127 Mick Doohan,
137 Alex Criville, NSR500. 138 Tadayuki Okada, NSR500. 139 Alex Criville, NSR500. 140 Loris Capiross, NSR500. 141 Alex Barros, NSR500. 142 Valentino Rossi, NSR500. 143 Alex Barros, NSR500. 144 Valentino Rossi, NSR500. 145 Valentino Rossi, NSR500. 146 Valentino Rossi, NSR500. 147 Valentino Rossi, NSR500. 148 Alex Barros, NSR500. 149 Valentino Rossi,
158 Tohru Ukawa, RC211V. 159 Valentino Rossi, RC211V. 160 Valentino Rossi, RC211V. 161 Valentino Rossi, RC211V. 162 Valentino Rossi, RC211V. 163 Valentino Rossi, RC211V. 164 Valentino Rossi, RC211V. 165 Valentino Rossi, RC211V. 166 Valentino Rossi, RC211V. 167 Valentino Rossi, RC211V. 168 Alex Barros, RC211V. 169 Valentino Rossi, RC211V. 170 Alex Barros, RC211V.
180 Valentino Rossi, RC211V. 181 Valentino Rossi, RC211V. 182 Max Biaggi, RC211V. 183 Valentino Rossi, RC211V. 184 Valentino Rossi, RC211V. 185 Valentino Rossi, RC211V. 186 Sete Gibernau, RC211V. 187 Sete Gibernau, RC211V. 188 Makoto Tamada, RC211V. 189 Max Biaggi, RC211V. 190 Sete Gibernau, RC211V. 191 Makoto Tamada, RC211V. 192 Sete Gib

MotoGP'06
A UNIQUE ANGLE ON RACING
XBOX 360
MotoGP'06
Game and Software ©2006 THQ Inc. MotoGP™ '06 and ©2006 Dorna Sports, S.L. MotoGP and related logos, characters, names, and distinctive likenesses thereof are the exclusive property of Dorna Sports, S.L. and/or their respective owners. Used under license. All Rights Reserved. Developed by Climax Racing. Climax Racing and its logo are trademarks and/or registered trademarks of Climax Racing Ltd. THQ and the THQ logo are trademarks and/or registered trademarks of THQ Inc. All Rights Reserved. All other trademarks, logos and copyrights are property of their respective owners. Microsoft, Xbox, Xbox 360, Xbox Live, and the Xbox, Xbox 360 and Xbox Live logos are either registered trademarks or trademarks of Microsoft Corporation in the United States and/or other countries.
WWW.MOTOGPTHEGAME.COM
3+
www.pegi.info
CLIMAX
THQ
Jump in.
XBOX 360

RIDERS' RIDER OF THE YEAR 2006

For the third year, every rider who competed in more than one race has voted in the MotoGP Season Review's poll to find the Riders' Rider of the Year. They were asked to name their six top riders of the season, in order, and not to vote for themselves. After the secret ballot, the scrutineers awarded six points for each first place down to one point for sixth. When the results were totalled up we had a new winner.

AS VOTED FOR BY

Loris Capirossi
Jose-Luis Cardoso
Carlos Checa
Colin Edwards
Toni Elias
James Ellison
Sete Gibernau
Nicky Hayden
Alex Hofmann
John Hopkins
Garry McCoy
Marco Melandri
Shinya Nakano
Dani Pedrosa
Randy de Puniet
Kenny Roberts Jnr
Valentino Rossi
Ivan Silva
Casey Stoner
Makoto Tamada
Chris Vermeulen

2nd
VALENTINO ROSSI
90 POINTS
3rd
DANI PEDROSA
81 POINTS
4th
NICKY HAYDEN
46 POINTS
5th
MARCO MELANDRI
42 POINTS
MICHELIN
DAINESE
agv
YAMAHA
FACTORY RACING
WLF
Red Bull

HATS OFF TO THE
Congratulations to Nicky Hayden
on his MotoGP World championship
from everyone at Arai. There
really *is* a difference.
Arai
HELMET®

It couldn't have been closer. When the votes were counted Loris Capirossi became the 2006 Riders' Rider of the Year by the margin of one single, solitary point from the man who won in 2005 and 2004 – Valentino Rossi. Both of Rossi's previous wins came with overwhelming points advantages – last year nobody placed him lower than second – but this year his peers obviously view him as fallible: although he still received more first-place nominations than anyone else, three of the electorate didn't vote for him at all.

Loris Capirossi had the same number of first-place nominations as Dani Pedrosa, four, but everybody had Loris somewhere on their ballot paper. Three other riders received a single nomination as top gun: Marco Melandri, Nicky Hayden and Casey Stoner. Pedrosa was a clear third overall, an amazing result for an amazing rookie, while fourth place went to Hayden by just four points from Melandri.

As we're dealing with motorcycle racers here, not everyone followed the rules to the letter. Quite a few decided they didn't want to, or couldn't, vote for more than three or four of their competitors. Colin Edwards' attempt to vote for Bradley Smith and Alvaro Bautista as his top two resulted in him being asked to try again.

Last year only one name in the top ten changed from the previous year, Tamada being replaced by Melandri. This year, however, the arrival of the new crop of MotoGP rookies has changed all that. As well as Pedrosa, Chris Vermeulen and Casey Stoner have made it into the top ten – and it hasn't all been about the youngsters. Kenny Roberts Jnr and Carlos Checa make their first appearances while Sete Gibernau, Shinya Nakano and Colin Edwards drop out (as do the absent Max Biaggi and Alex Barros).

In the first two polls, John Hopkins distinguished himself by being voted into a result far better than his finish in the championship. This year he has again achieved that but only by one place. Carlos Checa's ninth place is a whole six positions better than his World Championship classification, showing just how highly his efforts this year have been rated by his peers. The same must be said of our winner, Loris Capirossi, who ended up third in the championship just 23 points behind the new champion. What would have happened had he avoided that horrible crash in Barcelona? His injuries put him out of the Catalan GP and severely handicapped him for the next four races.

Loris's win in Brno gave him the longest winning career of any rider in the history of motorcycle Grand Prix racing, overtaking the previous mark set by Angel Nieto, an achievement that gave him great satisfaction. His wins later in the season extended the time between his first and most recent wins to well over 15 years. Given the enthusiasm with which he's looking forward to racing the 800cc Ducati in 2007, you just know there's more to come.

TECHNICAL REVIEW

NEIL SPALDING

THE GHOST BIKE

Developed in the cauldron of competition, the rarest RC211V was initially built for Biaggi and Gibernau as a Rossi-beater, but Hayden ended up with the ride – this is its story

When Rossi departed to Yamaha at the end of 2003 Honda's plans were thrown into confusion: they not only lost their top rider, but also lost their top crew chief and his team. HRC knew that Rossi was something special. They had a very clear idea of his abilities and were aware of the threat he would pose once he had sorted the Yamaha into something he could use.

That happened very quickly; Rossi won the first race of the 2004 season and never looked back. HRC had chosen to give the top ride in the Repsol team to a relatively old stager, Alex Barros. He did a sterling job of chasing Rossi but he didn't have the ability to beat him. While the racing team was marking time, HRC was reorganising itself. New team manager, new managing director – it was the start of the project to take the fight back to Rossi.

By late 2004 Honda had analysed precisely how they were being beaten. Where Rossi was managing to make the Yamaha work better and how they could improve their bike to give their riders at least a chance of matching the Italian where he was strongest. The analysis showed that the Honda was pretty good mid-corner, but under acceleration they had lost a lot of their initial advantage. Their bike also didn't have sufficient stability going into corners; indeed, Rossi was able to out-brake the Honda at will. Rossi's style on the Yamaha was to use his bike's superior ability into corners on the very last corner, where he couldn't be overtaken again before the line. Honda reasoned that if they could build a bike that could stay with Rossi in those situations they would have a chance of stopping him.

Below Hayden got a third at Jerez, but it was on a bike that was still far from right

Above The 'new-generation' RC211V at Assen; you can see all the cuts and rewelds needed to get the bike feeling right for the rider; making several chassis the same wasn't easy

Racing is not just about going fast; it's also about going faster than the rest where that's possible and being in the way when the others are faster. It's quite possible to win races with a bike that's acceptable in several areas of performance but has an advantage in one specific area, as long as the impact of that one advantage is maximised. Rossi's bike was slower but it had excellent corner-exit grip, and he was a demon on the brakes.

HRC set to work on a new-generation RC211V. The bike was to be ready early enough so that it would have an entire season near its peak of development. Honda wanted to stay loyal to their five-cylinder 75.5° vee layout, so the engine used mostly the same internals as their other bikes. The rest, however, was repackaged. The whole bike was reworked, the crankshaft placed higher, the gearbox and the clutch lower, and the output shaft moved forward. The engine layout was also modified with the water jacket packaged more closely around the cylinders and the whole vee rolled back; it's still a 75.5° but this change allowed the crankshaft to be moved forward in the chassis. The whole point of this development was to let Honda run a longer swingarm. Given Honda's analysis that they needed more stability into corners they had decided on a longer swingarm; this reduces the violence of the chain effect on the swingarm. Yamaha, with their in-line four, has certain disadvantages in terms of rolling into corners, and because of the width of their engine in ducting air out from behind the radiator, but the big advantage of an in-line four with a vertically stacked gearbox, like Yamaha's, is the length of swingarm that can be mounted to the bike.

Honda's challenge was ready in mid-2005 and was called the 'Brno bike' for a long time because three examples were built, two of which were brought to Brno for Gibernau and Biaggi to test. Unspecified maladies with the third bike, being run by the test team back in Japan, meant that Sete and Max didn't get out on the machines until midday on the second of two test days, by which time it was way too late to find out whether the new bikes were quicker and/or better than their current ones. These bikes weren't seen again in 2005 and Rossi romped home to a second World Championship on the Yamaha with four races still to run.

In early 2006 the 'Brno bike' was renamed the 'Hayden special', although it wasn't quite the same machine. Honda had kept working on it. The engine was different, with additional cooling fins sprouting all over the sump, making it look for all the world like something from an old MV. The chassis was different too. Where the 'Brno bike' had sported the usual sleek Honda finish, this one looked like somebody had attacked it with a hacksaw and then had a kids' welding competition to stick a few bits back on. It wasn't really like that, of course. All the modifications and work were designed to get the right flexibility and movement from the chassis, to give the rider the feel and the confidence to go quickly. At the same time new swingarms were fitted, with a smaller section at the axle end. (That new section of swingarm looked very familiar – just like the Yamaha, in fact!)

Hayden did his initial testing on a normal customer-style bike in mid-February, although the factory basically instructed him ('requested' was the word used by senior

HRC personnel) to concentrate on the new-generation bike. Hayden and his crew were eventually persuaded to use the bike for at least the first five GPs and, while the bike was not as good as Nicky wanted and needed it to be, it certainly did what Honda had designed it to do. It was very stable when braking and the front end inspired confidence. However, it had lost many of the attributes of the standard bike: its corner-exit behaviour wasn't good, and it changed direction unbelievably quickly; too quickly.

At the test immediately following the Jerez GP a lot of different settings were tried and Hayden ended up being fastest by nearly half a second. Just as Nicky was finding settings that he could trust on the new bike, Valentino Rossi was in deep trouble with a chassis that was suffering from enormous levels of chatter. At the same time, Dani Pedrosa was showing that he had the ability to fight at the front of the field, even in the first few races of his MotoGP career, and Ducati and Bridgestone seemed to have got their set-up right too. At the second race of the year, in Qatar, Hayden and the new bike showed that they could play at the front of the field but the American's form was erratic.

Once Rossi had decided that he was going to fight back, Hayden appeared to start feeling the pressure. Honda probably didn't help matters by turning up at Donington with a new chassis, produced in response to requests from the team for something to help tyre life during the race. The decision to test it during Friday practice at the British GP undoubtedly prevented Hayden's team getting a better finish. The new chassis placed the shock absorber lower and slightly off to the right-hand side of the bike, with the idea of achieving

Above Hayden had one new chassis at Donington using different, tidier construction, but it needed different settings and the middle of a GP wasn't the place to find them

Below Nicky Hayden and crew chief Pete Benson fought hard, having to develop the bike and keep grabbing points simultaneously

Above & below The plates are put back in after the clutch has been stripped and reassembled

Below The diaphragm variant of the Honda slipper clutch uses a turbine outer cover to get much needed cooling air down inside

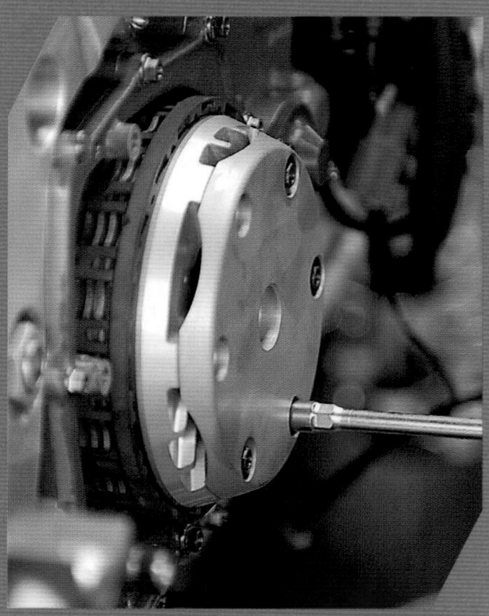

WHY DID NICKY HAYDEN HAVE SO MUCH TROUBLE WITH HIS SLIPPER CLUTCH?

Nicky Hayden is an old-fashioned dirt-track-style rider, his skills honed in a race series that doesn't use front brakes. Dirt track is all about kicking the back out going into corners and controlling the ensuing slide with a combination of balance and throttle. As a way of rider training it has had a lot of success over the past 20 or so years. But Nicky's riding is now unique, and tyres have changed since the days when backing the motorcycle into corners was the fastest way to get a bike round a circuit.

The new levels of front-tyre grip rely on increased pressure from a savagely applied front brake; the harder the front brake is applied the more the front tyre is squashed against the tarmac and the harder a rider can brake. It means that riders like Valentino Rossi are running their bikes much deeper into corners.

To be able to maximise speed through a corner, the current bikes have the rider applying the brakes late and hard, getting the bike to the apex, and using rider skill and traction control where necessary to get through and out of the corner as effectively as possible. One of the things that slows down this process is if the rear end is bouncing around and making it impossible for the rider to hold the bike accurately on line to the apex. The rear-wheel travel of a motorcycle is affected not only by its suspension, linkage and swingarm but also by chain force. The relationship between the sprockets, chain and swingarm pivot is usually designed so that, under acceleration, the chain forces the swingarm down and pushes the tyre firmly into the tarmac. On deceleration the rear wheel tries to turn over the engine and, as the geometry operates in exactly the opposite way to the under-power situation, this will try to lift the rear tyre off the ground. These days the resistance provided by the pistons being pushed over compression is partially eliminated by a well-set-up slipper clutch. To reduce that clutch's workload further the engine management system also increases the engine's effective tickover level. In combination these systems keep the tyre on the ground and available to stop any slides.

Hayden still seems to prefer the rear end of his bike to be loose, in other words moving all over the place. His machine carries a substantially heavier rear disc so that he can trigger this motion at will, but because he's using rear-wheel braking he doesn't typically make use of all the front-tyre traction, at least not in the same way that Rossi does. This meant that, in 2005, Hayden was one of the few riders to complain about the Michelin front tyre. This year's wider, grippier tyre is more to his liking, but that's only because he wasn't making maximum use of the old one.

What we have, therefore, is a Honda with a long swingarm, designed to react less violently to the effects of rear-wheel hop and to track more accurately towards the apex of corners, but the trouble is its rider actually prefers to have the rear of the bike loose. Hayden is clearly capable of trying to trigger slides by using the rear brake. Chances are, though, that Nicky will like more engine braking than most ex-two-stroke riders (this can be done by increasing the amount of drag reaching the tyre, by setting up the slipper clutch appropriately).

Slipper clutches last much longer if the clutch is disengaged under deceleration, for if the plates are apart and not transmitting any torque then they don't get hot and they don't wear out. If, however, the clutch is set up to provide more engine braking, with the plates held slightly together (and heavier main springs could easily do this), then more engine braking gets through to the bike and, in Nicky Hayden's case, he would achieve the loose rear-end feel he prefers. However, this means that the slipper clutch is being set up to get rid of the positive effect that Honda has designed into the bike with its long swingarm.

Hayden has suffered several different types of difficulty with his clutch this year. He had a bad experience when the 'rifled' clutch he used, preferred by Pedrosa, grabbed on the line in Qatar. After that he reverted to using the diaphragm clutch that has been on these bikes since 2003. In Brno he overheated the plates going off the line, and the warped plates prevented the clutch from disengaging during the race. Over the next few races several fixes were tried but Nicky had difficulty in balancing his desire for a fast launch against the need not to warp the plates.

By Motegi the Honda special parts department was well under way with a revised pressure plate for the rifled clutch, incorporating vanes that pulled in cool air. It still wasn't good enough, though, and the diaphragm clutch was back at Estoril; in conjunction with a rev-limited launch control it seemed to work all right for the short duration of Hayden's race. The clutch took a lot of criticism, and it's possible that there's a setting that will allow the clutch to drive smoothly off the line, work progressively and consistently for the duration of the race, and give Hayden the feel he wants, but the support systems Honda built around it do not make its life easy. The earlier arrival of the 'Gibernau' launch-control system might have made a difference, as would a bike that naturally wanted to let the rear end perform more loosely.

a much more repeatable construction. Unfortunately it didn't work in the same way as the old one and was going to need some time in testing to find the settings that made Hayden feel at home.

The new chassis was then parked until the Brno test. Useable settings were found there, but the old chassis was continually brought back out to check that the new one was, in fact, better. The new chassis did seem to be better, but each chassis was still different. Seemingly identical chassis simply working differently. It had been a problem all year, far from unexpected with the first 'cut and shut' chassis, but a surprise with the later 'industrialised' chassis.

Now, however, other problems came to the fore. Hayden had started the year using the same semi-coil spring/semi-rifled light-pull slipper clutch that had been designed to put Dani Pedrosa at ease. By round four, in China, it was back in the box and Hayden was employing the diaphragm design he was used to from previous years. At Brno this let him down badly, after a good launch off the line overheated the plates nearest the engine and caused them to warp. In a normal clutch that isn't good news; in a slipper clutch it's very bad news. With warped plates the slipper clutch action is inconsistent: every corner entry is different and every corner exit produces a bit of a lurch just when it's not wanted. Hayden immediately tried a modified clutch in testing, which seemed fine, but he hit problems again at the Malaysian and Australian rounds. At Phillip Island he managed to start, but with the clutch slipping almost all the way to the first corner.

At Motegi Honda had a revised version of the coil spring clutch. This still used the rifled design to servo on under power, but it also had additional ducting to try and drag cooling air inside. It was clear that this problem was really affecting Hayden. He kept commenting that his clutch wasn't receiving the cooling air that the other Hondas were, but, as can be seen from the pictures, in fact his bike received more cooling air than the other RC211Vs. After the Motegi race the media were treated to a series of practice starts from Hayden, with project leader Yoshii holding him on the starting grid for several seconds at a time to try and replicate the stress of a normal racing start.

By Portugal Honda had 'rediscovered' a revised launch-control system previously used only by Gibernau. This worked in a similar fashion to the Yamaha system in setting lower but ascending rev limits for the first few gears after launch, limiting power and revs and allowing the rider to be more cavalier in his clutch use. Amazingly, the normal Honda system reduces power at launch by retarding the ignition, though still allowing full revs. With the new system Hayden couldn't roast his plates off the line. He didn't get the best of starts at Estoril, but it was much better than some of his previous ones and at least he was in touch with the leaders. All that was left was Valencia, and there he got the start he needed.

Below left By Motegi, Honda were determined to solve the clutch problem; after the GP Hayden did numerous test starts from the end of pitlane

Below The electronics under the nose cone were standard works RCV but the air intakes were different, taking their intake from the centre of pressure at the tip of the nose

Bottom Hayden uses a rear disc about twice the size of that on other RCVs – it helps him make the rear end loose at will

Above Engine-change time at Honda; within half an hour the engine will be out and a fresh one back in; engine mileage is rigorously monitored and engines refreshed every 500 miles

Top right The last version of the chassis placed the shock absorber lower; this got in the way of the 'fifth' cylinder exhaust which meant that a new pipe had to route the exhaust out of the left side of the undertray

Right One chassis was modified with a revised swingarm position; note the weld where the swingarm pivot has been cut out and repositioned

THE INSIDE OF HONDA'S FINEST

Honda stripped down the new-generation RC211V at Motegi. This isn't just a little bit unusual – it's virtually unheard of! The last bike to be shown to the press in this way was the NR500. There's possibly a message here, for although the NR500 brought many ideas that are still around today, as a racing vehicle it wasn't considered a success. It was obvious from Honda's presentation that while there were many changes in the new-generation RC211V, it wasn't exactly receiving a glowing report from Honda's senior management. The bike clearly had basic design principles that are very important to Honda but in this case getting the set-up right proved to be far more of a struggle than they had expected. Honda always maintained that the internals of this engine were the same as those of the normal RC211V. On that basis there were some very interesting things to see indeed.

The Honda crankshaft is unique, almost like a two-stroke crankshaft in having full-circle crank cheeks and clearly using the fifth cylinder for a substantial amount of balancing. The layout of the cylinders and their heads was striking too, with the rear two cylinders a lot further apart than one would have thought they'd need to be, although with this crankshaft design some room does have to be left for the fifth cylinder on the front bank.

The Honda's firing order also gives a much better insight into the 'long-bang' concept (the process of having several different power impulses occurring quickly after one another so that the tyre is affected less by the acceleration and deceleration of the crank, as one piston and then another approaches top dead centre). Yoshi memorably described the effect of these firing pulses as being like a Space Hopper bouncing up the road, with big, soft pushes of power shoving the bike forward and allowing it to maintain grip.

The desire of Honda to minimise internal friction is quite apparent: the base circle of the cams has been machined away, even though they don't actually touch the buckets. The pistons are extremely short, with virtually no side skirts. The height of the crankshaft within the crankcases is also apparent, making certain that under no circumstances is power lost to windage. Honda call it a semi-wet sump and it's certainly a lot simpler than a car-type dry-sump system.

1 The new-generation RC211V motor. Note the deep, finned semi-wet sump and the widely spaced rear cylinders that allow a fifth cylinder to be added to the crankshaft below

2 The basic block shows just how simple the motor is, with the fifth cylinder, which has its own crankpin for balancing purposes, squeezed in the middle

3 The very short slipper pistons show evidence of a very flat valve angle and careful attention to the combustion chamber shape

4 Heavy-duty connecting rods, most probably of titanium

5 One of the most unusual crankshafts ever; light weight, high inertia with a removable, changeable flywheel. The crankpin layout is of a 360-degree V4 with a fifth cylinder crankpin spaced 104.5 degrees away

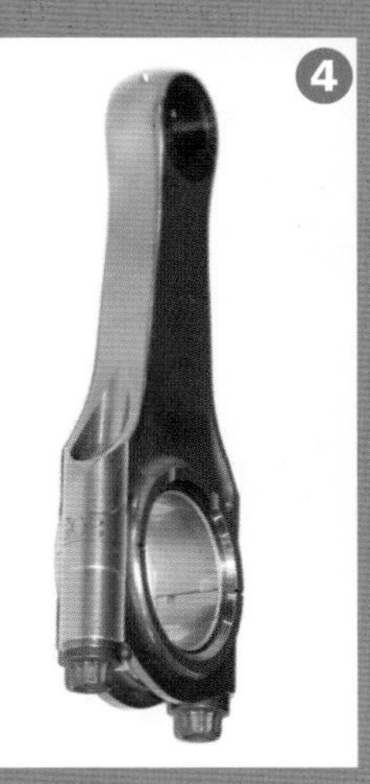

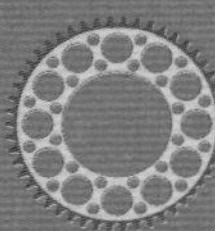

SO WAS THE NEW-GENERATION RC211V A PROTOTYPE 800?

Honda's new 800 is a further evolution of the V-format mass centralisation and longer swingarm concept born under such pressure this year. It may seem strange that Honda is going further with a system that gave problems this year, but it's obviously one with which Rossi and Yamaha are very comfortable. And despite the other factories on the grid, it's Rossi and Yamaha that Honda are determined to beat.

A short motor is good for mass centralisation, and that makes the bike more responsive. It turns quickly, and it also allows a long swingarm. The long swingarm dramatically reduces the bike's responses to chain-pull fluctuations under braking or acceleration, and that means the bike can operate well in the same areas as the Yamaha, deep into hard-braking corners. Honda learned a lot with this year's bike, saving valuable development time for the more extreme 800.

Above Hayden and his crew in the Valencia pitlane after winning the 2006 MotoGP World Championship at the final round

Above Honda's RC212V – the 800cc V4 challenger. It has an even shorter engine, a longer swingarm and radically different styling. This is already the second version seen in public

THE BIKES
2006 MotoGP MACHINERY

HONDA

RC211V

1 Pedrosa got a slightly different chassis before the first race; this had slightly more flexibility in the steering head

2 From Donington onwards Hayden had a revised rear pipe system with an increased diameter pipe, probably for more top-end power

3 Pedrosa also had this 'rifled' type clutch that used a combination of coil springs and ramps to servo on under power

4 Elias won the Portuguese GP with a standard customer bike, original chassis and all

Honda split their attack: Hayden would have the short-engine, long-swingarm 'proof of concept' bike, while the rest of the riders would have a slightly higher-engine version of the previous year's bike. This change was driven by arch 250 racer Max Biaggi while he was the Repsol team's top rider in 2005. The two approaches quickly became three, though, with a special chassis being made for Pedrosa. Melandri had problems with the handling of his 2006 bike and after Jerez, where he managed to get his 2005 chassis back, he was issued with a pair of Pedrosa replica chassis.

The new Honda didn't suffer from any problems with the new wider Michelins. In fact the additional grip was exactly what they needed with the Honda not having quite the same amount of mechanical traction as the Yamaha. More power was also on the agenda. Last year the RC211V was revving to 16,500rpm but suffered some reliability issues around Motegi and Qatar. This year there were no mistakes; reliability was superb.

By Sachsenring, Stoner inherited the same chassis as Pedrosa but his performances didn't obviously improve. However, he had transferred from a 250 to the front of the MotoGP field and rode with quite staggering displays of aggression.

The 2006 bike was a further careful development of the RC211V. The swingarm was the same as the one tested, for a few minutes only, by Biaggi at Brno in 2005. This swingarm was the major external difference between previous versions of the bike and this year's machine. It used the deep-section arms of the 2004 works bikes and the '04 and '05 customer bikes, but the shock absorber was in the original inverted position.

And then there was the Hayden special, the new-generation RC211V as reviewed elsewhere in this book. Hayden suffered all the problems of developing a one-off bike yet still led the championship for most of the year before clinching the title at the very last round.

YAMAHA
YZR-M1

1 At Le Mans Rossi had the use of a 2005 chassis; by Mugello another bike was prepared but after one session it was back to the 2005 version for qualifying and the race

2 Yamaha's 2006 engine had improved oil feeds to the crankshaft, shorter stroke and bigger bore – by the end of the year it could handle up to 16,800rpm

3 By Assen Yamaha had made a 2006-style airbox to fit the 2005-style chassis

4 Checa benefited from the bits Valentino didn't want, inheriting this hybrid bike – 2006 main frame, 2005 swingarm and fuel tank – at Assen

All Yamaha wanted to do was make their M1 concept a little more competitive, just enough to hold off Honda for another year and seize the moral high ground by winning three of the five World Championships of the 990cc era. So they played around a bit with the motor (bigger bore, shorter stroke) and a little with the chassis (just a trifle more rigidity and a new swingarm). And that's where it all went wrong.

Yamaha tested well in the winter, but not quite as much as the other factories because of Rossi's dalliance with Ferrari and Formula 1. Despite a couple of slight problems with chatter on a few corners in testing at Sepang and Qatar, the Yamaha squad cleaned up at the pre-season test at Catalunya. Then they went to the final test at Jerez where the bike chattered itself off the track.

The problem was a fundamental collision of harmonic frequencies (the frequency produced by the tyres when under pressure and the frequency of the revised chassis). The more grip that was available the worse the problem became, with qualifying tyres a particular issue. Yamaha and the team spent four races desperately looking for solutions, with some tests even including a rerun of the old 2005 bike. After a Michelin front tyre succumbed to the additional hammering of a charging Rossi in China, Yamaha reacted. For Le Mans there were 2005 chassis with 2006 engines grafted in for Valentino. They still suffered from chatter, but to a much lesser degree than before, and Rossi made it into the lead – and then the engine went.

The new/old chassis looked exactly like a 2005 bike. The swingarm was 2005, even the seat unit and airbox were 2005, but the engine was the short-stroke 2006 motor. By Mugello Edwards had a pair too. Several different versions were tried as experiments, Carlos Checa ending up with one that didn't react to the different frequencies created by the Dunlop tyre. That version had a 2006 main frame with a 2005 swingarm and fuel tank.

Yamaha had new chassis for the test after Brno. Rossi liked the one that still looked like a 2005 bike: it had chassis beams that were thinner than before and, once combined with new tyres developed for it by Michelin, Valentino returned to running at the front.

DUCATI
DESMOSEDICI-RR

1 Ducati built a lighter, stiffer 'birdcage' frame for 2006; this had the additional benefit of limiting the ability of the forks to bend back when braking hard

2 The 2006 Marelli ride-by-wire system was a big step forward; the rider 'request' was recorded by a unit on the side of the frame; the butterflies were moved by motors in the airbox

3 The Ducati swingarm was lighter and reinforced by this strengthening plate halfway down its length

4 Ducati tidied up their instrument binnacle and used smaller, lighter Marelli 'Marvel 4-2' equipment

Although it looked similar to the Ducati of the previous two years, the 2006 Desmosedici was a big step forward, with a new chassis and an uprated engine giving the 990cc 90-degree machine a serious shot at the title.

The motor received a serious upgrading in terms of its internal friction management and cooling system. The new thermal management meant that the bikes had to be laboriously bled every morning. Once that was done, however, the improved engine management system allowed the bike to sit ticking over at 3,000rpm while it warmed up. This redesigned system was Marelli-based, just like the Yamaha one, and used stepper motors mounted on the butterflies taking instructions from a potentiometer mounted under the fairing on the left-hand side.

The chassis redesign attempted to deal with the issue of excess flexibility under severe braking while trying to keep the steering head and fork deflection that allowed good grip at extreme lean angles. The swingarm was also new, lighter and sported a reinforcing web halfway down its length. It followed the current MotoGP fashion for keeping some lateral flexibility for good grip when leaned over, but it made the effect occur nearer the tip of the swingarm.

The Ducati still suffered from its excess length, though, needing improbable angles of lean for high corner speeds. The move to 800cc will allow a more compact cylinder-head design and a shorter wheelbase, but if Ducati can hang on to the advances they have made since they came into MotoGP they'll be very well placed in 2007.

SUZUKI
GSV-R

1 The 2006 bike used a far more space-conscious design that came apart in segments; here the bike is being warmed up using a small auxiliary fuel tank

2 Vermeulen preferred a swingarm with more fabricated parts than castings

3 Hopkins preferred the opposite; Suzuki denied there were any differences in feel between the two types

4 Suzuki continue to have the coolest pipes in the paddock

Suzuki produced an all-new bike for 2006, sporting a new 75-degree vee engine, a new chassis and spectacular exoskeleton-type bodywork. However, the bike wasn't without its birth pangs. Using pneumatic valves for the first time on a Japanese GP bike, the Suzuki immediately showed that it was fast, but a disastrous Qatar race saw both bikes suffer a multitude of valve-gear failures. Suzuki responded quickly and at the next GP, in Turkey, Vermeulen got his GSV-R on pole.

The new bike addressed serious packaging issues suffered by the previous 65-degree V4. The wider vee angle allowed the airbox to go down between the cylinder heads and the inlet ports to be at a better angle for best power. The old airbox height meant that the fuel tank had to go back under the rider into the seat hump, which undid all the mass centralisation benefits of the 65-degree V4.

Hopkins and Vermeulen had specific preferences on chassis flexibility, and both used different swingarm designs. During the mid-season Brno test three more swingarm designs were tried, along with machined-down outer upper tubes. By Estoril the new parts were standard equipment.

The bikes still never produced quite enough mid-range to get them in sight of the Hondas, Yamahas and Ducatis when conditions were good, but as soon as the weather was bad they lost their power advantage and the Suzukis were good enough to get among them. The Suzukis could shine in the dry, too, on Bridgestone's brilliant but short-lived qualifiers, but as soon as the edge grip went they were back with the crowd.

TEAM ROBERTS

KR-211V

1 From Motegi onwards Roberts used a higher front cowl for 'better aerodynamics'

2 The original chassis used the older Barnard-designed shock-mounted-on-the-swingarm system but it took 12 minutes to swap shocks

3 By Le Mans Roberts were experimenting with a shock mounted to the mainframe to speed shock-change times

4 The last Roberts chassis used different construction techniques and additional strengthening behind the engine spars

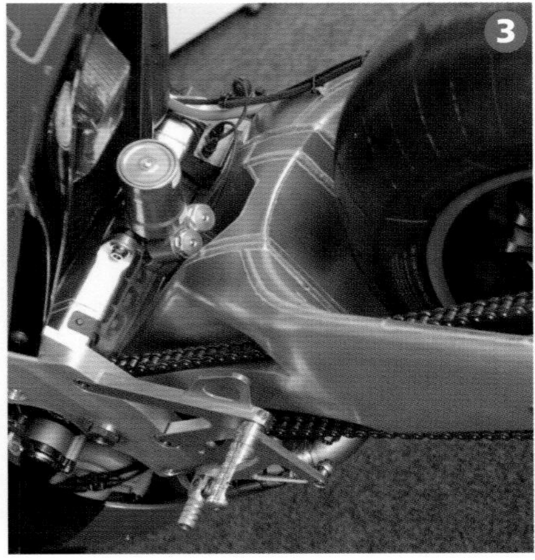

Kenny Roberts Snr at last achieved his dream, a MotoGP effort just like a Formula 1 team – the motor comes from someone else, build a chassis, and racetrack here we come. And what a motor! Roberts finally got Honda engines, and the latest RC211Vs at that. Honda have never let this sort of thing out of their control before – there were RC211V motors in the 2005 Moriwaki, of course, but they were first-year variants. Roberts, however, was actually given 2006 motors.

And Team Roberts did Honda proud. The first chassis was very similar to the final KTM powered bike from 2005 with modifications to suit the Honda engine and fit with a specific request from HRC, the front engine mounts were the elongated front spars that are now the MotoGP norm. As initial testing progressed the area around the headstock was progressively stiffened: first one pair of plates, then a total encapsulation of the old steering head machining.

The rear came under some scrutiny once the front was feeling good. Roberts' original design had a complex bracket for the shock top mount that made changing shocks a ten-minute job. A new frame and swingarm combination mounted the shock to a cross-member at the back of the main frame. This felt different to rider Kenny Jnr, though, and the last version of the 'shock to the swingarm' frame got used the most.

By Donington a new chassis with extended main beams and more conventional construction was ready, potentially faster but still not quite right. By Motegi, however, they had it cracked: a pair of reinforcing struts on the new chassis (that made it resemble, of all things, an RC211V!) and a swingarm originally designed for the 'shock on the swingarm' style of frame gave Kenny Jnr the feel he wanted. He finished on the rostrum in Portugal and for a time had really looked like a race winner.

KAWASAKI
ZX-RR

1 The new chassis runs higher over the head, and a separate airbox

2 New, more aerodynamic bodywork was added from Mugello onwards

3 The new engine tilted forward to ease the inlet and exhaust port designs. Initially it retained the B2 combustion timing but later a B4 design was used

4 Kawasaki campaigned this bike with a completely different engine (and probably a reverse-rotating crank) on one of their wild-card bikes at Motegi

Another new bike, new engine and all, but it came with the same B2 firing sequence that had been used for the previous year. Finally, in the last few races at the end of the season, Kawasaki came out with their own interpretation of a 'long-bang' engine, called B4. The delay in bringing in the 'long-bang' firing sequence meant that Kawasaki didn't achieve the success they deserved with their new bike; it clearly had the capacity from day one.

With the cylinders tilting forward around 15 degrees, the engine was an improved package, allowing better inlet port design and use of space behind the radiator. The new frame had main beams going over the top of the cylinder head but stayed with very similar geometry to the original SRT/Kawasaki chassis. The redesign brought a return to more conservative values in other ways; the new fuel tank was aluminium and had a separate airbox. Other changes included a clutch from new team sponsor FCC, and the Marelli ride-by-wire system got a pair of ECU-controlled throttle butterflies instead of the single one used in 2005.

Further evidence of Kawasaki's delayed ambitions surfaced at Motegi, where test rider Matsudo had two bikes, one with a reverse-rotating crank and the other with the prototype 'long-bang' engine. With just three races to go in the 990cc era, Kawasaki had finally arrived at the specification that would have given them the grip that might have made their year.

ILMOR
X3

Mario Ilien put his not inconsiderable reputation firmly on the line at Estoril. After a summer of rumours he arrived with his X3 team and a brand-new 800cc MotoGP bike to see how it fared in the last two races of the season. With Garry McCoy as rider the X3 therefore became the first 800 to race and, with 15th place, the first to win a World Championship point. The team is a partnership: Ilien builds the motor, Eskil Suter and his SRT organisation build the chassis, and others supply the team infrastructure.

The engine is a 70-degree V4, using a very unusual cam drive up the centre of the vee to keep the cylinder pairs as narrow as possible. Pneumatic valve springs mean that high revs aren't a problem. The crankcases are cast; bear in mind that the Yamahas still have their crankcases machined from solid chunks of ally. Ilmor and Suter clearly think that little change in this area is likely to be needed.

The engine has a dry sump with the oil tank integral with the motor; on the left-hand side of the motor you can see the circular housings for the scavenge pumps, and underneath them the single pressure pump. Oil cooling duties are carried out by a sandwich-construction heat exchanger mounted on the bottom of the engine. Separate oil supplies are used in the gearbox and engine.

Although specified for the original KTM V4 project (but never used) the McLaren Electronic Systems (formerly TAG McLaren) electronics are new to MotoGP. It would have been simpler to start with Marelli equipment but that would have limited the options to what Marelli build now and could have resulted in Ilmor's ideas becoming available to others in the paddock. Ilmor is planning to do a lot more with electronic control than we have been used to seeing in MotoGP and they don't want anyone else getting hold of their initiatives, let alone their solutions.

The chassis is a twin aluminium spar, both beams locating on the top of the crankcases. The crankcases appear able to support the swingarm directly but on this chassis the beams drop down outside the motor to support the swingarm pivot and allow its position to be adjusted.

The airbox and electronics unit sits on top of the heads; the electronics are easily to hand with the top cosmetic cover needing the removal of only four screws for access. The air inlets come around the sides of the forks and route air into the airbox through big air filters from each side.

The fairing is also novel. Serious thought has gone into a very narrow fairing design that forms a series of layers and routes hot air out of the bike, keeping heat away from the motor and internals. It's fiddly to get on but that'll improve with time, and if it can cover enough of the rider and allow a higher top speed then that seems a good compromise!

1 The radiator plugs straight on to the water pump with the heat exchanger immediately below it. You can also see how the rear section unplugs for easy maintenance

2 The engine uses a unique single train of gears up the centre of the vee to drive the cams and balance shaft

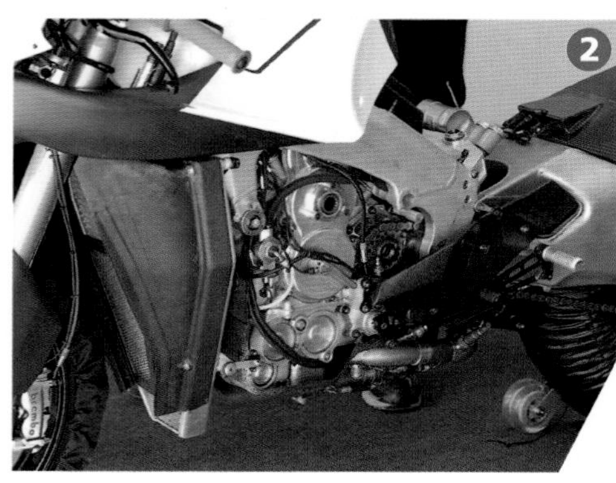

THE RIDERS
2006
GAS
REPSOL
HONDA

THE SEASON IN FOCUS

Every rider's season summed up in words and numbers, from Valentino Rossi to the wild cards whose races lasted less than a lap

The following nine pages detail the results of every rider who raced in MotoGP in 2006. They're arranged in final championship order with a data panel under each entry for the regular team riders. Wild-card and injury-replacement riders are dealt with on page 61.

The data strips have two numbers or a single number and a code letter or letters under each race. The first number is the rider's qualifying position, the second his finishing position. The letter 'i' means a rider was absent through injury, 'f' instead of a number in the results means a fall, and 'dnf' means 'did not finish' – usually due to a mechanical problem. The rider's points total for the season appears at the end of the strip. For further details, check each report's data pages.

NICKY HAYDEN 1

NATIONALITY American
DATE OF BIRTH 30 July 1981
TEAM Repsol Honda
2006 SEASON 2 wins, 1pole position, 2 fastest laps

The Nicky Hayden of 2006 was a very different animal from the one we have seen in previous years. Of course the consistency was still there but there was also the steel you just know an ex-dirt track champion must have. Would the old Nicky Hayden have attacked Edwards as he did on the last two laps at Assen? Would he have been as ruthless with his team-mate as he was at the Sachsenring? Not many people think so. There was also the matter of single-handedly developing the new-generation RCV, or the Ghost Bike as some HRC engineers refered to it, with a young and relatively inexperienced crew while he was trying to win a world title.

At Mugello he finished third despite his bike being 14th fastest through the speed trap; at Barcelona his lap record after poor qualifying was, according to Rossi, 'a small miracle'. Vale must have been impressed: he tried a few mind games on Nicky at the next race and The Doctor never wastes ammunition. As Nicky's only just starting to feel at home in the paddock, expect a spirited defence of the number-one plate.

SPA	QAT	TUR	CHI	FRA	ITA	CAT	NED	GBR	GER	USA	CZE	MAL	AUS	JAP	POR	VAL	POINTS
4-3	4-2	2-3	5-2	10-5	4-3	7-2	4-1	11-7	3-3	6-1	4-9	2-4	1-5	7-5	3-f	5-3	252

VALENTINO ROSSI 2

NATIONALITY Italian
DATE OF BIRTH 16 February 1979
TEAM Camel Yamaha
2005 SEASON 5 wins, 3 fastest laps, 5 pole positions

It's difficult to imagine that anyone other than Valentino Rossi could have been in a position to win the title at the final round having been 51 points down with six races to go. Yet this time his legendary luck ran out. It was as if fate was paying him back for his seven world titles, all of which he'd won from the front.

First there was the coming-together with Elias at the first corner of the first race, then there were back-to-back mechanical failures in China and France, then in Holland came his first real injury. After tyre and cooling problems put him out of the US GP, Vale was only fourth in the championship. Five races later he was leading it into the final round.

His race engineer Jerry Burgess's assessment is that Valentino and Nicky both finished on the rostrum ten times but, crucially, in the other seven races Nicky still piled up points while Valentino picked up only scraps. But when he got to Valencia the championship was still his to lose. The fact that he did proves he's human after all.

SPA	QAT	TUR	CHI	FRA	ITA	CAT	NED	GBR	GER	USA	CZE	MAL	AUS	JAP	POR	VAL	POINTS
9-14	6-1	11-4	13-dnf	7-dnf	3-1	1-1	18-8	12-2	11-1	10-dnf	1-2	1-1	3-3	2-2	1-2	1-13	247

JUST ADD GAS

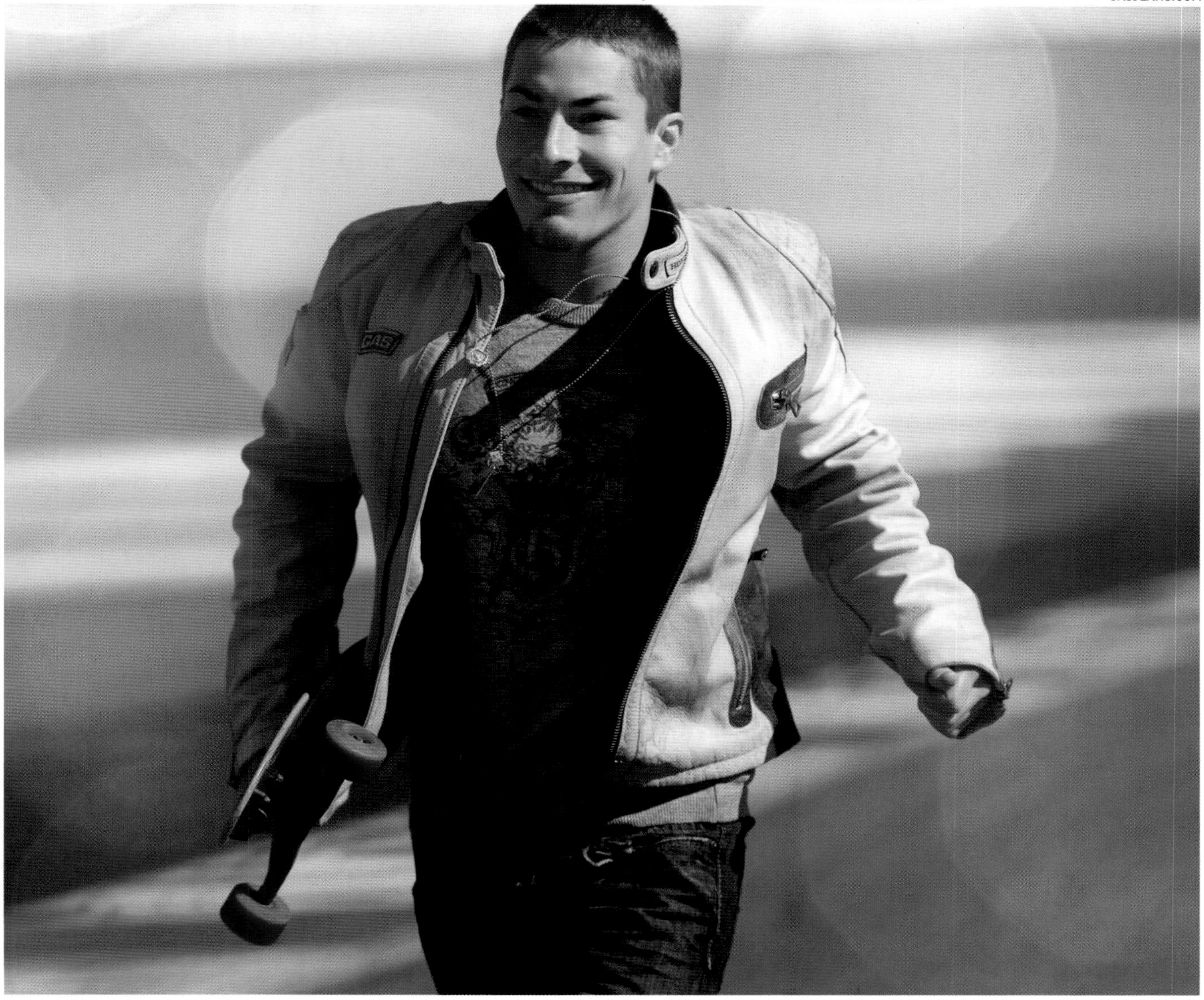

GAS
Keep it simple.

LORIS CAPIROSSI 3

NATIONALITY Italian
DATE OF BIRTH 4 April 1973
TEAM Ducati Marlboro Team
2006 SEASON 3 wins, 2 pole positions, 5 fastest laps

The question 'what if?' will always loom over Loris's 2006 season. When he went to the Catalan GP he was leading the championship, but the horror crash at the first corner put him out of that race and severely handicapped him for the next four races. He returned after the summer break fully fit and got on the rostrum in four of the remaining six events. At the other two his Bridgestone tyres let him down. However, the tyre choice that was viewed 12 months previously as a high-risk strategy was looking like a smart move by the end of the season, and it's now possible to envisage the title being won on a tyre other than Michelin.

He may have been unable to fight for the championship, but Loris's peers voted him their Rider's Rider of the Year and his win in Brno gave him the longest winning career in the history of Grand Prix motorcycle racing. Both achievements gave him real satisfaction.

Despite the tyre troubles and injuries, Loris was only 23 points behind Nicky Hayden at the end of the year. What if...?

SPA	QAT	TUR	CHI	FRA	ITA	CAT	NED	GBR	GER	USA	CZE	MAL	AUS	JAP	POR	VAL	POINTS
1-1	2-3	4-6	10-8	6-2	2-2	6-i	15-15	5-9	5-5	13-8	2-1	3-2	13-7	1-1	10-12	3-2	229

MARCO MELANDRI 4

NATIONALITY Italian
DATE OF BIRTH 7 August 1982
TEAM Fortuna Honda
2005 SEASON 3 wins

The championship runner-up of 2005 had a very mixed 2006. When he was good he was almost unbeatable but when he felt something wasn't right then he struggled. At the start of the year he couldn't get on with the 2006 chassis. However, he never finished a race outside the top ten and only lost out on third place in the championship to Capirossi at the final round.

Like Loris, Marco was a victim of the Barcelona crash. He seemed the worst injured at the time yet returned less than a week later, and in the following two races he rode to rostrum finishes with an undiagnosed break in a collarbone. In a paddock full of tough guys, there isn't anyone tougher than Marco Melandri.

Marco got over his Laguna Seca phobia but started hankering after Bridgestone tyres when he felt Michelin were more concerned with Rossi and Yamaha than with the Honda riders – this despite the fact that plenty of other Michelin-shod Honda riders, including his team-mate, were winning on the French rubber. Expect Fausto Gresini's team to switch suppliers for 2007.

SPA	QAT	TUR	CHI	FRA	ITA	CAT	NED	GBR	GER	USA	CZE	MAL	AUS	JAP	POR	VAL	POINTS
7-5	12-7	14-1	8-7	5-1	6-6	9-i	7-7	3-3	6-2	9-3	11-5	9-9	7-1	3-3	15-8	12-5	228

DANI PEDROSA 5

NATIONALITY Spanish
DATE OF BIRTH 29 September 1985
TEAM Repsol Honda
2005 SEASON 2 wins, 4 fastest laps, 4 pole positions

The reigning 250 World Champion came up to MotoGP with no fear. He won his fourth race in the top class from pole position, setting the fastest lap as well. Not surprisingly, he won Rookie of the Year with some ease.

His season wasn't without controversy or pain. He had a minor whinge after dicing with Rossi at Brno and complained about Rossi (again) and his team-mate after the German GP. Dani was at his best when out alone in front of the field, as in his magnificent display at Donington. However, there were doubts about his strength, especially under hard braking.

There was no doubt about his strength of character after Sepang when he got on the rostrum after a nasty knee injury. At that point he was still in conention for the title but his old aversion to rain resurfaced in Australia and effectively ended his chances. That didn't prevent Dani torpedoing his team-mate in Estoril, but what looked like one of the biggest foul-ups in GP history was made good in Valencia. That was in no small part due to Dani doing the right thing.

SPA	QAT	TUR	CHI	FRA	ITA	CAT	NED	GBR	GER	USA	CZE	MAL	AUS	JAP	POR	VAL	POINTS
5-2	5-6	16-14	1-1	1-3	8-4	11-f	5-3	1-1	1-4	4-2	9-3	5-3	10-15	9-7	4-f	6-4	215

KENNY ROBERTS Jnr 6

NATIONALITY American
DATE OF BIRTH 25 July 1973
TEAM Team Roberts
2006 SEASON 1 fastest lap, 2 podiums

The World Champion of 2000 re-established himself as one of the best riders in the world with the help of his dad's bike. Kenny Senior finally got to put a competitive motor in one of his own chassis and after a few pointers from HRC in China Kenny Junior and the bike were never far from the front. There was a run of three consecutive front-row starts in the middle of the year but the most impressive thing was how Kenny Junior was once again willing to fight for the points, the epic battle for fourth place in Brno being a case in point.

By his own admission, he rides at 95% nowadays, which the team likes just fine. They know that if Kenny goes faster then it's definitely due to something they've done to the bike, not Kenny getting the red mist. The story might have been even happier had Kenny not miscalculated the number of laps left at the end of the Portuguese GP, where a win was a definite possibility. That shouldn't detract from a great season from an experienced rider who many thought had ridden his last GP at the end of the 2005 season.

SPA	QAT	TUR	CHI	FRA	ITA	CAT	NED	GBR	GER	USA	CZE	MAL	AUS	JAP	POR	VAL	POINTS
13-8	10-10	10-13	18-13	15-dnf	11-8	3-3	10-5	9-5	2-f	3-4	3-4	4-7	4-14	14-9	13-3	14-8	134

COLIN EDWARDS 7

NATIONALITY American
DATE OF BIRTH 27 February 1974
TEAM Camel Yamaha Team
2006 SEASON 1 rostrum

It was not an easy year for the Texas Tornado. Like the other Yamaha riders, he found it difficult to get a base setting for the M1, but he also lost out on his first MotoGP win at the last corner. As if that wasn't bad enough, he was also deeply involved in Yamaha's expensive and futile attempt to stop Honda winning their tenth consecutive Suzuka 8 Hour race. It looked for a while as if Colin would be the man to pay for that failure with his job. Thankfully, Yamaha decided to keep him in MotoGP.

As always, Colin was a willing team player doing his best to help Valentino Rossi retain his title. That was plain to see in Portugal, where Colin protected Valentino for as long as he could. What was not so obvious were the hours of testing new parts in an attempt to stop the M1 chattering and the innumerable laps of Michelin's test track he did in this cause. Colin hasn't kept his job just because he gets on well with Valentino – he brings valuable skills and vast experience as well. He's also a godsend for any journalist in need of a good quote.

SPA	QAT	TUR	CHI	FRA	ITA	CAT	NED	GBR	GER	USA	CZE	MAL	AUS	JAP	POR	VAL	POINTS
10-11	8-9	9-9	3-3	9-6	14-12	12-5	3-13	10-6	15-12	2-9	8-10	11-10	5-f	10-8	2-4	10-9	124

CASEY STONER 8

NATIONALITY Australian
DATE OF BIRTH 16 October 1985
TEAM Honda LCR
2005 SEASON 1 pole position, 1 rostrum

The young Aussie hit the ground running with pole position in his second ever MotoGP event and a rostrum next time out. It looked as if he was on course for Rookie of the Year and a hatful of rostrums (at least), but then things got sticky.

Casey approached every new track at full throttle, rather than adopting the Pedrosa technique of building up to times. He was always entertaining to watch and usually a bit scary as well. Despite that pole position he didn't get on the front row again all year, usually preferring to spend his time on race set-up and trusting in his superb technique off the line – Casey says he never uses launch control. At Catalunya he got both holeshots from the third row of the grid!

The downside of a spectacular season was a rash of crashes, six in all, and always off the front tyre. By the end of the season Casey was voicing confusion as to why his bike could be perfect on Saturday and feel totally different on Sunday. None of these problems could obscure his raw talent, and Ducati snapped him up for 2007.

SPA	QAT	TUR	CHI	FRA	ITA	CAT	NED	GBR	GER	USA	CZE	MAL	AUS	JAP	POR	VAL	POINTS
15-6	1-5	7-2	7-5	11-4	9-f	8-f	12-4	8-4	8-i	7-f	12-6	10-8	8-6	11-f	5-f	7-f	119

TONI ELIAS

9

NATIONALITY Spanish
DATE OF BIRTH 26 March 1983
TEAM Fortuna Honda
2005 SEASON 1 win, 1 fastest lap

You couldn't keep Toni out of the headlines this year. He was the one who knocked Valentino Rossi off his bike at the first race and spent most of the slow-down lap apologising. Two races later he followed Rossi through the field in Turkey, setting a new lap record on the way. It looked as if the amiable Spaniard was taking to the RCV, but a fall at home at Catalunya and then a more serious, bone-cracking crash at Assen stopped his progress.

He missed two races with the Dutch injury and then took five races to get back in the top ten. It was now an open secret that he was out of a job at the end of the season.

Then came Portugal. From 11th on the grid Toni took the fight to Valentino Rossi and became one of the very few riders to beat The Doctor in a fair fight. More importantly, the five points that Rossi was deprived of at Estoril proved to be vital in the outcome of the championship two weeks later. Not surprisingly, Toni was given a new contract with Fausto Gresini's team on the Monday after the Portuguese race.

SPA	QAT	TUR	CHI	FRA	ITA	CAT	NED	GBR	GER	USA	CZE	MAL	AUS	JAP	POR	VAL	POINTS
6-4	3-8	12-5	15-11	16-9	12-7	14-f	–	–	16-11	12-15	6-11	14-f	14-9	6-6	11-1	13-6	116

JOHN HOPKINS

10

NATIONALITY American
DATE OF BIRTH 22 May 1983
TEAM Rizla Suzuki MotoGP
2006 SEASON 1 pole position

The numbers might not look that much better than in previous years, but the much-improved Suzuki allowed Hopper to run with the leaders regularly this year. He was particularly impressive in China where he scored his best ever result in MotoGP with fourth. There were still times when he was obviously over-riding the bike to stay in contention – as in France where he fell. However, he got it back to the pits and came out again to score a point. It was the only time in the first 13 races of the year that he finished outside the top ten.

You certainly couldn't fault Hopper's enthusiasm or his commitment. The team obviously thought so too. After a terrible weekend in Qatar peppered with engine failures, John gave his bike a good kicking after it expired in the race. The incident was hardly mentioned. John also coped with a new, young and very fast team-mate without showing any outward signs of irritation.

Although he missed out on his first rostrum finish, John did set his first pole position. It came at Assen, and was the Suzuki's first dry-weather pole.

SPA	QAT	TUR	CHI	FRA	ITA	CAT	NED	GBR	GER	USA	CZE	MAL	AUS	JAP	POR	VAL	POINTS
12-9	13-dnf	5-17	2-4	3-15	7-10	2-4	1-6	4-8	9-10	5-6	7-7	8-6	15-12	13-12	6-6	9-11	116

CHRIS VERMEULEN

11

NATIONALITY Australian
DATE OF BIRTH 19 June 1982
TEAM Rizla Suzuki MotoGP

Another very impressive MotoGP rookie. Chris took a wet-weather pole in Turkey and a dry one in the USA, and only a fuelling problem brought on by the extreme temperature stopped him getting on the rostrum at Laguna. Justice was done when he finished second at his home race despite being in serious trouble after qualifying.

There's no doubt that the ex-Supersport World Champion and World Superbike Championship runner-up impressed everybody, but in particular he impressed the people who work with him. Tom O'Kane, his race engineer, describes Chris in glowing terms and is convinced there's a good deal more to come. You hear the word 'intelligent' a lot when Chris is being discussed and he has totally justified his decision to jump to MotoGP before his ex-employers at Honda were ready.

SPA	QAT	TUR	CHI	FRA	ITA	CAT	NED	GBR	GER	USA	CZE	MAL	AUS	JAP	POR	VAL	POINTS
11-12	11-dnf	1-7	12-f	12-10	15-14	4-6	6-10	2-16	14-7	1-5	13-12	16-11	16-2	15-11	12-9	8-f	98

MAKOTO TAMADA

12

NATIONALITY Japanese
DATE OF BIRTH 4 November 1976
TEAM Konica Minolta Honda

The old, hard-riding, fearless Makoto Tamada wasn't seen very often in 2006. He was hamstrung by an inability to find a set-up he liked and was always having problems with feel at the front during qualifyng and grip at the back in races. One exception was the Chinese GP, where he cheerfully bashed fairings in a multi-bike duel that included the Ducatis, Stoner and Hopkins. There was another rare flash of the old talent in Portugal, but Makoto's best ride was cut short in Germany. He was right with the leaders and looking comfortable when Kenny Roberts crashed and took him out. However, it seemed that going back to standard settings had sorted out his problems, but it was an illusion. The team that was set up specifically for Makoto has replaced him with Shinya Nakano for 2007. Tamada will be in the Tech 3 Yamaha team on Dunlops.

SPA	QAT	TUR	CHI	FRA	ITA	CAT	NED	GBR	GER	USA	CZE	MAL	AUS	JAP	POR	VAL	POINTS
16-10	16-14	13-10	11-6	13-7	10-9	15-7	13-11	14-11	10-f	14-11	15-13	13-14	11-10	18-10	14-5	15-12	96

SETE GIBERNAU

13

NATIONALITY Spanish
DATE OF BIRTH 15 December 1972
TEAM Ducati Marlboro Team

You really wouldn't want Sete Gibernau's luck. His season with new employers Ducati seemed to be going brilliantly for all of two laps, after which his electrics played up and put him out from what looked like a certain rostrum finish at Jerez. He did upset a few Italians by setting pole in Italy, but a bizarre boot failure led to him losing touch with the leaders. Then came the Barcelona crash which rebroke an already plated collarbone, complicating what's normally the simplest of injuries. The break didn't heal and the new plates fatigued when he rode in Germany and the USA. He returned in Malaysia to start a run of three top-five finishes that was brought to an end when he got tangled up in Casey Stoner's Portuguese crash and did further damage to the collarbone. To add insult to injury, the young Aussie was then announced as Sete's replacement for 2007.

SPA	QAT	TUR	CHI	FRA	ITA	CAT	NED	GBR	GER	USA	CZE	MAL	AUS	JAP	POR	VAL	POINTS
2-dnf	7-4	3-11	6-9	8-8	1-5	13-i	–	–	7-8	16-10	–	6-5	12-4	5-4	8-f	–	95

SHINYA NAKANO

14

NATIONALITY Japanese
DATE OF BIRTH 10 October 1977
TEAM Kawasaki Racing Team

This was Shinya's third, and, it would transpire, final season with Kawasaki. It was also his least successful in terms of the end-of-season result as in the previous two years he had finished in the top ten. Conversely, this season featured his career-best result – second at Assen.

There's no doubt that the Kawasaki became more rideable as the season went on but equally the rate of progress that made the ZX-RR Ninja the most improved bike of 2005 wasn't maintained. Shinya was often able to use his qualifying tyres to secure a good grid slot and after the more useable motor arrived he didn't finish a race outside the top ten. Unfortunately, he developed an unhealthy tendency to crash early in races which saw him fail to score in three of the last five outings. For 2007 he will be on a Honda for the Konica-Minolta team.

SPA	QAT	TUR	CHI	FRA	ITA	CAT	NED	GBR	GER	USA	CZE	MAL	AUS	JAP	POR	VAL	POINTS
3-7	9-11	8-8	4-10	2-12	5-11	5-EX	2-2	7-dnf	4-6	8-dnf	5-8	12-f	2-8	4-f	7-f	4-7	92

CARLOS CHECA

15

NATIONALITY Spanish
DATE OF BIRTH 15 October 1972
TEAM Tech 3 Yamaha

The unsung hero of the season. Took on the thankless task of developing Dunlop's MotoGP tyres almost from scratch for what was rumoured to be no wages because he couldn't stand the thought of sitting at home watching Jerez on the TV. There's no better man if you have a lost cause that needs rescuing.

Carlos started with tyres that were marginal at best and by the end of the season his work with the Tech 3 squad and Dunlop had seen a best finish of seventh in Portugal and a best qualifying position of sixth in Australia. Carlos also achieved the distinction of being overall fastest in one practice session and fastest Yamaha in another.

His season of hard graft earned him a Honda for 2007; he will replace Casey Stoner at LCR. Not bad for a 34-year-old who no-one wanted to employ at the start of the season.

SPA	QAT	TUR	CHI	FRA	ITA	CAT	NED	GBR	GER	USA	CZE	MAL	AUS	JAP	POR	VAL	POINTS
14-13	14-12	15-15	14-14	14-11	13-15	16-8	8-9	13-10	12-9	11-7	17-15	15-12	6-f	17-14	9-7	16-10	75

RANDY DE PUNIET

16

NATIONALITY French
DATE OF BIRTH 14 February 1981
TEAM Kawasaki Racing Team

Kawasaki's MotoGP rookie had a tough start to his career in the top class. He was injured in practice for the first race, fell on the first lap of the second and was the innocent victim of the now traditional domino effect at the chicane on the first lap at Le Mans. It took Randy until Portugal, the penultimate round of the season, to register a top-ten finish but he looked much better than that in qualifying for much of the year. He was able to use the extra grip of a qualifying tyre to great effect and was fourth on the grid at Le Mans, a circuit he professes not to like even though it hosts his home race. He never started from the front row but was on the second row three times and the third row three times.

There was only one crash in the second half of the year and when he saw the chequered flag he was always in a points-scoring position.

SPA	QAT	TUR	CHI	FRA	ITA	CAT	NED	GBR	GER	USA	CZE	MAL	AUS	JAP	POR	VAL	POINTS
8-dnf	15-f	6-12	9-12	4-f	16-13	10-f	11-14	6-12	13-dnf	15-12	10-14	7-13	9-11	8-f	16-10	11-f	37

ALEX HOFMANN

17

NATIONALITY German
DATE OF BIRTH 25 May 1980
TEAM Pramac d'Antin MotoGP

The likeable German plugged away manfully on the d'Antin Ducati and was rewarded with three replacement rides on the factory bike when Sete Gibernau was injured – Holland, Britain and the Czech Republic.

His team manager's public criticism of their Dunlops probably didn't help the situation too much and Alex frequently likened his experience during a race to a rodeo ride. In among the hard work and struggle there were a couple of seriously impressive rides. He was heading for the top ten at Laguna Seca before running off track at the very last corner, and he was the first Ducati to finish in Portugal. In Australia his tyre was missing chunks of tread at the finish but he brought his bike home in the points and without being lapped. He has never been lapped in any level of competition and used that as motivation.

SPA	QAT	TUR	CHI	FRA	ITA	CAT	NED	GBR	GER	USA	CZE	MAL	AUS	JAP	POR	VAL	POINTS
19-15	18-15	17-16	16-15	18-13	18-f	17-10	9-12	15-13	17-dnf	17-14	14-16	17-15	17-13	20-16	18-11	17-f	30

JAMES ELLISON

18

NATIONALITY British
DATE OF BIRTH 19 September 1980
TEAM Tech 3 Yamaha

After his mightily convincing 2005 season on the outgunned WCM, British fans were hoping that James would be just as impressive on a factory Yamaha. Unfortunately, it didn't happen. He was stuck for the whole season with the original chattering Yamaha chassis as the factory concentrated on trying to keep the title and develop the new 800. James understood why he wasn't getting the bits but that didn't make the situation any less frustrating. Those who could be bothered to look could find evidence of his old form in some section times, notably late in the race at Laguna Seca and the fearsome final part of Phillip Island. Was his fate sealed early on when he was considerably slower than his team-mate Checa on equal machinery? Should James have risked more? 'I wouldn't do anything differently,' he says. He will probably race in the USA in 2007.

SPA	QAT	TUR	CHI	FRA	ITA	CAT	NED	GBR	GER	USA	CZE	MAL	AUS	JAP	POR	VAL	POINTS
18-16	17-13	19-18	17-16	17-14	17-16	18-9	14-f	16-14	18-13	18-13	16-17	18-16	18-16	19-15	17-13	19-14	26

JOSE LUIS CARDOSO

20

NATIONALITY Spanish
DATE OF BIRTH 2 February 1975
TEAM Pramac d'Antin MotoGP

The urbane ex-250 rider from Seville used his considerable personal wealth and charm to secure a ride on the d'Antin Ducati for the 2006 season. Jose has had ten top-ten finishes in the 250cc class over the years, including a fifth place at Jarama back in 1988. His form on the 500s wasn't quite so good: just two top-ten finishes in four years of trying, both in 2001 on a Yamaha. Unfortunately it was his 500 form that followed him to MotoGP for his 2006 season.

He scored points four times, his best result being 11th at Catalunya when eight of the field either crashed or were excluded. His best qualifying position was 16th at Assen, where he had the satisfaction of seeing both his team-mate and Valentino Rossi behind him on the grid.

With the d'Antin team now receiving funding from Pramac, it's unlikely Jose Luis will return.

SPA	QAT	TUR	CHI	FRA	ITA	CAT	NED	GBR	GER	USA	CZE	MAL	AUS	JAP	POR	VAL	POINTS
17-dnf	19-16	18-dnf	19-17	19-dnf	19-17	19-11	16-17	18-15	19-14	19-16	18-dnf	19-17	19-17	21-f	19-14	18-dnf	10

Thanks!
LeoVince Staff
Spain's Nº1
Honda
OFFICIAL SPONSOR
Italian Technology
LeoVince.com
EXHAUST SYSTEMS

WILD CARDS & REPLACEMENT RIDERS

MotoGP regulations stipulate that when a team's regular rider is injured he can be replaced. It's also possible for wild-card entries to be nominated race-by-race by Dorna (MotoGP rights holders), IRTA (the teams' organisation), and the FIM (the sport's governing body) and its local affiliates. These are the men who couldn't give up the day job this time round.

TROY BAYLISS 19

25 POINTS

One ride as a replacement for the injured Sete Gibernau produced one of the most dominant victories of the year. The reigning World Superbike Champion led every lap of the final race of the year and immediately announced that he wouldn't ride in a MotoGP race again. Not a bad way to sign off, especially given the way he was sacked by Ducati at the end of 2004 and then suffered on a Honda in 2005. A popular winner.

KOUSUKE AKIYOSHI 21

3 POINTS

Suzuki's veteran All-Japan Championship star and the GSV-R test rider was rewarded for his good work with a wild-card entry at the Japanese GP. Kousuke Akiyoshi impressed in both qualifying and the race (he was 12th on the grid and 13th in the race), matching both of his team-mates for pace and showing scant respect for the MotoGP regulars. Not bad at all for your first appearance in a Grand Prix.

GARRY McCOY 22

2 POINTS

Three times a GP winner on 500 Yamahas, McCoy left MotoGP for Superbike at the end of the 2003 season. In 2006 his racing was confined to a few supermoto events until the Ilmor team hired him to test their new 800 and ride as a wild card at Estoril and Valencia, two tracks on which he won GPs. Garry qualified for both races without any problems and picked up the final point in both as well, making him the first 800cc MotoGP points scorer.

NAOKI MATSUDO

Best known for his eight years in the 250cc class during which he achieved two rostrum finishes on Yamahas, Matsudo-san is now Kawasaki's MotoGP development rider. His only wild-card ride of the year – indeed, his only race of the year – was as at Motegi for the Japanese GP. He qualified 16th, ahead of five MotoGP regulars, but his race only lasted eight laps before he was forced to retire with mechanical problems.

MICHEL FABRIZIO

Michel Fabrizio, who caught the attention of several teams when he rode for WCM in 2004, was scheduled to replace the injured Toni Elias at Donington Park. However, a highside crash at Goddards in practice broke the young Italian's collarbone. The ride was originally scheduled to go to ex-World Superbike Champion James Toseland but a clash of sponsors put paid to that plan and what would have been Toseland's MotoGP debut.

IVAN SILVA

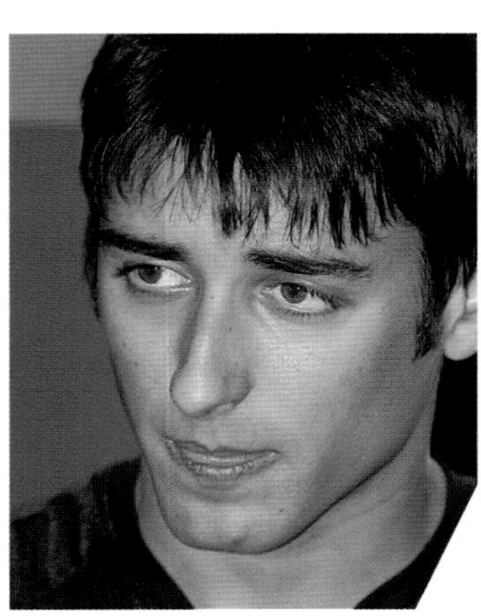

The young Spaniard was promoted from the d'Antin Spanish Championship team to stand in for Alex Hofmann for three races while Hofmann was in turn deputising for Sete Gibernau in the factory Ducati team. Silva finished 16th at Assen, retired from Donington Park due to an injury and finished 18th at Brno. It was the first time he'd ever seen any of the circuits and he'd also never before ridden the Desmosedici Ducati.

THE RACES
MotoGP 2006

SPANISH GP

JEREZ

ROUND 1

RED MIST

Just the start to the season that everyone wanted – with the exception of Valentino Rossi. The champ hit the floor at the first corner, leaving Capirossi and Ducati to fight off Pedrosa for the win

The Spanish Grand Prix didn't go according to the script. Everyone was expecting a dominating performance from Valentino Rossi at a track where he had won four races in the senior class; everyone was anticipating another record race time and a Michelin victory. No-one expected a class rookie to fight for the win or for Bridgestone to fill the front row and be victorious; and certainly no-one thought that the factory Yamaha would be afflicted by such serious chatter that the World Champion couldn't exploit the grip of a qualifying tyre.

As if starting from the back of the third row wasn't bad enough for Rossi, when he arrived at the first corner he was skittled by an errant Toni Elias.

After a few moments of arm-waving in the direction of the fast-disappearing Spaniard, Valentino realised his bike was still just about rideable and recommenced racing, albeit three-quarters of a minute behind the leaders. Not surprisingly, he never troubled them. And those leaders were the Ducatis, just as they'd been in qualifying. Loris Capirossi led the first lap – and all the subsequent 26 laps as well. It looked for a short while as if his new team-mate, Sete Gibernau, would be the one to make a challenge but it was quite another Spaniard who emerged from the pack. Sete's bad luck seemed to have followed him from Honda: this time it was an electrical fault in the gearchange system.

Rossi's legendary good luck appeared to have deserted him after the test session at Catalunya three weeks before the first GP. There the Yamahas had looked immaculate but at the final test, alarmingly at Jerez, they developed serious chatter and it was still there for the race. Pictures beamed from his Yamaha were so

Opposite Dani Pedrosa prepares to do battle at the front of a MotoGP field for the first time

Left Rossi hits the deck and only just avoids being hit by Elias before running to his bike

Below Scraped fairing, bent brake pedal and lever, twisted handlebar – but Valentino didn't slow down much

blurred it looked as if the on-board camera's mounting had come loose. Indeed, it was so serious that Valentino would say later that never in the whole weekend did he think he could have won the race, claiming that fighting for the rostrum was the limit of his ambitions. But he never even got the chance to do that.

In fact, Rossi was lucky to avoid injury after he was sent sprawling on the tarmac in the middle of the pack. Elias only just avoided him and Colin Edwards had to take to the grass to avoid his team-mate, rejoining with only Valentino behind him. Once Gibernau had stopped on the second lap the picture was clear: Capirossi was in command, as he'd been right through practice and qualifying. The question now was whether his Bridgestone tyres would last the distance. The company had never won a race in Europe and the perceived wisdom was that Michelin's ability to build and deliver new tyres overnight in their Clermont-Ferrand factory gave them the upper hand. Not this time. A pack of Michelin-shod Hondas pursued Capirossi's Desmosedici and, although they got close, he was never troubled. Actually only one of them got really close – the astounding Dani Pedrosa.

Everyone knew Dani had talent – three world titles in three years is proof enough of that – but not many thought he could be this competitive this quickly on a MotoGP bike. His stature, or lack of it, was the main talking point: how could a guy who weighs 51kg have the strength to muscle a big bike around and the stamina to do it for 45 minutes? From the stands it looked as though he didn't have any problems, but he did admit afterwards that he was grateful when Capirossi slowed the pace slightly mid-race and that

REPSOL

Above Casey Stoner inpressed hugely on his MotoGP debut

he had been troubled by front-end slides towards the end. When Capirossi reapplied the pressure with half-a-dozen laps to go it was instantly apparent that Pedrosa was unable to respond. Ducati and Capirossi got their best-ever start to a season, but just as much attention was lavished on Dani Pedrosa in second place. He'd qualified on the second row and finished the first lap in seventh place, so he hardly had an easy race. It was an astonishingly smooth transition from 250cc champion to MotoGP contender, and he wasn't alone. Fellow rookie Casey Stoner, with no pre-season testing, ran with the leaders and finished a comfortable sixth.

For once Nicky Hayden didn't seem too distressed with another third place, even though it involved being beaten by his team-mate. After the travails of pre-season testing on the development Honda V5 it was a relief to be anywhere near the front. Hayden almost lost third place on the last lap to, of all people, Toni Elias. The Spaniard, in his first ride on a Honda V5, charged through the field after his tangle with Rossi and did get a wheel in front of Hayden at the last hairpin, only to be retaken. A contrite Toni then stopped on the slow-down lap to apologise profusely to Rossi, and when he got back to pit lane he crawled under the Camel team's pit garage door to offer further apologies. He's a difficult man to dislike.

Below Toni Elias so nearly took third after riding through the field following his first-corner tangle with Rossi

Jerez set several trends that would run through the season, not least the difficulty Rossi would have in qualifying his Yamaha anywhere near the front row. It was also apparent that Bridgestone were going to be more competitive at more tracks than had previously been the case. The most significant development, though, was the stellar showing of MotoGP rookies Pedrosa and Stoner: they were the thin end of what would prove to be a very large wedge. It was noticeable, too, that the names of Max Biaggi, Alex Barros and the other MotoGP refugees were never mentioned in the paddock.

While Capirossi and Ducati left the first race of the year leading their championships for the first time, Valentino Rossi contemplated a new experience. His previous titles had been won from the front; now he was going to have to chase down some very good opposition. The Doctor himself would doubtless have disagreed, but spectators and TV viewers alike now looked forward to exactly what they wanted to see – Valentino Rossi having to work hard for every point.

WHAT IS HONDA DOING?

Above Nicky Hayden listens carefully to his crew chief Pete Benson

One of the longest-running sub-plots of any recent season is which of the Honda riders is getting the best treatment and the latest machinery. This time it looked a more pointed question than ever. Only Stoner, Tamada and Elias appeared to have the base-model bike. Pedrosa, as befits a factory team rider, benefited from chassis and electronics iterations, but the Spaniard's team-mate, Nicky Hayden, now the most experienced Honda rider, had the job of developing a brand-new machine that appeared to be a rolling test-bed for the 2007 800cc bike. It was smaller, narrower and different in every dimension from Dani's bike. Just to complicate the issue, Marco Melandri had failed to come to terms with the handling of the 2006 model in pre-season testing and had been given special dispensation by HRC to ride the '05 bike for one race only. None of the rookies had problems, but the veterans of the '05 bike, Marco and Makoto, were not happy with feedback from the front.

If you were Nicky Hayden you could look at this situation in two ways. The first was the flattering option – that HRC had trusted you and you alone, their most experienced rider, to bring on the new bike, and anyway the old bike was surely at the end of its development life. The second could be called the paranoid option – that in a team financed by Spanish money you're doing the donkey work of developing a 'super 250' for your team-mate, who seems to be Honda's favoured son and has twice been a 250cc World Champion. Originally the plan was that Nicky would ride the new model for four or five races before getting the same bike as Pedrosa, but actually he stayed with it for much longer.

The paranoid option looked the more realistic after pre-season testing, but Hayden qualified for the first GP of the year as top Honda (and Michelin) rider and then had a far better race than anyone could have predicted. Maybe the optimistic outlook was the right one after all?

Below MotoGP rookie Pedrosa made sure that Capirossi had to work for his victory

SPANISH GP

JEREZ

ROUND 1

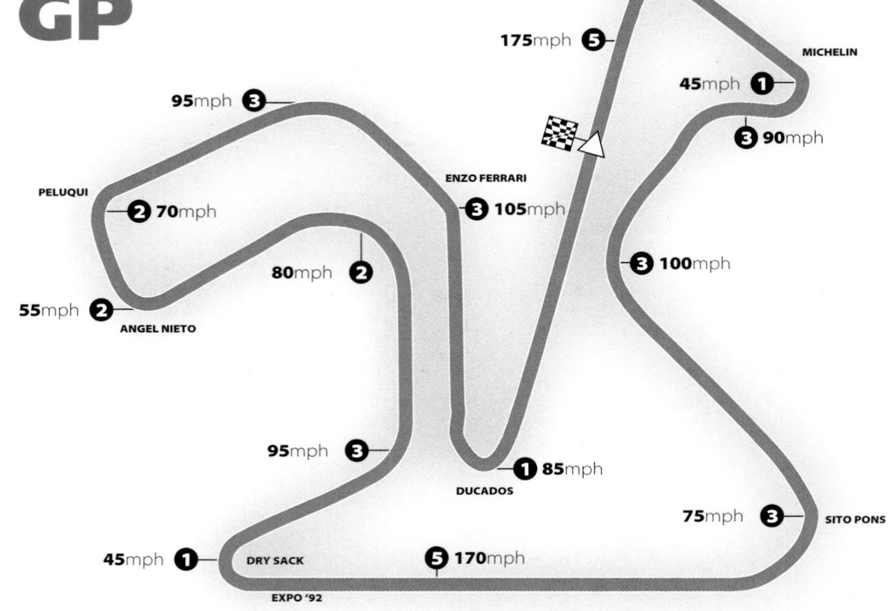

RACE RESULTS

RACE DATE March 26th
CIRCUIT LENGTH 2.748 miles
NO. OF LAPS 27
RACE DISTANCE 74.196 miles
WEATHER Dry, 22°C
TRACK TEMPERATURE 33°C
WINNER Loris Capirossi
FASTEST LAP 1m 41.248s, 97.724mph, Loris Capirossi
PREVIOUS LAP RECORD 1m 40.596s, 98.136mph, Valentino Rossi, 2005

QUALIFYING

	Rider	Nationality	Team	Qualifying	Pole +	Gap
1	Capirossi	ITA	Ducati Marlboro Team	1m 39.064s		
2	Gibernau	SPA	Ducati Marlboro Team	1m 39.285s	0.221s	0.221s
3	Nakano	JPN	Kawasaki Racing Team	1m 39.526s	0.462s	0.241s
4	Hayden	USA	Repsol Honda Team	1m 39.666s	0.602s	0.140s
5	Pedrosa	SPA	Repsol Honda Team	1m 39.734s	0.670s	0.068s
6	Elias	SPA	Fortuna Honda	1m 39.875s	0.811s	0.141s
7	Melandri	ITA	Fortuna Honda	1m 39.932s	0.868s	0.057s
8	De Puniet	FRA	Kawasaki Racing Team	1m 40.146s	1.082s	0.214s
9	Rossi	ITA	Camel Yamaha Team	1m 40.160s	1.096s	0.014s
10	Edwards	USA	Camel Yamaha Team	1m 40.181s	1.117s	0.021s
11	Vermeulen	AUS	Rizla Suzuki MotoGP	1m 40.215s	1.151s	0.034s
12	Hopkins	USA	Rizla Suzuki MotoGP	1m 40.340s	1.276s	0.125s
13	Roberts	USA	Team Roberts	1m 40.497s	1.433s	0.157s
14	Checa	SPA	Tech 3 Yamaha	1m 40.851s	1.787s	0.354s
15	Stoner	AUS	Honda LCR	1m 40.982s	1.918s	0.131s
16	Tamada	JPN	Konica Minolta Honda	1m 41.119s	2.055s	0.137s
17	Cardoso	SPA	Pramac d'Antin MotoGP	1m 41.749s	2.685s	0.630s
18	Ellison	GBR	Tech 3 Yamaha	1m 42.267s	3.203s	0.518s
19	Hofmann	GER	Pramac d'Antin MotoGP	1m 42.341s	3.277s	0.074s

FINISHERS

1 LORIS CAPIROSSI The perfect weekend: pole, fastest lap and the win. The only other occasion Loris collected the full set was at Motegi in 2005. Now he had the added bonus of leading the championship table for the first time and seeing Ducati top the constructors' standings, again for the first time.

2 DANI PEDROSA A remarkable debut in the top class: Dani became the first rookie to finish on the rostrum since the opening race of the 1998 season, when Max Biaggi and Noriyuki Haga finished first and third. He also became the second-youngest rider ever to score top-three finishes in all three classes. The youngest? Mike Hailwood.

3 NICKY HAYDEN A fifth successive rostrum, but third place behind your team-mate doesn't sound too good until you factor in the development bike Nicky was on. Two weeks earlier, at the final test, he didn't think he'd see which way the opposition went, let alone stand on the podium. For once, he looked happy with third.

4 TONI ELIAS After coming to a near-stop in the first-turn mêlée, which he'd instigated, Toni charged through the field, overtaking his team-mate along the way, to his best-ever result in the premier class. Not bad for his Honda debut in MotoGP. Offered profuse apologies to Rossi on the slow-down lap and ducked under the Camel team's garage door later to apologise there as well.

5 MARCO MELANDRI Still suffering from a total lack of feel with the 2006 RCV, so HRC took the unprecedented step of allowing him to race the '05 bike. He was still uncomfortable with the front-end feel and decided not to risk the points he had when his team-mate came past.

6 CASEY STONER Another remarkable debut, in which the only weakness appeared to be an inability to take full advantage of qualifying tyres. Casey profited from the first-turn fracas which enabled him to latch on to the leaders – and that's where he stayed.

7 SHINYA NAKANO Disappointed not to back up his superb front-row qualifying performance with a better result in the

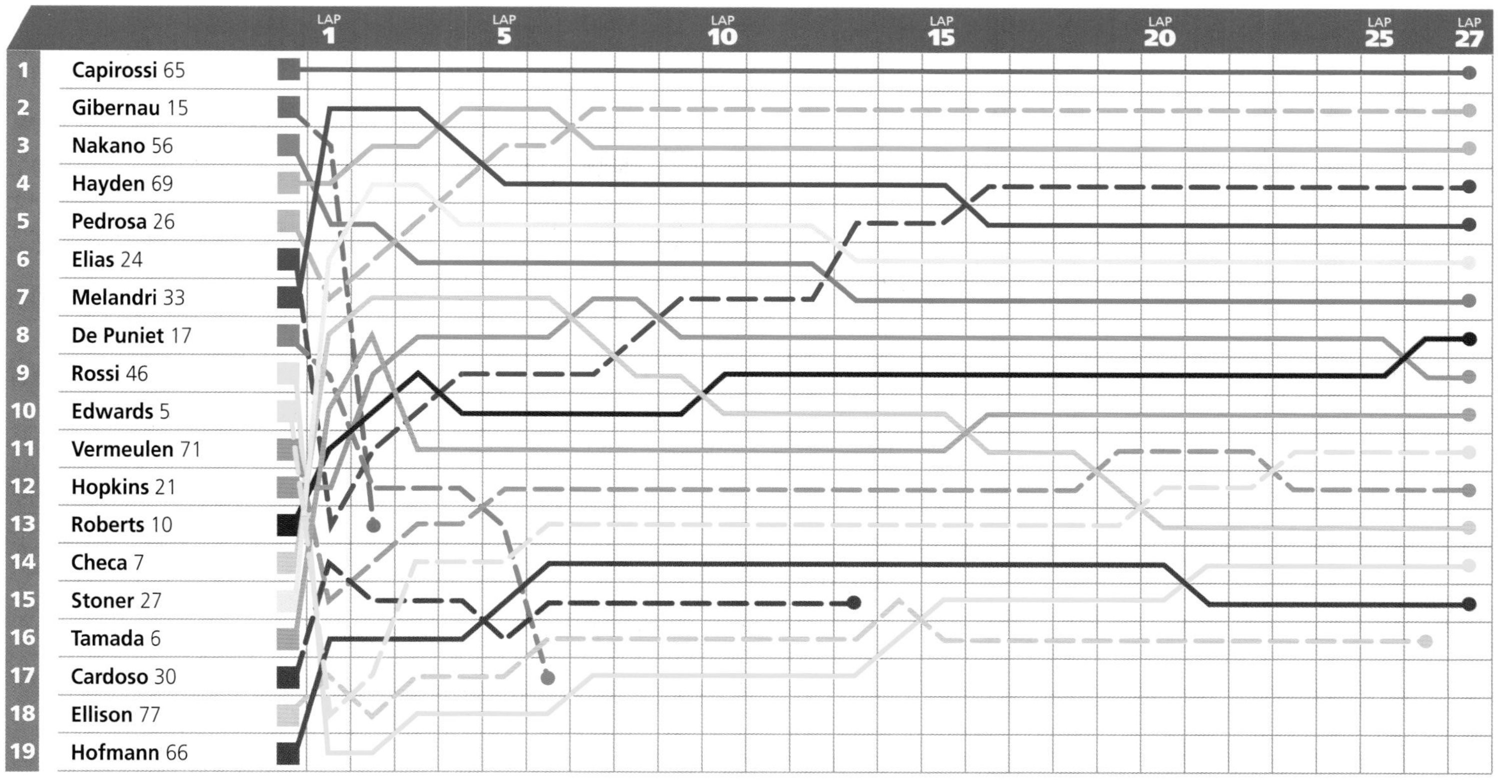

RACE

	Rider	Motorcycle	Race Time	Time +	Fastest Lap	Average Speed
1	Capirossi	Ducati	45m 57.733s		1m 41.248s	96.810mph
2	Pedrosa	Honda	46m 02.108s	4.375s	1m 41.297s	96.657mph
3	Hayden	Honda	46m 07.729s	9.996s	1m 41.412s	96.460mph
4	Elias	Honda	46m 07.868s	10.135s	1m 41.743s	96.455mph
5	Melandri	Honda	46m 17.280s	19.547s	1m 41.794s	96.129mph
6	Stoner	Honda	46m 18.970s	21.237s	1m 41.723s	96.070mph
7	Nakano	Kawasaki	46m 19.105s	21.372s	1m 42.017s	96.065mph
8	Roberts	KR211V	46m 30.147s	32.414s	1m 42.109s	95.685mph
9	Hopkins	Suzuki	46m 30.392s	32.659s	1m 41.598s	95.677mph
10	Tamada	Honda	46m 33.716s	35.983s	1m 42.344s	95.563mph
11	Edwards	Yamaha	46m 35.663s	37.930s	1m 42.545s	95.497mph
12	Vermeulen	Suzuki	46m 37.247s	39.514s	1m 42.648s	95.443mph
13	Checa	Yamaha	46m 40.562s	42.829s	1m 42.161s	95.330mph
14	Rossi	Yamaha	47m 03.499s	1m 05.766s	1m 42.184s	94.555mph
15	Hofmann	Ducati	47m 21.033s	1m 23.300s	1m 44.076s	93.971mph
16	Ellison	Yamaha	46m 08.428s	1 lap	1m 44.430s	92.864mph
	Cardoso	Ducati	22m 53.296s	14 laps	1m 44.280s	93.603mph
	De Puniet	Kawasaki	10m 41.370s	21 laps	1m 43.296s	92.502mph
	Gibernau	Ducati	3m 37.233s	25 laps	1m 48.223s	91.040mph

CHAMPIONSHIP

	Rider	Team	Points
1	Capirossi	Ducati Marlboro Team	25
2	Pedrosa	Repsol Honda Team	20
3	Hayden	Repsol Honda Team	16
4	Elias	Fortuna Honda	13
5	Melandri	Fortuna Honda	11
6	Stoner	Honda LCR	10
7	Nakano	Kawasaki Racing Team	9
8	Roberts	Team Roberts	8
9	Hopkins	Rizla Suzuki MotoGP	7
10	Tamada	Konica Minolta Honda	6
11	Edwards	Camel Yamaha Team	5
12	Vermeulen	Rizla Suzuki MotoGP	4
13	Checa	Tech 3 Yamaha	3
14	Rossi	Camel Yamaha Team	2
15	Hofmann	Pramac d'Antin MotoGP	1

race. Thwarted by the change in grip levels and a lack of grunt that wouldn't let him get in a position to challenge the two men right in front of him on the brakes.

8 KENNY ROBERTS Discovered the team's tyre and suspension choices, informed by experience with Yamaha and Ohlins, didn't cross over directly to their own chassis and the RCV motor: the front end tucked at nearly every corner. Amazed by the Honda engine, which he said was the first he'd ever used that felt exactly the same at the end of a race as it did at the start.

9 JOHN HOPKINS Got a great start from the fourth row but was another victim of the first-turn incident, where he nearly ran Rossi over. His subsequent charge back through the field was halted when he developed arm pump – the first time he'd suffered from it. He was in sixth when it struck.

10 MAKOTO TAMADA A high-speed highside in pre-season testing at Phillip Island hadn't helped Makoto's search for confidence, especially in the front end. Despite a good start his lack of pace into corners meant he had an unsatisfactory race.

11 COLIN EDWARDS Bitterly disappointed with his weekend. Unhappy after qualifying and even unhappier when he was forced to take evading action at the first corner and ran off the track. Given that he was last but one on the first lap, 11th wasn't the worst possible outcome.

12 CHRIS VERMEULEN A bad start meant Chris was also held up by the Rossi crash and he never got in touch with the leaders. Said afterwards that he thought his inexperience with race set-up might have contributed to the result.

13 CARLOS CHECA The main beneficiary of the first-turn turmoil, which saw him as high as eighth half-way round the first lap, despite starting in 14th. First Dunlop finisher, and able to lap at similar times to Edwards at the end of the race.

14 VALENTINO ROSSI Afflicted by chatter all through practice and unable to use a qualifier because of the vibration, then clipped in the first corner by Elias and dumped on the track where he was lucky to avoid being hit by the pack. Got back on after waving angrily at the disappearing Spaniard and, despite a bent right footrest, inoperable rear brake, broken front brake lever and sundry other damage, scored a couple of points.

15 ALEX HOFMANN Had the pleasure of racing with Rossi for a chunk of the race but otherwise reported a lonely and boring ride to secure the final point.

16 JAMES ELLISON Suffered the embarrassment of being lapped in his first race on the Yamaha after lack of experience with the machinery and tyres led to serious set-up errors. A doubly disappointing debut after things had looked so good at the Barcelona test three weeks before.

NON-FINISHERS

JOSE LUIS CARDOSO Pulled in citing lack of grip from his rear tyre as the problem.

RANDY DE PUNIET Forced to retire when the wrist he hurt in a practice crash became too painful for him to continue.

SETE GIBERNAU His run of bad luck from the previous season continued when the electronics that tell the engine management what gear the bike is in failed

QATARI GP

LOSAIL

ROUND 2

FLATTERING TO DECEIVE

Normal service was resumed with a Rossi win, but Hayden ran him close and Casey Stoner showed that Pedrosa wasn't the only rookie who was going to make an impression in 2006

The two bikes that gave most cause for alarm in testing and at the first race of the year came good at the second round. Valentino Rossi and his crew ironed out most of the problems of their Yamaha M1 to take the win, while Nicky Hayden and the development Honda showed the sort of fight that everyone had been waiting to see from the ex-dirt track champ. The Doctor was particularly delighted that he'd set the fastest lap because it proved how well the bike was now working. Valentino has always valued the fastest lap of a race above pole position and before this race had set 45 of them in his 500cc/MotoGP career as against 30 poles. Over in the Honda camp, any lingering worries Nicky Hayden had about being the lone rider on the development bike must have been reduced to a minimum. Another second-row start and a very competitive race saw him a close second – and well in front of his team-mate. More importantly, Nicky was able to fight with Rossi after he was passed. They swapped places five times on the sixth lap as Nicky responded instantly to the Doctor's moves with the aggression to be expected from a man raised in the tough

NOLAN
NOLAN
NOLAN
CARRERA
CARRERA
CARRERA
WOLFTANK
RA-MA
HONDA
HONDA
DENSO
IRIDIUM POWER
Lee
Xpd
PIVETTI
PIVETTI
Amor di farina
N94
GP Pro
DENSO

school of the American dirt ovals. The real surprise is that they weren't dicing for the lead.

Rossi and Hayden were chasing the man who started from pole – Casey Stoner. It was hard to remember that the young Aussie was only riding in his second MotoGP race – Valentino was later moved to remark that Stoner rode as if he'd been in the class for ten years. Mind you, Rossi tempered his praise with the observation that Casey was at a bit of a loss once the tyres wore significantly. Stoner is as likely to ignore that sort of perceived criticism as his illustrious fellow countrymen Wayne Gardner and Mick Doohan; he would remember the slight. And his performance was even more remarkable given that he missed all pre-season testing because of a shoulder operation and had had a nightmare journey to Qatar that involved two nights sleeping in airports and had only arrived in the country an hour before first practice. Not surprisingly, he didn't feel very well either. His pole position was no fluke: he was fast throughout practice and he was able to use his qualifiers, something he couldn't do in Spain two weeks earlier – a quick learner, this kid.

Given his condition it was no surprise that Stoner slipped back to fifth after half-distance. In fact it could

Above Casey Stoner leads a MotoGP race for the first time

Opposite Stoner started from pole for what was only his second MotoGP race

Below John Hopkins and the Rizla Suzuki team had a weekend to forget

be considered a major surprise that he led nearly half the race and only got passed by Rossi, Hayden and the factory Ducatis.

Gibernau had to work hard to catch Stoner but no-one else was able to jump the gap after Hopkins' Suzuki started spraying its oil over the pack, causing more than a few riders to lose time while considering evasive action. John's dnf was no surprise, given that the team had performed more than a dozen engine changes over the weekend, and Vermeulen's bike had also let go on the front straight in warm-up, bringing out the red flag. The Aussie's GSV-R only lasted three more race laps than Hopper's. The Suzuki team's disastrous weekend was rounded off when John Hopkins was caught by TV cameras throwing a hissy fit and giving his steaming bike a good kicking beside the track. The problem? Overheating caused by the failure of the plastic water impeller, a component that had never caused a hiccup before.

Once Stoner had dropped back from the front four he had enough of a gap not to fall into the hands of the Pedrosa/Melandri dice that enlivened the second half of the race. Neither man troubled the leaders as Melandri was still unhappy with the 2006 RCV and Pedrosa had made a hash of the start thanks to clutch problems. The Italian was able regularly to outbrake Dani at the first corner but was equally regularly passed again before the end of the lap. Their fight was resolved on the penultimate lap when Melandri tried an optimistic round-the-outside move and Pedrosa showed him the Astroturf at the edge of the track.

The pleasant surprise of the third Qatar GP was that the Ducatis, or to be more precise their tyres, stayed competitive for the whole weekend. In 2005 Capirossi had arrived in Losail after back-to-back victories and proceeded to set a third consecutive pole position, but in the race his Bridgestones never worked, coming round on him as he went into corners and not allowing him to put any power down coming out. It was one of the Japanese tyre company's worst weekends of the year. Yet less than half a season later Loris was able to maintain his pace for the whole distance and set his fastest lap on the 11th out of the 22 laps. If Bridgestone could get on the rostrum at Losail, why shouldn't they be just as competitive at their other bogey tracks, like Donington and Catalunya? The third tyre company, Dunlop, also gleaned some hope from the fact that both the Tech 3 Yamaha riders beat Makoto Tamada's Michelin-equipped Honda.

Against most people's expectations, Rossi did not escape from Hayden and Capirossi and the Honda rider went back to the front with four laps to go. It was the classic outbraking move at Turn 1, but Rossi didn't appear unduly worried: he sat up and took a long look over his shoulder to check on the Ducati. He obviously thought Loris was a little close for comfort and a lap later he repaid Nicky's compliment. Hayden mustered another comeback but a slide half-way round the last lap prevented a real challenge for the victory.

Valentino Rossi appeared to have restored order to the proceedings, but it wasn't quite that clear-cut. He was still unable to use the new-generation wider front Michelin, and while the team had managed the chatter cleverly, they hadn't eliminated it. Worse, they weren't at all sure what was causing it.

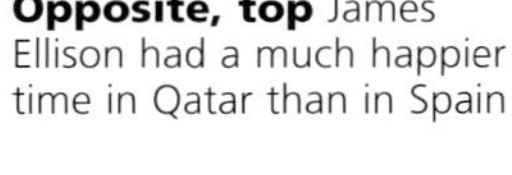

Opposite, top James Ellison had a much happier time in Qatar than in Spain

Below Nicky Hayden showed some real fight and never let Rossi escape

LIGHT FANTASTIC

The idea of MotoGP under floodlights has been around since the Qatar GP was first announced. Indeed, it was thought for a while that the first event would be held under lights. The idea may not be as far-fetched as it sounds. At the behest of the promoter of the Losail race, who believes he'd get a significant crowd if the race was run later in the day, the first three corners of the track were illuminated with high-tech floodlights and the three riders who sit on the Safety Commission went out to test the idea. Rossi, Roberts and Capirossi circulated on street bikes to test the facilities, and while work needs to be done they didn't rule out the idea.

Loris identified the way a rider sees shadows on his inside going into corners as a big problem: 'You don't know if it is another rider overtaking or just your shadow.' The Suzuka 8 Hours and 24-hour endurance races have used floodlights for years but, as Capirossi points out, 'If you lose three seconds in an endurance race, nobody cares; if you lose three seconds in a Grand Prix...'

Rossi agreed that the overall level of lighting needed improving but he pinpointed the problems in seeing things off the track, like braking markers and marshals' flags, as needing attention. Given the money already spent on what we were told was the best equipment available, installing coloured lights at marshals' posts and illuminated numbers counting the distance to corners wouldn't seem too much to ask. The organisers certainly weren't disheartened and promised to have some improvements ready for another test in 2007.

QATARI GP

LOSAIL

ROUND 2

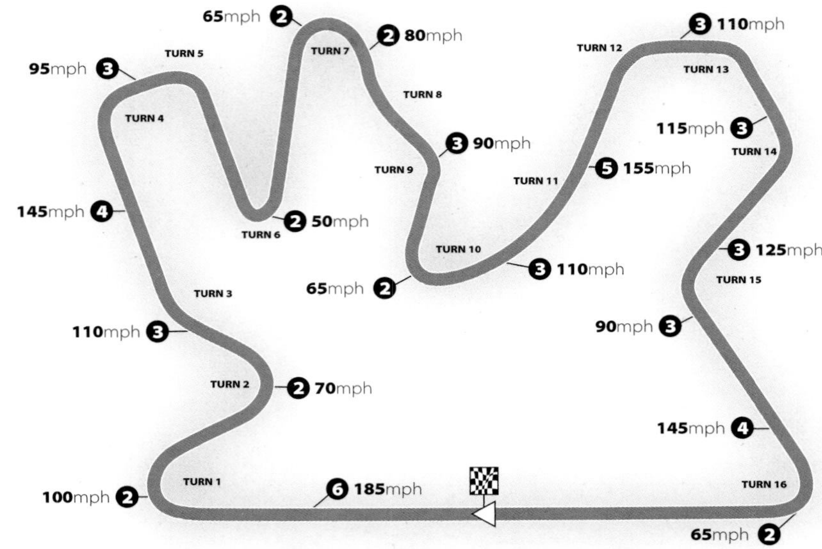

RACE RESULTS

RACE DATE April 8th
CIRCUIT LENGTH 3.343 miles
NO. OF LAPS 22
RACE DISTANCE 73.546 miles
WEATHER Dry, 26°C
TRACK TEMPERATURE 41°C
WINNER Valentino Rossi
FASTEST LAP 1m 57.305s, 102.598mph, Valentino Rossi
PREVIOUS LAP RECORD 1m 56.917s, 102.706mph, Loris Capirossi, 2005

QUALIFYING

	Rider	Nationality	Team	Qualifying	Pole +	Gap
1	Stoner	AUS	Honda LCR	1m 55.683s		
2	Capirossi	ITA	Ducati Marlboro Team	1m 55.721s	0.038s	0.038s
3	Elias	SPA	Fortuna Honda	1m 55.735s	0.052s	0.014s
4	Hayden	USA	Repsol Honda Team	1m 55.793s	0.110s	0.058s
5	Pedrosa	SPA	Repsol Honda Team	1m 56.008s	0.325s	0.215s
6	Rossi	ITA	Camel Yamaha Team	1m 56.076s	0.393s	0.068s
7	Gibernau	SPA	Ducati Marlboro Team	1m 56.177s	0.494s	0.101s
8	Edwards	USA	Camel Yamaha Team	1m 56.230s	0.547s	0.053s
9	Nakano	JPN	Kawasaki Racing Team	1m 56.237s	0.554s	0.007s
10	Roberts	USA	Team Roberts	1m 56.272s	0.589s	0.035s
11	Vermeulen	AUS	Rizla Suzuki MotoGP	1m 56.356s	0.673s	0.084s
12	Melandri	ITA	Fortuna Honda	1m 56.822s	1.139s	0.466s
13	Hopkins	USA	Rizla Suzuki MotoGP	1m 56.981s	1.298s	0.159s
14	Checa	SPA	Tech 3 Yamaha	1m 57.299s	1.616s	0.318s
15	De Puniet	FRA	Kawasaki Racing Team	1m 57.822s	2.139s	0.523s
16	Tamada	JPN	Konica Minolta Honda	1m 57.891s	2.208s	0.069s
17	Ellison	GBR	Tech 3 Yamaha	1m 58.674s	2.991s	0.783s
18	Hofmann	GER	Pramac d'Antin MotoGP	1m 59.591s	3.908s	0.917s
19	Cardoso	SPA	Pramac d'Antin MotoGP	1m 59.733s	4.050s	0.142s

FINISHERS

1 VALENTINO ROSSI Back to winning ways for the first time in four races, and with the fastest lap, to equal Mick Doohan's career total of 54 victories in the top class. Had to deal with a very determined Hayden and, in the final laps, a charging Capirossi. The overwhelming impression was one of relief that his team had rediscovered how to make the M1 work.

2 NICKY HAYDEN Anyone who thought Hayden lacked a little aggression had to think again after this race. It took Rossi at his best to shake him off after a gloves-off dice. Nicky was depressed at coming so close to winning, but to wring such a performance from the development Honda was truly impressive.

3 LORIS CAPIROSSI A stunning result at a track where his Bridgestones simply didn't work at the end of the 2005 season. This time he was able to conserve his tyres and make a late charge up to the leaders, finishing less than 1.5s down on the winner to keep himself at the top of the points table.

4 SETE GIBERNAU Reckoned he was losing half a second a lap with chatter at the left-hand hairpin, the slowest corner on the track. Also disconcerted by the effort needed to keep the Desmosedici in a straight line on the windswept front straight, but it was an impressive way to score his first points for Ducati.

5 CASEY STONER First of the rookies: the remarkable young Aussie started from pole and led the first nine laps of his second MotoGP race despite being unwell and only just arriving at the circuit in time for first practice after lengthy flight delays. Unable to up his pace when the fuel load lightened, as Rossi later noted.

6 DANI PEDROSA Clutch trouble off the start and spray from the Suzuki saw Dani lose over five seconds to the leaders in the opening couple of laps. Having lost touch with the front, he then had a splendid battle with Melandri.

7 MARCO MELANDRI Still unhappy with his chassis, especially on corner entry, but got a good start and then had an entertaining dice with Pedrosa. The Spaniard had more speed on to the straight but Marco was able to outbrake him at

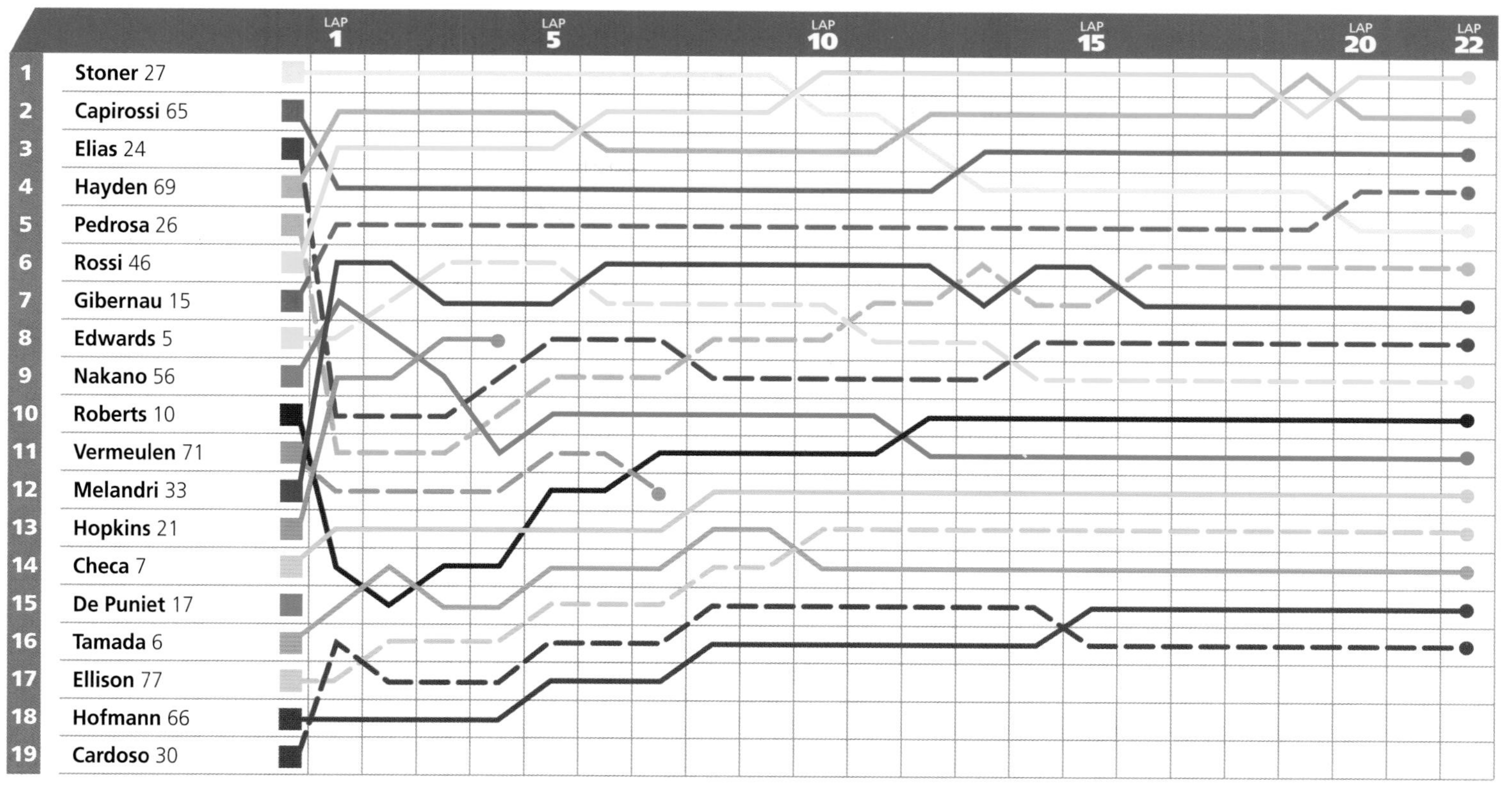

RACE

	Rider	Motorcycle	Race Time	Time +	Fastest Lap	Average Speed
1	Rossi	Yamaha	43m 22.229s		1m 57.305s	101.684mph
2	Hayden	Honda	43m 23.129s	0.900s	1m 57.577s	101.649mph
3	Capirossi	Ducati	43m 23.723s	1.494s	1m 57.648s	101.625mph
4	Gibernau	Ducati	43m 26.867s	4.638s	1m 57.523s	101.503mph
5	Stoner	Honda	43m 29.804s	7.575s	1m 57.777s	101.389mph
6	Pedrosa	Honda	43m 33.049s	10.820s	1m 57.381s	101.263mph
7	Melandri	Honda	43m 34.013s	11.784s	1m 57.881s	101.225mph
8	Elias	Honda	43m 41.710s	19.481s	1m 57.758s	100.928mph
9	Edwards	Yamaha	43m 45.149s	22.920s	1m 57.640s	100.796mph
10	Roberts	KR11V	43m 56.515s	34.286s	1m 58.202s	100.361mph
11	Nakano	Kawasaki	43m 57.545s	35.316s	1m 58.913s	100.322mph
12	Checa	Yamaha	44m 11.474s	49.245s	1m 58.785s	99.795mph
13	Ellison	Yamaha	44m 23.698s	1m 01.469s	1m 59.388s	99.338mph
14	Tamada	Honda	44m 33.007s	1m 10.778s	1m 59.640s	98.991mph
15	Hofmann	Ducati	44m 44.280s	1m 22.051s	2m 00.367s	98.576mph
16	Cardoso	Ducati	44m 56.047s	1m 33.818s	2m 00.722s	98.145mph
	Vermeulen	Suzuki	14m 08.367s	15 laps	1m 58.824s	99.241mph
	Hopkins	Suzuki	8m 04.022s	18 laps	1m 58.765s	99.396mph
	De Puniet	Kawasaki				

CHAMPIONSHIP

	Rider	Team	Points
1	Capirossi	Ducati Marlboro Team	41
2	Hayden	Repsol Honda Team	36
3	Pedrosa	Repsol Honda Team	30
4	Rossi	Camel Yamaha Team	27
5	Elias	Fortuna Honda	21
6	Stoner	Honda LCR	21
7	Melandri	Fortuna Honda	20
8	Nakano	Kawasaki Racing Team	14
9	Roberts	Team Roberts	14
10	Gibernau	Ducati Marlboro Team	13
11	Edwards	Camel Honda Team	12
12	Tamada	Konica Minolta Honda	8
13	Hopkins	Rizla Suzuki MotoGP	7
14	Checa	Tech 3 Yamaha	7
15	Vermeulen	Rizla Suzuki MotoGP	4
16	Ellison	Tech 3 Yamaha	3
17	Hofmann	Pramac d'Antin MotoGP	2

Turn 1. Made a mistake on the final lap, but a good result after difficult practice and qualifying.

8 TONI ELIAS Paid the price for a bad start after qualifying on the front row for the first time in his MotoGP career. Caught up behind Hopkins and slowed when his visor was covered in what he presumed to be oil. Very disappointed not to have backed up his third place on the grid.

9 COLIN EDWARDS Incandescently angry after the race and refused to speak to journalists for the first time anyone could remember. Happy until lap six when he lost the front three times in consecutive corners and nearly crashed each time. His last race lap was three seconds slower than in the simulation he ran in practice. There was speculation he was using the new, wider Michelin for the first time.

10 KENNY ROBERTS Still making big changes to base settings in practice, and another rider to be hampered by the leaking Suzuki early on. Also got boxed in at the first corner.

11 SHINYA NAKANO The Doha track has never been kind to Kawasaki and, sure enough, Team Green experienced problems all weekend getting the power down. Shinya nearly salvaged a top-ten finish with a superb start to be fourth into Turn 1 (off the third row!) but found other riders could simply drive by him even on the short back straight.

12 CARLOS CHECA Hampered by de Puniet's crash, the gusting wind and his injured shoulder from Jerez, but a more encouraging race than the season opener for rider, team and their tyre manufacturer, Dunlop.

13 JAMES ELLISON Hugely relieved to score points after the nightmare of Jerez. Delighted to have caught, overtaken and escaped from Tamada on a Honda V5, but was stuck behind the Japanese rider for longer than he'd have liked. Also caught up in the de Puniet crash.

14 MAKOTO TAMADA A rider with his confidence at an all-time low. Tested after Jerez and found a tyre he liked only to be highsided while using it right at the end of the day. As Ellison later reported, Makoto's corner entry was tentative in the extreme.

15 ALEX HOFMANN Got a good start only to be forced off track when de Puniet crashed on the first lap. The flying Kawasaki actually brushed Alex's helmet, and it took five laps for him to stop being blazing mad. Happy with another point, but thought he could have beaten the other Dunlop runners.

16 JOSE LUIS CARDOSO Happy in the early laps but hit problems before mid-distance. Consoled himself with a finish and collecting useful data.

NON-FINISHERS

CHRIS VERMEULEN Lost time when de Puniet crashed, then got past Roberts only to be caught in his team-mate's fluid leak. Three laps later Chris pulled in with the same problem. The bike overheated when a plastic impeller shaft failed.

JOHN HOPKINS Going like a train when yet another mechanical problem stopped his Suzuki (it was overheating like his team-mate's bike due to the shaft that carries the coolant impeller failing). Gave his machine a good kicking when it came to a rest, but his team-manager refused to criticise him after such a disastrous weekend.

RANDY DE PUNIET Crashed on the first lap and nearly took a few others down too. Fortunately unhurt, but the bike was too badly damaged for him to continue.

TURKISH GP
ISTANBUL

ROUND 3

Thanks to variable weather in qualifying, we had a mixed-up grid and an unpredictable race. The result was a fabulous fighting win for Marco Melandri on what's already proving to be a classic track

Anyone who thought the trends set by the first two races of the year – Rossi's set-up problems and the competitiveness of the rookies – were mere blips that would be ironed out as the season unfolded had to think again after Istanbul. Once again Valentino couldn't use his qualifiers and ended up nearer the back of the grid than the front, while Casey Stoner came within a fifth of a second of winning a MotoGP race at his third attempt. Just to add to the mix, the Suzukis both came good, with Vermeulen dominating wet qualifying and Hopkins running at the front of the race until he hit tyre problems. The 'tuning' Hopper performed with his boot in Qatar had obviously worked.

The mixed weather on Friday and Saturday turned the grid upside-down, with Melandri and Pedrosa starting on the fifth and sixth rows respectively, while Rossi lined up on the fourth. Randy de Puniet qualified in front of team-mate Nakano and Gibernau was ahead of Capirossi. Not normal. The result was three storming rides through the field, but only after Gibernau had reminded us how good he can be and Hopkins had displayed his talent. Both men suffered from the performance of their Bridgestones dropping off precipitately mid-race, which the tyre company blamed on lack of dry-weather track time. They had to content themselves with Vermeulen's stunning pole.

Above Yet another rookie shone in qualifying – Chris Vermeulen put his Suzuki on pole

Opposite Valentino Rossi had a tough time in his 100th MotoGP start – not even a rostrum finish

Below This isn't the 125 race: Gibernau leads with Melandri, Pedrosa and Hayden in close attendance; Stoner waits his turn

No-one spent longer in the lead than Gibernau, but at the half-way point he was shuffled from the front to the back of the five-man leading group in one lap, and next time round Hopkins came in to change his rear tyre. That left an all-Honda fight at the front, and it was a real battle. Istanbul Park gives riders more passing opportunities than all the other new tracks put together, and Melandri, Stoner, Pedrosa and Hayden used every one. Even the left/right/left double chicane that ends the lap manages to be interesting. In fact, it's so wide that a rider passed on the brakes in the first left has ample opportunity to take his revenge before getting on to the main straight. 'It was a wild race,' said Nicky Hayden, echoing just about everyone's thoughts and again speaking for the whole grid when he added, 'Nobody was doing any bone-headed stuff.'

Melandri's ride to the front was eclipsed only by Pedrosa's. The Italian made up nine places in the first two laps, the Spaniard seven; Marco took the lead for the first time on lap 11, Dani a lap later. The lack of dry track time and paucity of data should have given the advantage to the much more experienced Melandri but, apart from revisiting his aquaphobia in qualifying, Pedrosa had no machinery problems. Much credit is due to his Austrian race engineer, Mike Leitner, who'd come up to MotoGP with Dani after running his pit crew in the 250cc class.

Valentino Rossi didn't make such an instant impact. He'd observed the first-corner pile-up in the 250 race and decided to take a precautionary inside line. The tactic got him boxed in, however, and although he immediately regained more than a few places, on lap two he ran off track and started the third lap seven

46
TEAM
YAMAHA
agv
TRIBU DEI CHIHUAHUA
MOTUL YAMAHA
ÖHLINS

THE FRAME GAME

Above Jerry Burgess contemplates the vices of the M1 Yamaha's chassis

Now there was no disguising it – the 2006 Yamaha M1 had a serious problem and not even the combined talents of Valentino Rossi and Jerry Burgess's crew could sort it out. The culprit looked to be the new chassis, which was prone to chatter on both new and worn tyres. In fact, it seemed to behave better the less grip there was. At Istanbul, James Ellison managed to talk to Rossi and Edwards about it and discovered that, like him, they wanted the '05 frame back. It was altogether more forgiving, allowing the bike to push and slide and generally be ridden loose into a corner. The new model reacted badly to such tactics and didn't allow any gradual sliding: it didn't give any feedback and would snap back without any warning. Unfortunately, the 2006 M1 engine wouldn't fit into the '05 chassis.

There was also the matter of the new, wider Michelin front tyre. Every Michelin runner had now raced the new design except Valentino Rossi, who preferred the old slim-line tyre both because it was a known quantity and because, while it might give less grip, it was more precise. It was thought that Edwards' problems in the Qatar race stemmed from using the wide tyre.

While the team was usually able to give Valentino a decent race set-up, they had so far been unable to give him a bike that could use the grip of a qualifying tyre, with the result that he had yet to make it on to the front row of the grid in 2006. The test session on the Monday after the Turkish GP resulted in some modifications being put in train, but they wouldn't be available for the next race – a 'flyaway' in China. They were promised for the first round of the European season at Le Mans, in three weeks' time.

seconds down on the leaders. That, he said later, was the end of his chance of a rostrum place. Nevertheless, he fought back to fourth and did his personal best lap of the race last time round. He was shadowed all the way by Toni Elias, who set the fastest lap of the race on the penultimate lap, and who was moved to applaud the Doctor for his riding on the slow-down lap. 'I have the only bike which is better on used tyres than new ones,' Rossi half-joked afterwards. It was now clear that Yamaha had a serious problem and much hope was invested in the test day scheduled for the Monday after the race.

Rossi's pace could have put him on the podium, but the man who assuredly could have won this race was Pedrosa. He was a close third coming to the end of the penultimate lap but made a mistake braking for the final chicane; he immediately tried to get some ground back but folded the front at the first corner of the last lap. Dani got back on again to salvage a couple of points, but was seriously upset with himself for crashing both in the race and in practice: 'Two mistakes and two crashes – this is a lot for me!' The Spanish rider is a perfectionist in the true sense of the word, for he simply detests making mistakes. His team-mate Hayden inherited third place and revealed that his race had been disrupted by a juddering brake thanks to a tyre warmer melting on to a disc on the grid. Nicky dropped off the leaders in the closing stages and was almost caught by the Rossi/Elias double act, so the last-lap duel was between Melandri and Stoner.

Like Pedrosa, Stoner had cause to regret his practice crashes – two of them at the end of the back straight. They'd made him slightly unsure in the last sector of the track, and Marco took advantage. Coming down the top-gear hill to the braking zone for the final chicane, the Italian was able to take the inside line into the left-hander and then drop his bike over the Aussie's nose in the right-hander. Casey admitted that he'd been a little wary at that point on the track, and he knew Marco would make a move there, but he was far from disappointed with a rostrum finish in only his third MotoGP race. He did feel the need to remind some people about what they'd said after Qatar, about his not being so good on worn tyres. Stoner pointed out he'd been with the leaders for the whole race and led the last four-and-three-quarter laps under pressure from two other Hondas, which tended to suggest he knew what he was doing on worn tyres. Qatar, he maintained, had been down to his physical condition. It was exactly the sort of feisty rejoinder to be expected from an Aussie in any sport, and given extra edge by the fact that the originator of the opinion was Valentino Rossi.

During the meeting a rumour surfaced that MotoGP would not be returning to Istanbul Park. In two years the track has provided brilliant racing in all classes and this time there was an encouraging crowd of nearly 40,000 to watch it. It isn't just Marco Melandri, winner of both the Turkish GPs held so far, who hopes the rumour is false.

Above left Casey Stoner again led a race but this time he got to stand on the rostrum as well

Right Marco Melandri celebrates two wins out of two at the Istanbul Park circuit

TURKISH GP
ISTANBUL

ROUND 3

TURN 9
TURN 8
TURN 7
TURN 6
TURN 5
TURN 4
TURN 3
TURN 2
TURN 1
TURN 10
TURN 11
TURN 12
TURN 13
5 165mph
2 100mph
60mph 2
2 55mph
3 135mph
3 105mph
95mph 4
165mph 5
2 65mph
150mph 5
160mph 5
2 50mph
180mph 6
45mph 1
105mph 3
1 50mph
3 60mph
50mph 2
5 170mph

RACE RESULTS

RACE DATE April 30th
CIRCUIT LENGTH 3.311 miles
NO. OF LAPS 22
RACE DISTANCE 72.838 miles
WEATHER Dry, 16°C
TRACK TEMPERATURE 21°C
WINNER Marco Melandri
FASTEST LAP 1m 52.877s, 105.830mph, Toni Elias (record)
PREVIOUS LAP RECORD 1m 53.111s, 105.373mph, Marco Melandri, 2005

QUALIFYING

	Rider	Nationality	Team	Qualifying	Pole +	Gap
1	Vermeulen	AUS	Rizla Suzuki MotoGP	2m 04.617s		
2	Hayden	USA	Repsol Honda Team	2m 04.823s	0.206s	0.206s
3	Gibernau	SPA	Ducati Marlboro Team	2m 05.003s	0.386s	0.180s
4	Capirossi	ITA	Ducati Marlboro Team	2m 05.540s	0.923s	0.537s
5	Hopkins	USA	Rizla Suzuki MotoGP	2m 05.700s	1.083s	0.160s
6	De Puniet	FRA	Kawasaki Racing Team	2m 06.102s	1.485s	0.402s
7	Stoner	AUS	Honda LCR	2m 07.277s	2.660s	1.175s
8	Nakano	JPN	Kawasaki Racing Team	2m 07.294s	2.677s	0.017s
9	Edwards	USA	Camel Yamaha Honda	2m 07.344s	2.727s	0.050s
10	Roberts	USA	Team Roberts	2m 07.345s	2.728s	0.001s
11	Rossi	ITA	Camel Yamaha Team	2m 07.552s	2.935s	0.207s
12	Elias	SPA	Fortuna Honda	2m 07.763s	3.146s	0.211s
13	Tamada	JPN	Konica Minolta Honda	2m 08.143s	3.526s	0.380s
14	Melandri	ITA	Fortuna Honda	2m 08.393s	3.776s	0.250s
15	Checa	SPA	Tech 3 Yamaha	2m 10.322s	5.705s	1.929s
16	Pedrosa	SPA	Repsol Honda Team	2m 10.956s	6.339s	0.634s
17	Hofmann	GER	Pramac d'Antin MotoGP	2m 11.241s	6.624s	0.285s
18	Cardoso	SPA	Pramac d'Antin MotoGP	2m 11.456s	6.839s	0.215s
19	Ellison	GBR	Tech 3 Yamaha	2m 12.298s	7.681s	0.842s

FINISHERS

1 MARCO MELANDRI A fine, hard-fought victory and the first by a Honda rider in any class of GP racing in 2006. It was also Marco's third win in the last five races, his second at the Istanbul Park track and, even more remarkably, he came from 14th place on the grid.

2 CASEY STONER Despite two practice crashes Casey was fastest in one dry session and always in contention for the win. Became the youngest Australian rider ever to stand on the podium of racing's top class, taking that honour from Darryl Beattie, and proving to anyone who ever doubted it he could ride on worn tyres.

3 NICKY HAYDEN Leading the championship for the first time after his seventh successive rostrum in his 50th start in MotoGP, but any chance of victory went when his tyre warmer melted on to a brake disc on the grid and dented Nicky's confidence in the stoppers.

4 VALENTINO ROSSI Unable to celebrate his 100th start in 500cc/MotoGP with a rostrum, never mind a win, although he did become the leading all-time points scorer. Boxed in at the first turn after another lacklustre qualifying session, then ran off track on the second lap. Passed seven rivals during an inspired charge back to the front of the field, lapping at the same pace as the leaders.

5 TONI ELIAS Set his first fastest lap of a MotoGP race as he shadowed Rossi's charge through the field. Tried a pass on the last lap but couldn't make it stick: fulsome in his praise of the champion after the race. Dissatisfied with his pace in the early laps so far this season.

6 LORIS CAPIROSSI Lost his championship lead but was first Bridgestone runner again, as he has been in every race so far this year. His race didn't live up to the promise of practice and qualifying mainly because the mixed conditions curtailed testing of dry-weather rubber.

7 CHRIS VERMEULEN First pole position in his fifth MotoGP race, and the first for Suzuki since Rio in 2004. After the disaster

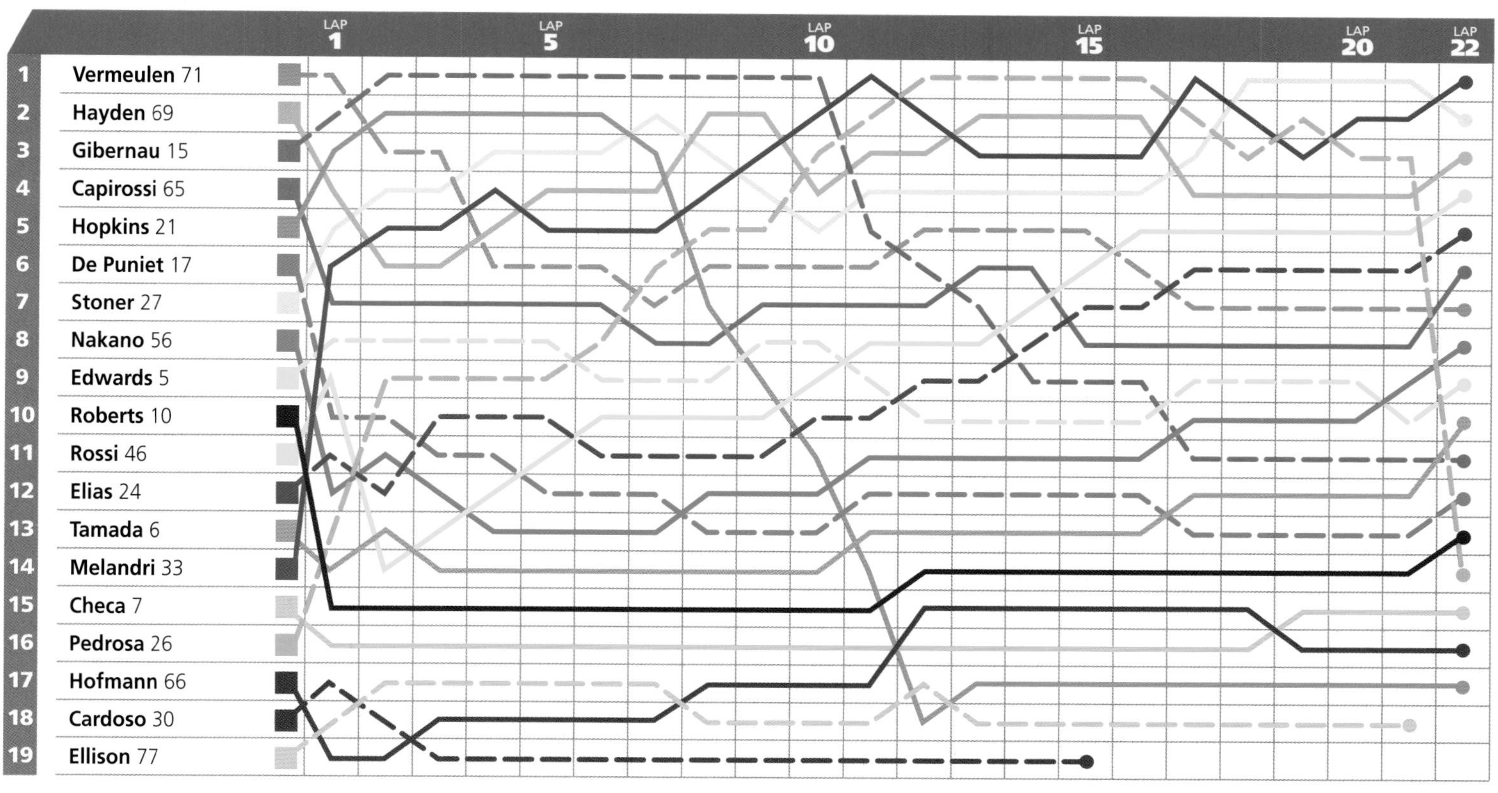

RACE

	Rider	Motorcycle	Race Time	Time +	Fastest Lap	Average Speed
1	Melandri	Honda	41m 54.065s		1m 53.261s	104.467mph
2	Stoner	Honda	41m 54.265s	0.200s	1m 53.274s	104.459mph
3	Hayden	Honda	41m 59.523s	5.458s	1m 53.473s	104.241mph
4	Rossi	Yamaha	42m 00.274s	6.209s	1m 53.238s	104.210mph
5	Elias	Honda	42m 00.652s	6.587s	1m 52.877s	104.194mph
6	Capirossi	Ducati	42m 10.747s	16.682s	1m 54.365s	103.778mph
7	Vermeulen	Suzuki	42m 10.842s	16.777s	1m 54.151s	103.775mph
8	Nakano	Kawasaki	42m 15.602s	21.537s	1m 54.523s	103.578mph
9	Edwards	Yamaha	42m 16.912s	22.847s	1m 54.513s	103.526mph
10	Tamada	Honda	42m 24.548s	30.483s	1m 54.896s	103.217mph
11	Gibernau	Ducati	42m 24.608s	30.543s	1m 53.909s	103.213mph
12	De Puniet	Kawasaki	42m 28.349s	34.284s	1m 54.610s	103.062mph
13	Roberts	KR211V	42m 39.177s	45.112s	1m 55.476s	102.626mph
14	Pedrosa	Honda	42m 47.590s	53.525s	1m 53.305s	102.289mph
15	Checa	Yamaha	42m 53.920s	59.855s	1m 56.018s	102.036mph
16	Hofmann	Ducati	42m 55.306s	1m 01.241s	1m 56.149s	101.983mph
17	Hopkins	Suzuki	43m 32.693s	1m 38.628s	1m 53.978s	100.527mph
18	Ellison	Yamaha	43m 27.080s	1 lap	1m 56.686s	96.161mph
	Cardoso	Ducati	42m 25.898s	7 laps	1m 57.275s	70.337mph

CHAMPIONSHIP

	Rider	Team	Points
1	Hayden	Repsol Honda Team	52
2	Capirossi	Ducati Marlboro Team	51
3	Melandri	Fortuna Honda	45
4	Stoner	Honda LCR	41
5	Rossi	Camel Yamaha Team	40
6	Pedrosa	Repsol Honda Team	32
7	Elias	Fortuna Honda	32
8	Nakano	Kawasaki Racing Team	22
9	Edwards	Camel Yamaha Team	19
10	Gibernau	Ducati Marlboro Team	18
11	Roberts	Team Roberts	17
12	Tamada	Konica Minolta Honda	14
13	Vermeulen	Rizla Suzuki MotoGP	13
14	Checa	Tech 3 Yamaha	8
15	Hopkins	Rizla Suzuki MotoGP	7
16	De Puniet	Kawasaki Racing Team	4
17	Ellison	Tech 3 Yamaha	3
18	Hofmann	Pramac d'Antin MotoGP	2

of Qatar this was a major step forward for rider, team and factory. Only lost out on sixth on the last lap when he and Capirossi swapped places several times.

8 SHINYA NAKANO Also handicapped by lack of dry testing but found a tyre that went the distance and allowed him to lap consistently enough to outbrake Edwards a lap and a half from the flag. Not exactly happy with eighth, but realistic enough to admit the result exceeded his expectations after practice.

9 COLIN EDWARDS One of those weekends when he never figured at the fast end of the field: Colin was starting to get very frustrated about his and the team's inability to get the M1 set up. One bright spot in an otherwise depressing meeting was out-qualifying his team-mate for only the second time since he joined Yamaha.

10 MAKOTO TAMADA Another weekend in which he was almost invisible. Still unable to find a set-up he felt comfortable with and only made it into the top ten on the last lap after Pedrosa crashed in the final stages and he caught a grip-free Gibernau.

11 SETE GIBERNAU Led the first ten laps in fine style before his rear tyre's performance dropped off dramatically. Reported feeling a vibration as early as lap four and considered pitting for a new tyre, but decided to plug on for any points he could get.

12 RANDY DE PUNIET Out-qualified his team-mate, raced with him and Tamada in the early stages, then tried to follow Nakano but made a mistake passing a slowing Hopkins and lost touch. Happy and relieved to finish a MotoGP race for the first time and to score points.

13 KENNY ROBERTS Still experimenting with radical adjustments to chassis settings and so seriously handicapped by the lack of dry time in practice and qualifying.

14 DANI PEDROSA Suffered in wet qualifying so only started from 16th yet led after early leader Gibernau faded with tyre problems. Held the lead for five laps – only Sete led for more. Started the last lap in third but crashed going into the first corner. Picked the bike up to salvage a couple of points.

15 CARLOS CHECA Lost the front on the third lap and ran off track, then lost the rear. Realised his set-up was all at sea, so established a rhythm that he thought would conserve his tyres. Judged the situation well, set his fastest lap on the 20th of 22 laps and snared the last point.

16 ALEX HOFMANN Given that all the Dunlop runners had a weekend to forget, finishing two seconds behind Checa has to be considered a decent ride. Asked Dunlop to give him tyres developed for the Ducati as opposed to the Yamaha.

17 JOHN HOPKINS Ran second to early leader Gibernau before his tyres went off at one-third distance. Forced to pit and change wheels but not before he had demonstrated how far Suzuki had come since the Qatar disaster three weeks earlier.

18 JAMES ELLISON After the promise of Qatar it was back to the pain of Jerez. Never got near a usable set-up and had to pit for a change of rear tyre.

NON-FINISHERS

JOSE LUIS CARDOSO Sent back to the pits by electrical problems and took the chance to change tyres. However, the work took so long that he didn't complete the number of laps necessary to be classified as a finisher.

CHINESE GP
SHANGHAI
ROUND 4

VICTORY – AND SOON!

Pedrosa took the win in only his fourth MotoGP outing to make it four different winners in the first four races. Rossi suffered a tyre failure...

The Spanish magazine *Solo Moto* revived the Castroist slogan from the Cuban revolution, *Hasta la victoria siempre!*, usually translated as 'Victory and Soon!', and put it on their T-shirts, but with Dani Pedrosa's face superimposed on that iconic image of Che Guevara. Did even the most fervent Catalan supporter think the MotoGP rookie's maiden win would come this quickly? Pedrosa's race victory was impressive enough, coming as it did after an exchange of lap records with his team-mate, the championship leader Nicky Hayden, but to do it from pole position as well as setting the fastest lap marked this as a very special achievement indeed.

The victory had all the hallmarks of Pedrosa's 125 and 250cc career. He wasn't panicked by a mistake at the first corner, after Hopkins went up the inside and pushed him wide; he worked his way to the front, took the lead just before half-distance and was never headed again, although he was shadowed throughout by his team-mate. Hayden had nearly as bad a start but he got behind Dani half-way round the second lap, and from

then until the chequered flag they were never separated by much more than a second. The young Spaniard set a new record two laps after he hit the front, then two laps later Nicky put in back-to-back lap records but only closed the gap by a little over a tenth of a second. Another two laps and Nicky gave it his best shot, closing the gap to half a second: that was on lap 18 of 22. In another flashback to his two-stroke days, Pedrosa responded immediately with the fastest lap of the race and raised the gap to over a second. It was the decisive moment of the race, an astonishingly mature display but totally in character for this amazing racer.

Dani did manage to look excited when he crossed the line but afterwards he seemed more surprised than delighted. He'd been surprised to be on pole as well, because he reckoned it was the first time he'd been quick on qualifiers; he refused to get excited about that either, pointing out that Casey Stoner had been on pole in only his second MotoGP outing and this was the fourth round. That's typical Pedrosa as well.

Nicky Hayden didn't look happy about being beaten by his team-mate again, but he did allow that Dani deserved credit for not cracking under the pressure. 'I kept going faster and faster,' said the American, 'trying to put some heat on him. He rode a really strong race.' Nicky had to content himself with an increased lead at the top of the points table and the first Repsol Honda one–two finish since Rossi and Ukawa at Barcelona in 2002. The race was watched by Takeo Fukui, the President and CEO of Honda, who managed to fit in a visit to Shanghai after the opening of Honda's first plant in China. It was also viewed by 60,000 fans back home in Barcelona, watching at the Catalunya circuit. They were actually there for the F1 GP, but the organisers opened the gates early and laid on breakfast for those who wanted to follow the MotoGP race on the track's 23 giant screens before cheering another local hero, Fernando Alonso, on to victory.

The Repsol Honda team's dominant performance came after another two days of mixed weather that saw only Saturday morning's session completely dry. The first 20 minutes of qualifying were also lost to rain. Once again Valentino Rossi was the main victim of these circumstances. The dreaded chatter returned, at the same level as during Jerez and on three-quarters

Above No bias in the Spanish media! *Solo Moto* magazine's crew show where their loyalty lies

Opposite Sete Gibernau demonstrating the efficacy of Ducati's traction control and Bridgestone's wet-weather grip

Below Valentino Rossi was closing in on fourth-placed John Hopkins and the much-improved Suzuki when he hit tyre problems

Above Makoto Tamada had his best race for a long time, bashing fairings with the Ducatis and Nakano

Below Colin Edwards led until the Repsol Hondas came past, then fended off a feisty John Hopkins

of the corners. The team's test after the Turkish GP was thought to have solved the problem, but new parts wouldn't be ready until the next race, in France. However, Colin Edwards was able to put his Yamaha on the front row for only the second time. The Texan credited Rossi with solving a lot of his problems at the Turkish test but he decided to go his own way with set-up as copying the Doc's settings hadn't done him much good so far in 2006. Colin promptly led the race for the first nine laps before the Repsols came past him 'like a freight train'. Edwards was also dealing with chatter, and managing it limited his pace. It looked as if his third spot on the rostrum might be under threat from his team-mate, but for the second time in four races the Rossi luck ran out.

The man whose luck looked to have taken a turn for the better was John Hopkins. Istanbul wasn't a fluke. Hopper put the Suzuki on the front row and glued himself to the back of Edwards' M1 for most of the race. It was undoubtedly John's best outing since he'd come to GPs. The Suzuki was still obviously down on ultimate top speed, but the American made up for that with such bravery on the brakes and breathtaking corner entry speed that he didn't appear to be losing out down the kilometre-long straight. He only gave up on third place four laps from the flag but it was noticeable that his Bridgestone tyres stayed with him for the whole distance, Hopkins even reporting that he had more edge grip than Edwards.

Colin's first podium since Laguna Seca in 2005 was Camel Yamaha's only bright spot of the weekend. As part of their experiments to deal with the chatter, Rossi raced with the new, wider Michelin front tyre for the first time. It looked like it was working – he was able to make his way through the field and it seemed as if third place was well within his grasp – but then his bike shed its front mudguard on the big straight. Valentino felt the vibration but assumed it was his rear tyre that had lost some tread. He entered pit lane, pointing at the back of his bike, and the crew duly changed the back wheel. One mechanic had spotted the missing mudguard but was told there was no need to replace it. As soon as he left the pits Rossi realised the problem was still there and cruised round to retire five laps from the end. Michelin's subsequent analysis revealed the front tyre was faulty.

DANI BY NUMBERS

Pedrosa's victory in only his fourth MotoGP race made him the joint second-youngest winner ever in the top class. Only Freddie Spencer (winning at Spa in 1982) was younger while Norick Abe was exactly the same age, to the day, when he won at Suzuka in 1996. It made Dani the youngest rider to win in three classes of GP racing; the man from whom he took that distinction was Mike Hailwood. The Spaniard is also the youngest rider ever to win three world titles – and this time the previous holder of that honour was Valentino Rossi.

Dani's 250 career saw him become the youngest ever race winner, the youngest ever World Champion and the youngest ever to take back-to-back titles in that class. His first 250 win, at Welkom in 2004, also made him the youngest ever rider to have won GPs in two separate classes. It was the first time a reigning 125cc World Champion had won the first race of the 250 season since Bill Ivy in 1968, and Pedrosa's first 250 title made him the first 125 champion to take the 250 crown since Carlo Ubbiali back in 1960.

Pedrosa's career statistics, at 20 years of age, outshine even those of Valentino Rossi and mark him out as a very special talent indeed. Which makes it even more amazing that he was discovered through a radio and press campaign to find young riders for a one-make championship with the ultimate prize of a place in a 125cc GP team. Pedrosa never won the Telefonica Movistar Cup but the man who organised it, and is now his manager, Alberto Puig, decided that whatever happened the youngster would go to the GPs. Puig's latest protégé is the Oxfordshire teenager Bradley Smith, who made his debut in 125 GPs this season.

CHINESE GP

SHANGHAI

ROUND 4

TURN 1
TURN 2
TURN 4
1 50mph
TURN 5
4 155mph
TURN 3
180mph 5
1 50mph
130mph 4
TURN 6
1 45mph
TURN 7
4 95mph
TURN 8
55mph 2
2 75mph
TURN 12
TURN 9
80mph 2
50mph 1
TURN 13
130mph 3
TURN 16
TURN 15
2 70mph
TURN 10
4 145mph
TURN 11
35mph 1
3 80mph
TURN 14
6 195mph

RACE RESULTS

RACE DATE May 14th
CIRCUIT LENGTH 3.281 miles
NO. OF LAPS 22
RACE DISTANCE 72.182 miles
WEATHER Dry, 31°C
TRACK TEMPERATURE 26°C
WINNER Dani Pedrosa
FASTEST LAP 1m 59.318s, 99.011mph, Dani Pedrosa (record)
PREVIOUS LAP RECORD 2m 13.716s, 88.150mph, Alex Barros, 2005

QUALIFYING

	Rider	Nationality	Team	Qualifying	Pole +	Gap
1	Pedrosa	SPA	Repsol Honda Team	1m 59.009s		
2	Hopkins	USA	Rizla Suzuki MotoGP	1m 59.373s	0.364s	0.364s
3	Edwards	USA	Camel Yamaha Team	1m 59.383s	0.374s	0.010s
4	Nakano	JPN	Kawasaki Racing Team	1m 59.570s	0.561s	0.187s
5	Hayden	USA	Repsol Honda Team	1m 59.574s	0.565s	0.004s
6	Gibernau	SPA	Ducati Marlboro Team	1m 59.639s	0.630s	0.065s
7	Stoner	AUS	Honda LCR	1m 59.890s	0.881s	0.251s
8	Melandri	ITA	Fortuna Honda	2m 00.014s	1.005s	0.124s
9	De Puniet	FRA	Kawasaki Racing Team	2m 00.044s	1.035s	0.030s
10	Capirossi	ITA	Ducati Marlboro Team	2m 00.078s	1.069s	0.034s
11	Tamada	JPN	Konica Minolta Honda	2m 00.176s	1.167s	0.098s
12	Vermeulen	AUS	Rizla Suzuki MotoGP	2m 00.304s	1.295s	0.128s
13	Rossi	ITA	Camel Yamaha Team	2m 00.720s	1.711s	0.416s
14	Checa	SPA	Tech 3 Yamaha	2m 01.052s	2.043s	0.332s
15	Elias	SPA	Fortuna Honda	2m 01.275s	2.266s	0.223s
16	Hofmann	GER	Pramac d'Antin MotoGP	2m 01.972s	2.963s	0.697s
17	Ellison	GBR	Tech 3 Yamaha	2m 02.088s	3.079s	0.116s
18	Roberts	USA	Team Roberts	2m 02.311s	3.302s	0.223s
19	Cardoso	SPA	Pramac d'Antin MotoGP	2m 02.948s	3.939s	0.637s

FINISHERS

1 DANI PEDROSA All the firsts in one race: pole (he'd not managed the front row before), fastest lap and race win – just like he did in 250s, letting a challenger within range, then pushing again to demoralise the opposition. The victory made him the youngest rider ever to win in all three GP classes, taking that record from Mike Hailwood.

2 NICKY HAYDEN Gracious enough to admit he gave it his best shot and came up short, but at least extended his run of consecutive podiums to eight. Fifth in qualifying was Nicky's worst grid position since Qatar 2005. Extended his championship lead to 13 points but didn't look at all happy being beaten by his new team-mate.

3 COLIN EDWARDS First rostrum of the year, and first since Laguna Seca 2005. Led for nine laps, off only the second front-row start of his MotoGP career, until the Repsol Hondas went past together. Fended off Hopkins in the closing stages thanks to making his own choice of tyre rather than following Rossi's ideas.

4 JOHN HOPKINS His best ride and his best result in MotoGP. Worked so hard going into corners and on the brakes to make up for lack of ultimate top speed that he didn't lose ground on the longest straight in the MotoGP calendar. Ran the whole race at the front and proved that the Hopper/Bridgestone/Suzuki package is ready for the rostrum – at least.

5 CASEY STONER Another remarkable ride that included an off-track excursion on lap 15, then came back from 11th to fifth place in just three laps. Earlier he'd been held up behind Gibernau and then had rear grip problems but, as Casey noted, so did all the other Hondas except the factory bikes that finished first and second.

6 MAKOTO TAMADA A welcome return to form and his best result since taking third in Japan in 2005 – not a bad way to celebrate his 50th MotoGP start. Involved in the entertaining race-long brawl that included the Ducatis, Melandri and Stoner.

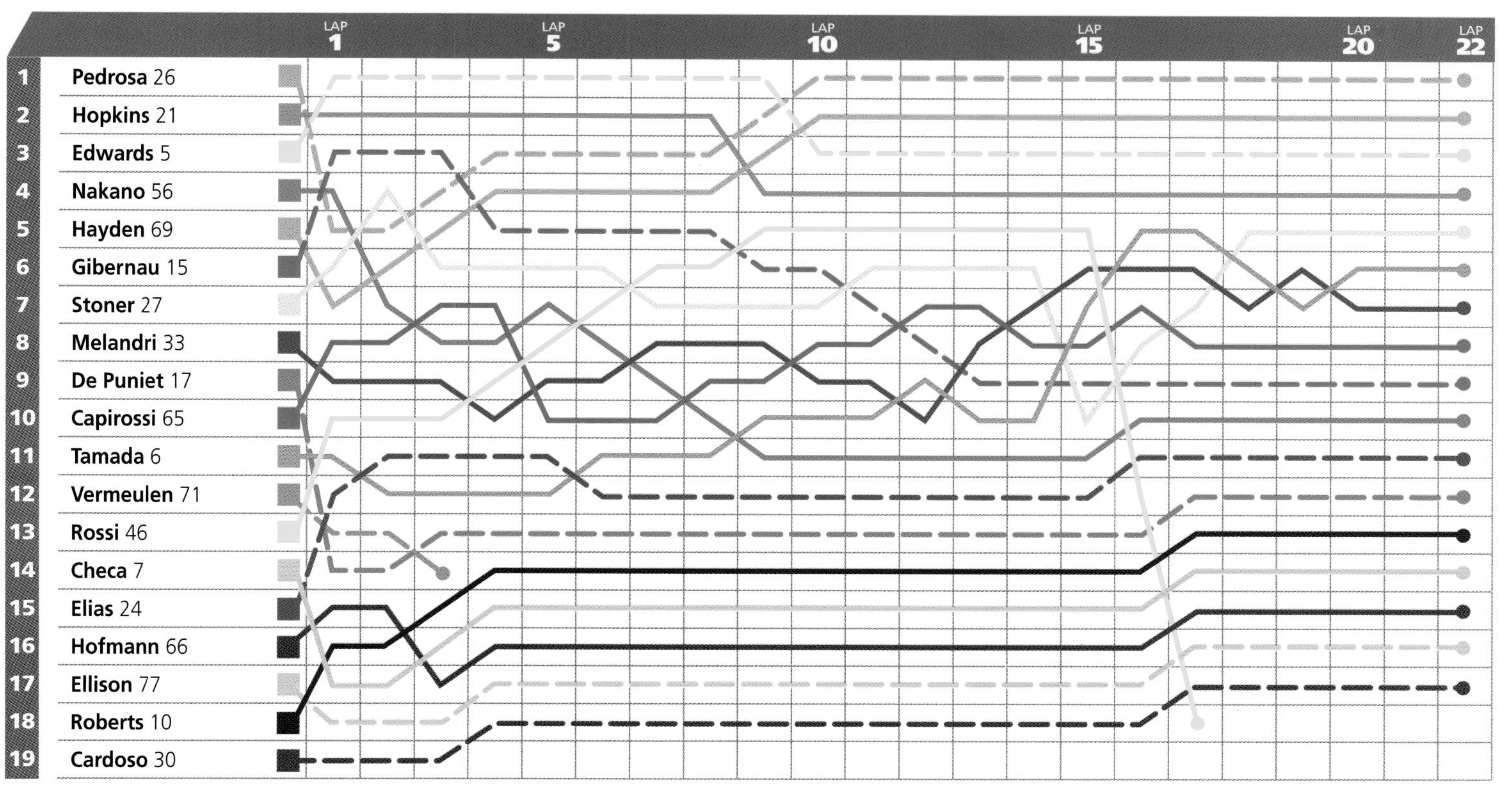

RACE

	Rider	Motorcycle	Race Time	Time +	Fastest Lap	Average Speed
1	Pedrosa	Honda	44m 07.734s		1m 59.318s	98.097mph
2	Hayden	Honda	44m 09.239s	1.505s	1m 59.474s	98.042mph
3	Edwards	Yamaha	44m 22.368s	14.634s	2m 00.469s	97.558mph
4	Hopkins	Suzuki	44m 26.999s	19.265s	2m 00.474s	97.389mph
5	Stoner	Honda	44m 30.795s	23.061s	2m 00.333s	97.250mph
6	Tamada	Honda	44m 31.613s	23.879s	2m 00.326s	97.221mph
7	Melandri	Honda	44m 31.835s	24.101s	2m 00.270s	97.213mph
8	Capirossi	Ducati	44m 32.201s	24.467s	2m 00.163s	97.199mph
9	Gibernau	Ducati	44m 36.092s	28.358s	2m 00.708s	97.058mph
10	Nakano	Kawasaki	44m 41.549s	33.815s	2m 01.191s	96.860mph
11	Elias	Honda	44m 43.050s	35.316s	2m 00.841s	96.806mph
12	De Puniet	Kawasaki	44m 59.738s	52.004s	2m 01.752s	96.208mph
13	Roberts	KR211V	45m 04.027s	56.293s	2m 02.086s	96.055mph
14	Checa	Yamaha	45m 11.309s	1m 03.575s	2m 02.610s	95.797mph
15	Hofmann	Ducati	45m 18.906s	1m 11.172s	2m 02.879s	95.530mph
16	Ellison	Yamaha	45m 30.809s	1m 23.075s	2m 03.139s	95.113mph
17	Cardoso	Ducati	45m 42.884s	1m 35.150s	2m 03.297s	94.694mph
	Rossi	Yamaha	36m 11.885s	5 laps	2m 00.131s	92.410mph
	Vermeulen	Suzuki	6m 11.848s	19 laps	2m 02.075s	95.250mph

CHAMPIONSHIP

	Rider	Team	Points
1	Hayden	Repsol Team Honda	72
2	Capirossi	Ducati Marlboro Team	59
3	Pedrosa	Repsol Honda Team	57
4	Melandri	Fortuna Honda	54
5	Stoner	Honda LCR	52
6	Rossi	Camel Yamaha Team	40
7	Elias	Fortuna Honda	37
8	Edwards	Camel Yamaha Team	35
9	Nakano	Kawasaki Racing Team	28
10	Gibernau	Ducati Marlboro Team	25
11	Tamada	Konica Minolta Honda	24
12	Hopkins	Rizla Suzuki MotoGP	20
13	Roberts	Team Roberts	20
14	Vermeulen	Rizla Suzki MotoGP	13
15	Checa	Tech 3 Yamaha	10
16	De Puniet	Kawasaki Racing Team	8
17	Ellison	Tech 3 Yamaha	3
18	Hofmann	Pramac d'Antin MotoGP	3

7 MARCO MELANDRI An unsatisfactory weekend for the winner of the previous race: problems on Friday were never solved thanks to lack of dry track time and all he could do was race for points. Not shy about bouncing off the Ducatis and Tamada's Honda in the first turn, though.

8 LORIS CAPIROSSI For the first time this season wasn't the fastest Bridgestone runner. Suffered from lack of dry time to test new tyres and raced with rubber he'd only tried in Sunday morning warm-up (which turned out not to be the best choice). Definitely a weekend that didn't live up to expectations.

9 SETE GIBERNAU Exactly the same problems as his team-mate and chose a rear tyre that never got enough heat into its left side. 'It was our mistake,' he said. Involved in the hectic midfield dice, but was struggling too much to enjoy the experience.

10 SHINYA NAKANO Another great run in qualifying but unable to back it up on race tyres. Yet again lack of testing time led to racing with a rear tyre that started to spin up on corner exits early in the race, enough for him to lose contact with the battling group in front.

11 TONI ELIAS In even bigger trouble than his team-mate but for the same reasons, despite the fact that Fausto Gresini's team had had both their riders setting the pace at the 2005 race.

12 RANDY DE PUNIET Messed up his start by keeping his hand on the clutch during a gear change and confusing the electronics: five bikes went past as he shut off and reselected the gear. Stuck behind Vermeulen for a while before finding himself alone for the rest of the race.

13 KENNY ROBERTS With no experience at the Shanghai circuit the team were lost, and Kenny found himself dissatisfied with just about every area of his bike's performance – except the engine.

14 CARLOS CHECA Although the result doesn't look very different from previous races, Carlos was much happier with his tyres. The Dunlops maintained their consistency throughout and put him within striking distance of Roberts and the slower works bikes.

15 ALEX HOFMANN Happy to have a choice of race tyres at last and put them to good use by splitting the Tech 3 Yamahas.

16 JAMES ELLISON Like his team-mate, very happy with the improvement in his Dunlops' durability, but lost ground when the side grip decreased towards the closing stages.

17 JOSE LUIS CARDOSO Severely beaten up by three crashes in practice but made it to the flag.

NON-FINISHERS

VALENTINO ROSSI Another qualifying that didn't go as planned, followed by another brilliant ride through the pack until, at two-thirds' distance, he felt a vibration. Assuming it was a rear tyre problem he pitted to change it, only to realise as he exited the pits that it was his front tyre that had chunked.

CHRIS VERMEULEN Crashed on the brakes trying to pass de Puniet, which impressed Hofmann (following him), who was under the impression it was impossible to crash off the front on Bridgestones.

FRENCH GP
LE MANS

ROUND **5**

LIGHTNING STRIKES AGAIN

Just when Rossi thought things couldn't get any worse, they did – and Valentino's misfortune allowed Melandri to become the first man to win two races in 2006

It seemed like the defining image of the season, or at least the season so far: Valentino Rossi sitting slumped in the back seat of a photographers' shuttle bus, helmeted head in hands. He had just coasted to a halt seven-and-a-half laps from what looked like certain victory, for at the time he was over four seconds clear of Pedrosa after the first direct on-track confrontation between the two. The champ might have won that fight decisively, but Dani had taken pole for the second successive race, inevitably making him the youngest rider to have taken back-to-back pole positions in the top class.

It had looked as if most, if not all, of Rossi's problems were over. All through practice both he and Edwards displayed good pace on race tyres. Only when the very stickiest qualifiers were put on did the chatter that had bedevilled them all season return. Although Yamaha strenuously denied it, their management continually referred to the 'new' chassis; the cure seemed to be the 2005 frame with revised bracketry to enable it to accept the '06 motor and most of the current bodywork. Here

Above Randy de Puniet was the principal victim of the mêlée at the first chicane

Opposite On Saturday night Loris Capirossi didn't think he had a chance; he changed his mind on race day

Below John Hopkins led the chasing pack but asked too much of his front tyre; he crashed but got back on again to secure one point

at Le Mans the bike was good enough to put Valentino on the front of the third row, which he thought was 'a little disappointing but not a disaster'. Colin was two places further back, on the 'old' chassis. And Rossi again stuck with the older, narrower Michelin front for the race.

Valentino set about making up for any disappointment he may have felt in the first corner – it might have been revised, but the Dunlop chicane is still a serious bottleneck – where he arrived fast and on the inside for the first, left-handed element, but then had to pick up when Pedrosa cut across his nose. That set off a domino effect which saw de Puniet, who has never had any luck at his home race, on the floor and Gibernau and Edwards ploughing through the gravel trap to rejoin at the back of the field.

Melandri led the shuffled pack but was soon passed by John Hopkins, continuing the form he'd shown in China. Hopper led the first four laps before a vengeful Rossi came past, setting the fastest lap of the race as he did so. It was painfully obvious that Hopkins was over-riding the Suzuki to keep Rossi in sight while also aiming to keep the Hondas of Pedrosa and Melandri behind him. The inevitable happened on lap ten, when John asked too much of his front tyre at the Garage Vert hairpin, but he was determined enough to pick up the bike, get it back to the pits for running repairs and go out again to salvage the last point. That left Rossi leading Pedrosa by a mere quarter-second but, until the Italian's bike stopped, the gap was opening steadily; in fact Dani didn't circulate faster than Valentino once in the ten laps he was behind the Doctor. The young Spanish star said later that he knew he was in trouble just a few laps into the race: he had decided to go with a soft tyre which turned out to be a mistake. After two big moments on one lap he realised he was 'going slowly while on the limit' and decided to ride for the finish. It was, he said, a lucky rostrum.

Pedrosa's difficulties put him in the clutches of Loris Capirossi whose ride was the big surprise of the day, not least to the man himself. On Saturday night Loris had declared that it was 'impossible to win', a reflection of a lack of confidence in his dry-weather Bridgestone tyres. He should have been more optimistic. The Japanese tyre company had four men out of six on the front two rows, dominated Sunday morning warm-up and, with

SUOMY
ADVANCE
Alice
BREIL
65
DUCATI
axo

Hopkins, showed just how competitive their race tyres could be. To his delight Capirossi ran in fourth for most of the race and inherited third when Rossi stopped. Realising he was within range of Pedrosa, he pushed and got past on the last lap, finishing less than two seconds behind the winner. Loris looked happier than he'd done after many of his wins. Team manager Livio Suppo reckoned this rostrum was of more value to the morale of Marlboro Ducati than a wet-weather win would have been.

Kawasaki might have joined in celebrating with the other Bridgestone teams had they not had the race day from hell. Shinya Nakano only just missed out on pole position and Randy de Puniet had by far his best qualifying of the season, only to find himself in the wrong place at the wrong time on the first lap. Nakano was with the leading group when he was called in to do a ride-through penalty for jumping the start.

Casey Stoner had yet another impressive race, making up for a troubled qualifying with a determined charge once some fuel was burnt and his RCV felt manageable. For the last eight laps of the race he was in close company with Nicky Hayden, who was suffering from what he thought was a bad cold but was later diagnosed as bronchitis: no wonder his run of rostrums came to an end. Stoner's fourth place made it five top-six finishes in his first five MotoGP races, and he felt the need to revisit what he felt was the slur on his riding from the Qatar race: 'I've answered people who said I couldn't ride on worn tyres.' An Aussie sportsman nursing a grudge? Who'd have thought it?

Surprisingly, Rossi wasn't that downhearted. Once

the dust had settled he was happy to look on the bright side, preferring to emphasise the fact that, for the first time this year, the M1 had been working exactly as he wanted in race trim and he'd actually enjoyed riding the bike. As in Qatar, setting the fastest lap gave him particular pleasure.

Not as much pleasure, though, as Melandri got from his win. He admitted that he hadn't really been expecting it, especially when his choice of a hard rear Michelin made the early laps difficult and he dropped back to fifth with the bike sliding everywhere. Marco kept calm and timed his moves on both Capirossi and then Pedrosa to perfection. When he found himself in second he was over three seconds back but the fastest man out there. 'Little by little the grip came and I could attack. When I saw Valentino at the side of the track I thought to myself that I could win this race. I knew Dani was in difficulties and I could get him. Valentino gave me a nice present!'

Opposite top Shinya Nakano got himself excluded after jumping the start

Opposite bottom Colin Edwards was another victim of the pile-up at the first chicane but came through the pack to finish sixth

Right Valentino Rossi rolls to a silent, despairing halt with engine failure

MARCO'S STEADY PROGRESS

Marco Melandri's stuttering start to the year and his difficulty in adapting to the 2006 Honda tended to disguise the fact that he had been very much the man in form over the previous half-season and more. Since the 2005 Turkish GP, that season's penultimate race, Marco had won four out of seven races. The last man other than Rossi to achieve that sort of win-to-start ratio in that number of races was Alex Criville in his World Championship-winning year, 1999. Go back another three races and Marco is the top scorer over that period of time with 173 points, followed by Hayden (168) and Rossi (146). Go back even further, to the start of 2005 when he first raced a Honda in MotoGP, and Marco has never finished a race lower than seventh in 22 starts. The three races he didn't finish last year were due to crashes at Donington and Laguna and being torpedoed by Rossi at Motegi.

While he's undoubtedly racing well, the same cannot be said of his qualifying – he has never achieved pole position in MotoGP. His wins this year have come from fifth (France), 14th (Turkey) and seventh (Australia) places on the grid. In the previous 30 Grands Prix the only other rider to have won after starting behind the front row is Valentino Rossi. And it's also worth remembering that Marco is three-and-a-half years younger than Valentino.

FRENCH GP
LE MANS

ROUND 5

RACE RESULTS

RACE DATE May 21st
CIRCUIT LENGTH 2.597 miles
NO. OF LAPS 28
RACE DISTANCE 72.716 miles
WEATHER Wet, 20°C
TRACK TEMPERATURE 29°C
WINNER Marco Melandri
FASTEST LAP 1m 35.087s, 98.339mph, Valentino Rossi
PREVIOUS LAP RECORD 1m 33.678s, 99.594mph, Valentino Rossi, 2005

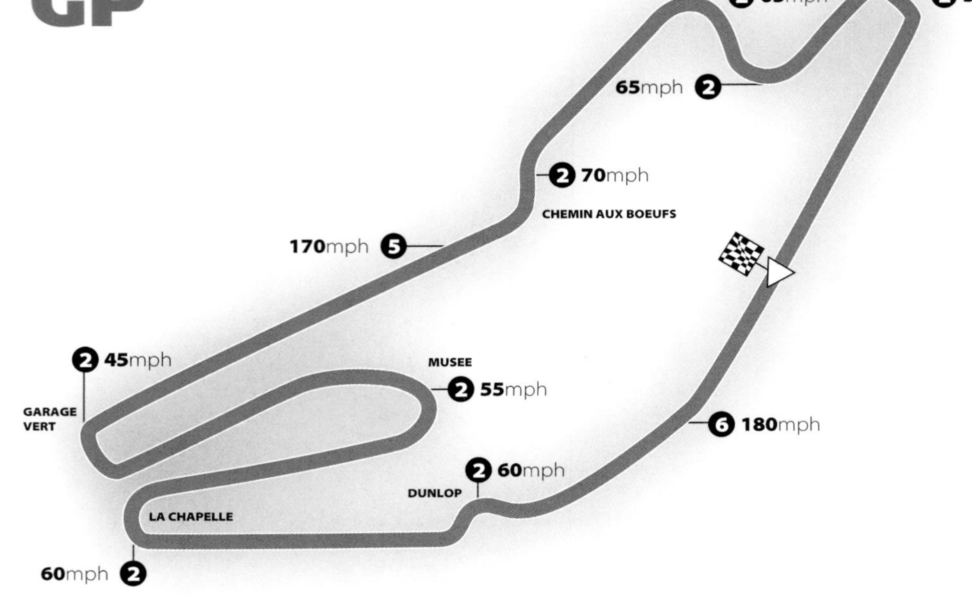

QUALIFYING

	Rider	Nationality	Team	Qualifying	Pole +	Gap
1	Pedrosa	SPA	Repsol Honda Team	1m 33.990s		
2	Nakano	JPN	Kawasaki Racing Team	1m 34.201s	0.211s	0.211s
3	Hopkins	USA	Rizla Suzuki MotoGP	1m 34.636s	0.646s	0.435s
4	De Puniet	FRA	Kawasaki Racing Team	1m 34.780s	0.790s	0.144s
5	Melandri	ITA	Fortuna Honda	1m 34.795s	0.805s	0.015s
6	Capirossi	ITA	Ducati Marlboro Team	1m 34.802s	0.812s	0.007s
7	Rossi	ITA	Camel Yamaha Team	1m 34.840s	0.850s	0.038s
8	Gibernau	SPA	Ducati Marlboro Team	1m 34.870s	0.880s	0.030s
9	Edwards	USA	Camel Yamaha Team	1m 34.970s	0.980s	0.100s
10	Hayden	USA	Repsol Honda Team	1m 34.988s	0.998s	0.018s
11	Stoner	AUS	Honda LCR	1m 35.430s	1.440s	0.442s
12	Vermeulen	AUS	Rizla Suzuki MotoGP	1m 35.705s	1.715s	0.275s
13	Tamada	JPN	Konica Minolta Honda	1m 36.058s	2.068s	0.353s
14	Checa	SPA	Tech 3 Yamaha	1m 36.260s	2.270s	0.202s
15	Roberts	USA	Team Roberts	1m 36.501s	2.511s	0.241s
16	Elias	SPA	Fortuna Honda	1m 36.582s	2.592s	0.081s
17	Ellison	GBR	Tech 3 Yamaha	1m 37.019s	3.029s	0.437s
18	Hofmann	GER	Pramac d'Antin MotoGP	1m 37.267s	3.277s	0.248s
19	Cardoso	SPA	Pramac d'Antin MotoGP	1m 37.812s	3.822s	0.545s

FINISHERS

1 MARCO MELANDRI An intelligent race: he maintained a good pace then timed his attack perfectly to become the first man to win two races in the season. Has won four of the previous seven races, and scored more points than anybody from the last ten races. Fifth place on the grid was his best qualifying position so far this year.

2 LORIS CAPIROSSI On Saturday he was praying for rain and went so far as to say he couldn't win. On Sunday his Bridgestones performed much better in the dry than expected – he tracked Melandri through the leading pack to catch and pass Pedrosa on the last lap.

3 DANI PEDROSA Pole position made him the youngest rider ever to set back-to-back poles in the top class. Lost the first head-to-head encounter with Rossi decisively, and was grateful to finish on the rostrum. Blamed himself for making a bad tyre choice.

4 CASEY STONER Couldn't run with the leaders at the start, mainly due to losing time on the brakes, then had a good dice with Hayden, making the decisive pass seven laps from the flag. Again pointed out that he didn't do a bad job on worn tyres.

5 NICKY HAYDEN Ended his run of eight consecutive rostrum finishes when what he thought was a touch of flu was later diagnosed as bronchitis. Under the circumstances, useful points and the retention of the championship lead wasn't a bad outcome.

6 COLIN EDWARDS Ran off the track at the first chicane when de Puniet crashed and ended the first lap in last place, then worked his way through the field in fine style. Was happy with his bike but deeply frustrated not to have been on the rostrum.

7 MAKOTO TAMADA Not quite up to the form of the last race but at least he showed spirit in his dice with Edwards and Gibernau.

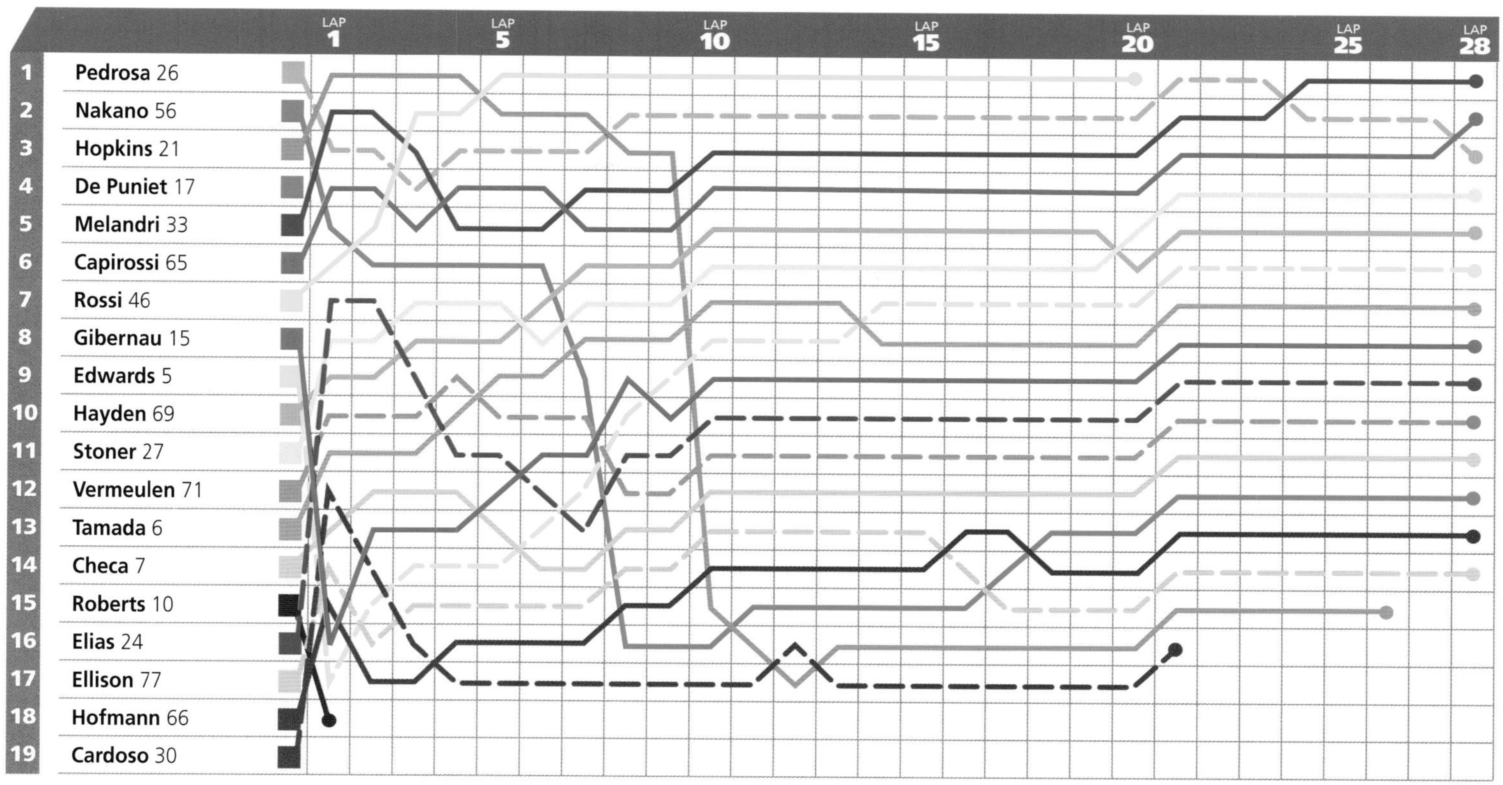

RACE

	Rider	Motorcycle	Race Time	Time +	Fastest Lap	Average Speed
1	Melandri	Honda	44m 57.369s		1m 35.332s	97.003mph
2	Capirossi	Ducati	44m 59.298s	1.929s	1m 35.548s	96.934mph
3	Pedrosa	Honda	44m 59.638s	2.269s	1m 35.156s	96.922mph
4	Stoner	Honda	45m 02.863s	5.494s	1m 35.637s	96.806mph
5	Hayden	Honda	45m 03.078s	5.709s	1m 35.621s	96.798mph
6	Edwards	Yamaha	45m 08.888s	11.519s	1m 35.671s	96.591mph
7	Tamada	Honda	45m 14.061s	16.692s	1m 35.791s	96.406mph
8	Gibernau	Ducati	45m 15.511s	18.142s	1m 35.969s	96.355mph
9	Elias	Honda	45m 21.014s	23.645s	1m 36.055s	96.161mph
10	Vermeulen	Suzuki	45m 36.731s	39.362s	1m 36.618s	95.608mph
11	Checa	Yamaha	45m 45.099s	47.730s	1m 36.781s	95.317mph
12	Nakano	Kawasaki	45m 45.151s	47.782s	1m 36.008s	95.315mph
13	Hofmann	Ducati	46m 06.461s	1m 09.092s	1m 37.456s	94.581mph
14	Ellison	Yamaha	46m 13.541s	1m 16.172s	1m 37.572s	94.339mph
15	Hopkins	Suzuki	45m 17.059s	2 laps	1m 35.249s	89.421mph
	Cardoso	Ducati	37m 25.234s	7 laps	1m 38.077s	87.403mph
	Rossi	Yamaha	32m 02.389s	8 laps	1m 35.087s	97.221mph
	Roberts	KR211V	2m 10.374s	27 laps		
	De Puniet	Kawasaki				

CHAMPIONSHIP

	Rider	Team	Points
1	Hayden	Repsol Honda Team	83
2	Melandri	Fortuna Honda	79
3	Capirossi	Ducati Marlboro Team	79
4	Pedrosa	Repsol Honda Team	73
5	Stoner	Honda LCR	65
6	Edwards	Camel Yamaha Team	45
7	Elias	Fortuna Honda	44
8	Rossi	Camel Yamaha Team	40
9	Gibernau	Ducati Marlboro Team	33
10	Tamada	Konica Minolta Honda	33
11	Nakano	Kawasaki Racing Team	32
12	Hopkins	Rizla Suzuki MotoGP	21
13	Roberts	Team Roberts	20
14	Vermeulen	Rizla Suzuki MotoGP	19
15	Checa	Tech 3 Yamaha	15
16	De Puniet	Kawasaki Racing Team	8
17	Hofmann	Pramac d'Antin MotoGP	6
18	Ellison	Tech 3 Yamaha	5

8 SETE GIBERNAU Suffered the same fate as Edwards at Turn 1, then came through the field with the American. His ride back towards the front of the field reinforced his assertion that he'd made another step forward in understanding the Ducati.

9 TONI ELIAS Problems with rear grip meant he started 16th on the grid and, despite a good start, couldn't maintain the pace he wanted. Never happy on the circuit where he suffered serious injuries in testing after the 2005 race.

10 CHRIS VERMEULEN Lack of dry practice didn't help Chris in his first race at Le Mans. Not happy with his pace but did improve on his 12th in qualifying in what turned out to be a lonely race.

11 CARLOS CHECA Ran with Vermeulen and Elias in the first dozen laps, then had to fend off Nakano when his tyre started to move around. Enjoyed having someone to race for the whole distance and was much happier than after Turkey and China.

12 SHINYA NAKANO Second on the grid was Shinya's best qualifying since joining Kawasaki for 2004. Unfortunately he then jumped the start and had to come in for a ride-through penalty, rejoining the race dead last.

13 ALEX HOFMANN Happy with the points but unhappy with what he regarded as the inadequate choice of tyres offered by Dunlop.

14 JAMES ELLISON Much happier with his lap times and his race. Closer than any race so far to both team-mate Checa and the leaders; did lose out to Hofmann in the closing laps, though.

15 JOHN HOPKINS Lost the front while visibly over-riding the Suzuki to try and stay with the leaders. Got the bike back to the pits, kicked it straight and went out to salvage a point. There was some talk of clutch trouble contributing to the crash, but it's likely that Hopper's hard riding caused any problems there were.

NON-FINISHERS

JOSE LUIS CARDOSO Came in to change his rear tyre, went out again, but retired rather than get in the way of the guys racing for points.

VALENTINO ROSSI Everything looked to be going so well until three-quarter distance. Took the lead on lap five, setting the fastest lap of the race as he did so, then pulled steadily away from Pedrosa. Had a commanding lead when his engine cut out.

KENNY ROBERTS Hit electrical problems on the warm-up lap and came into the pits to change bikes. Unfortunately, his second machine was fitted with cut slick tyres so he retired after one lap. The first examination of the bike diagnosed fuel pump maladies.

RANDY DE PUNIET On the rostrum of the French 250cc GP for the previous four years without winning his home race. This time, he was an innocent victim of the domino effect in the crowded first chicane. Suffered concussion and wrecked his bike. Just to add to the pain, he was starting from his best grid position in MotoGP.

ITALIAN GP

MUGELLO

ROUND 6

NESSUN DORMA

Valentino Rossi made it five wins in a row at Mugello, sent an entire country wild and re-ignited his World Championship challenge – and he did it in one of the best races of recent years

It was hard work, it was bloody hard work, but Valentino Rossi repulsed challenges from all his main competitors on one of the world's most demanding race tracks to win at home again. Worse still, from the other guys' point of view, he announced after months of speculation about a move to F1 that not only was he staying with bikes for 2007 but also that his Yamaha was now capable of putting him on the rostrum at all 11 remaining races. A frightening thought.

Things even went well in practice and qualifying, despite the now usual rain on Friday, and Vale started from the front row of the grid for the first time this season. He hit the front at Turn 3 on lap one, at the highest point of the circuit, right in front of the massed ranks of his fan club, but there was to be no easy

Above The choir on its way to give the rowdiest rendition of the Italian national anthem ever heard

Opposite Roberts, Elias and Tamada climb every mountain

victory because he lost the lead after running wide on lap two. From then on it was really tough.

In the first half of the race his challenger was the mightily impressive Sete Gibernau, who'd become the first Ducati rider to set pole position at Mugello. 'I know it's only qualifying but this is like a victory to me,' he said. Loris Capirossi was less than a tenth of a second slower to make it a Ducati one–two on the front row, but he wasn't impressed, judging by a snide aside to Rossi in parc fermé – it's a team-mate thing. Ducati celebrated with a special retro livery for the race to mark not one but three anniversaries: the 80th birthday of the company, their 60th year of motorcycle production and 50 years of using their hallmark desmodromic valve gear. Just for fun, they also unveiled the first MotoGP replica for the road. It's a small company but they keep busy.

Gibernau's challenge ended under the strangest of circumstances. The toe-slider from his right boot came off, and in the two laps it took to adjust his style to avoid abrading his foot on the tarmac he lost touch with the leading group. Sete finished in fifth place, with blood on his boot. His Ducati team-mate turned out to be Rossi's most serious rival after the others had dropped away: Loris went for a hard tyre so he was unable to push in the early laps and had to work his way through from as far back as eighth on lap four. He spent the first two-thirds of the race chipping away at the lead that Sete and Valentino had opened up, and was aided by Casey Stoner crashing spectacularly out of third place. When he was within range of the leaders Rossi made what could have been a costly error. After seeing Capirossi's name on his pit board he decided to let him through, but he braked so deep at Turn 1 that both the Ducatis, Hayden and Melandri all came past. There followed nine of the most spectacular laps you could hope to see.

Rossi passed Melandri and Hayden on consecutive laps at Casanova and then Sete hit his problem. The two Hondas had their own dogfight, which was resolved in Nicky's favour when Marco ran off the track attempting an instant retake. Six laps to go and now only Capirossi was in front of Rossi. The Doctor himself later admitted that going into the last lap he didn't know who would win and that he'd never been in a race where things were so evenly matched – riders, bikes, tyres. Loris and Valentino seemed to be side by side in every corner but neither of them used an inside line to push the other man on to the dirty part of the track. 'We overtook each other many times,' said Loris, 'but always in a correct manner; it's always so nice to ride with Valentino. I enjoy races like that even if I don't win!' It was as hard a race as you could hope to see but completely fair as well and it went right down to the last lap. Rossi made it past on the brakes for the final time at the end of the front straight and immediately opened a small but significant gap; it was enough.

One measure of Rossi's dedication to the task in hand was that he hadn't wasted any energy on planning stunts for the slow-down lap: there was just the customary special crash helmet paint job. He did park his bike, but only so he could stand and gaze at a steep hillside covered in a boiling mass of humanity screaming their approval of the epic they'd just witnessed. The one real surprise of the race was that the lap record survived; it still belongs to Max Biaggi.

fortuna
Castrol
HONDA
alpinestars
KONICA MINOLTA
HONDA

at the front for most of the time. He was pushed back to eighth on the last lap by a charging Toni Elias, but it was the first sign that the Honda-engined Team KR bike was coming good thanks to some advice imparted by HRC in China. The one unpleasant note of the weekend was sounded by Luis d'Antin, who claimed that his team was not being treated properly by Dunlop and threatened legal action. The tyre manufacturer did not respond, at least not in public.

Had Rossi played a clever strategic game? Not at all, he said, there was no way he was in a position to do that. He knew he was fastest in some corners and that Capirossi had the advantage elsewhere. 'The race is like a game of cards, and you know your cards only and you try and use them in the best possible way; today I won the game.' Given the presence of Michael Schumacher and Rossi's decision not to go to F1, inevitably he was asked if he'd made the right decision. His answer was accompanied by a wide smile: 'I do not think that many people fell asleep in front of their televisions this afternoon.'

Above Pedrosa never really threatened his team-mate; Gibernau led early but faded

Opposite Hayden is the bewigged interloper on the otherwise all-Italian rostrum

Below Special anniversary paint for Capirossi's Ducati, and the now traditional one-off paint job for Rossi's crash helmet

Third place went to Hayden, who was never far away from the Italians but couldn't quite lay a glove on them – hardly surprising as his RCV had been the slowest Honda through the speed traps all weekend and the 14th fastest overall. 'They say it's got potential,' he remarked grimly, 'but potential gets people fired.' At least he beat his team-mate. Dani Pedrosa has never liked Mugello, yet in his first visit on a MotoGP bike he managed to hang on to the leaders for fourth.

The crowd had plenty of downfield action to add to the entertainment. Five men disputed seventh place all through the race, with Kenny Roberts

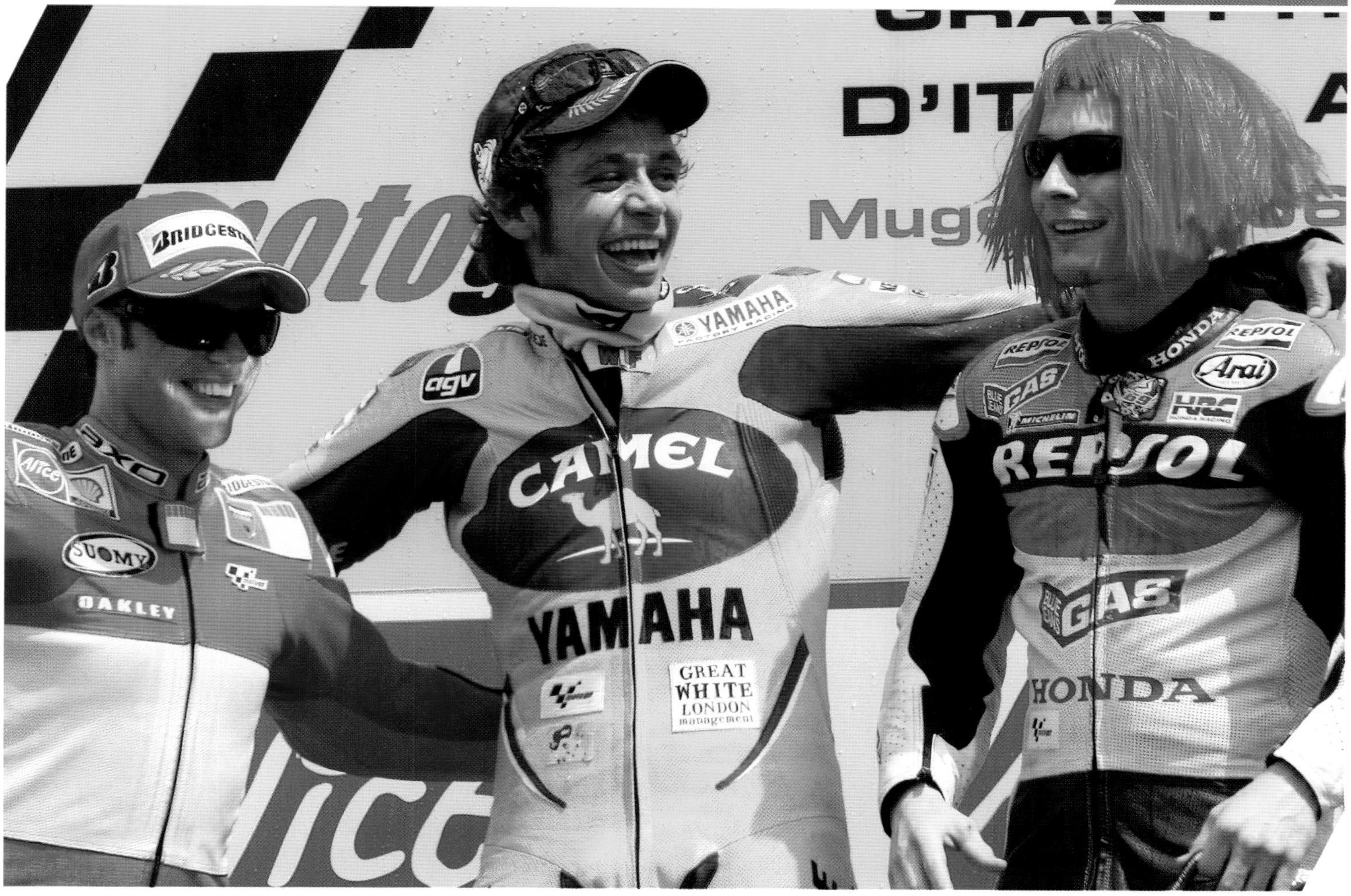

NOW THAT'S WHAT I CALL RACING

Why did Valentino Rossi decide to stay with bikes and reject F1? Because, he said, he realised that in F1 a driver isn't allowed to be a racer; he has to do what he's told by the strategists in pit lane. He'd thought long and hard after his last Ferrari test at Valencia before making up his mind, but it was that lack of freedom to be a racer that seems to have been the biggest influence on his decision. There were, of course, other factors in play that were outside Rossi's control. Michael Schumacher had yet to decide what he was doing in 2007 and Ferrari had interests in other drivers that would be expensive to scrap. No less an authority than John Surtees, the only man to win world titles on two and four wheels, was of the opinion that the final decision in these matters was always made by the stopwatch. Mick Doohan wondered why Valentino would entertain the possibility of diluting his legacy as one of the greatest bike racers we've ever seen.

Valentino's decision, and the main reason for it, gladdened the hearts of bike fans everywhere. They also enjoyed the perceived irony of Schumacher's presence at Mugello. He was there for a ride on the back of Ducati's MotoGP two-seater, piloted by Randy Mamola, who later admitted it was the only time he'd gone at 100 per cent with a passenger on the back. Michael said he'd tapped Randy on the back a couple of times to remind him there was an F1 race at Silverstone the following weekend.

Schumacher had ridden his Harley-Davidson from his home in Switzerland and was only scheduled to stay for the start of the race before leaving early to beat the traffic. He stayed for the whole distance, though, hanging over the Armco like any race fan. He must have enjoyed all that overtaking.

ITALIAN GP

MUGELLO

ROUND 6

80mph 2 SAN DONATO
2 70mph CORRENTAIO
100mph 3
BIONDETTI
70mph 2 LUCO
70mph 2 POGGIO SECCO
70mph 2 SCARPERIA
PALAGIO
80mph 2
MATERASSI
2 75mph
BORGO SAN LORENZO
2 80mph
95mph 3 ARRABBIATA 2
BUCINE
2 60mph
SAVELLI
3 85mph
3 80mph CASANOVA
100mph 3 ARRABBIATA 1

RACE RESULTS

RACE DATE June 4th
CIRCUIT LENGTH 3.259 miles
NO. OF LAPS 23
RACE DISTANCE 74.794 miles
WEATHER Dry, 20°C
TRACK TEMPERATURE 29°C
WINNER Valentino Rossi
FASTEST LAP 1m 50.195s, 106.477mph, Loris Capirossi
PREVIOUS LAP RECORD 1m 50.117s, 106.312mph, Max Biaggi, 2005

QUALIFYING

	Rider	Nationality	Team	Qualifying	Pole +	Gap
1	Gibernau	SPA	Ducati Marlboro Team	1m 48.969s		
2	Capirossi	ITA	Ducati Marlboro Team	1m 49.058s	0.089s	0.089s
3	Rossi	ITA	Camel Yamaha Team	1m 49.167s	0.198s	0.109s
4	Hayden	USA	Repsol Honda Team	1m 49.212s	0.243s	0.045s
5	Nakano	JPN	Kawasaki Racing Team	1m 49.328s	0.359s	0.116s
6	Melandri	ITA	Fortuna Honda	1m 49.343s	0.374s	0.015s
7	Hopkins	USA	Rizla Suzuki MotoGP	1m 49.478s	0.509s	0.135s
8	Pedrosa	SPA	Repsol Honda Team	1m 49.516s	0.547s	0.038s
9	Stoner	AUS	Honda LCR	1m 49.915s	0.946s	0.399s
10	Tamada	JPN	Konica Minolta Honda	1m 50.084s	1.115s	0.169s
11	Roberts	USA	Team Roberts	1m 50.181s	1.212s	0.097s
12	Elias	SPA	Fortuna Honda	1m 50.196s	1.227s	0.015s
13	Checa	SPA	Tech 3 Yamaha	1m 50.347s	1.378s	0.151s
14	Edwards	USA	Camel Yamaha Team	1m 50.405s	1.436s	0.058s
15	Vermeulen	AUS	Rizla Suzuki MotoGP	1m 50.430s	1.461s	0.025s
16	De Puniet	FRA	Kawasaki Racing Team	1m 50.597s	1.628s	0.167s
17	Ellison	GBR	Tech 3 Yamaha	1m 51.866s	2.897s	1.269s
18	Hofmann	GER	Pramac d'Antin MotoGP	1m 52.100s	3.131s	0.234s
19	Cardoso	SPA	Pramac d'Antin MotoGP	1m 52.780s	3.811s	0.680s

FINISHERS

1 VALENTINO ROSSI Said it was the hardest victory of his career. It was also five in a row at Mugello and his 55th career victory, making him the second most successful 500/MotoGP rider of all time. Mugello is the first circuit on which he's scored three wins on the Yamaha M1.

2 LORIS CAPIROSSI Can never have ridden so hard and finished second: any chance of the win disappeared when he made a mess of the start. More upset about losing pole to his team-mate than coming second to Valentino.

3 NICKY HAYDEN Back on the rostrum despite not being fully recovered from bronchitis. Didn't get a good start, then battled with Melandri before closing on the leaders in the final laps. As usual had 'no excuses' for not winning but did keep the championship lead, although now shared with Capirossi.

4 DANI PEDROSA Despite Mugello's extremely physical nature (and a track he has never much liked) Dani rode a calculated race to finish just a couple of seconds down on the winner. A better result than he expected: he was even moved to describe it as 'a perfect result for me.'

5 SETE GIBERNAU Started from his first pole on a Ducati, then led for three laps. Shadowed Rossi for the next 11 laps until he lost the toe-slider from his right boot. It took him two laps to recover from rubbing his toes on the tarmac, by which time the leaders had gone.

6 MARCO MELANDRI Ran off track while trying to take third from Hayden six laps from the flag, and there was no time left to salvage a rostrum position. Complained of having to make up ground on the brakes to compensate for a bike that didn't want to change direction.

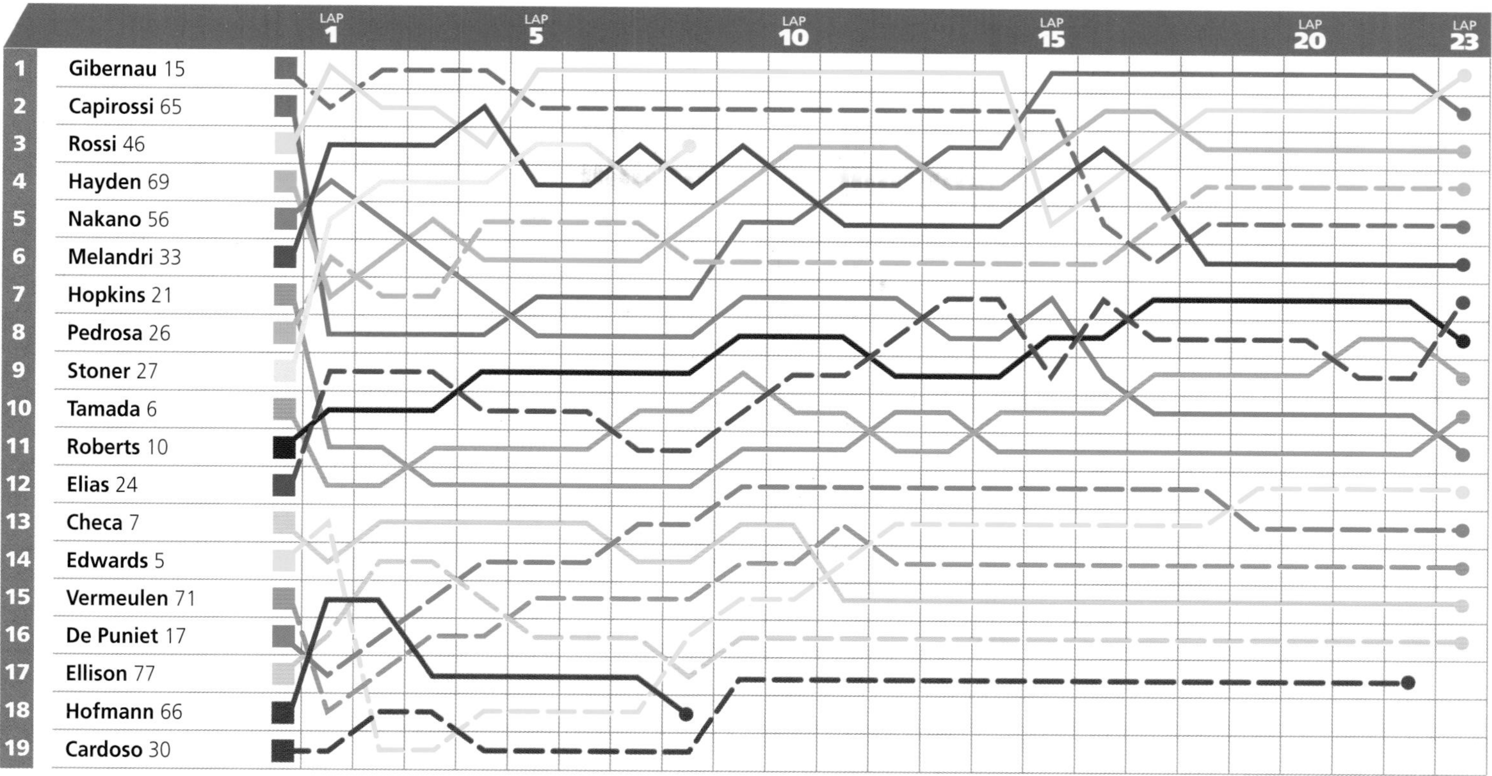

RACE

	Rider	Motorcycle	Race Time	Time +	Fastest Lap	Average Speed
1	Rossi	Yamaha	42m 39.610s		1m 50.357s	105.364mph
2	Capirossi	Ducati	42m 40.185s	0.575s	1m 50.195s	105.340mph
3	Hayden	Honda	42m 40.345s	0.735s	1m 50.522s	105.334mph
4	Pedrosa	Honda	42m 41.617s	2.007s	1m 50.300s	105.281mph
5	Gibernau	Ducati	42m 42.680s	3.070s	1m 50.255s	105.238mph
6	Melandri	Honda	42m 51.403s	11.793s	1m 50.304s	104.881mph
7	Elias	Honda	42m 58.609s	18.999s	1m 50.930s	104.587mph
8	Roberts	KR211V	42m 58.782s	19.172s	1m 51.130s	104.581mph
9	Tamada	Honda	42m 58.841s	19.231s	1m 50.907s	104.578mph
10	Hopkins	Suzuki	42m 59.431s	19.821s	1m 51.322s	104.555mph
11	Nakano	Kawasaki	42m 59.473s	19.863s	1m 50.895s	104.553mph
12	Edwards	Yamaha	43m 10.288s	30.678s	1m 51.283s	104.116mph
13	De Puniet	Kawasaki	43m 16.808s	37.198s	1m 51.395s	103.855mph
14	Vermeulen	Suzuki	43m 21.322s	41.712s	1m 52.086s	103.675mph
15	Checa	Yamaha	43m 35.866s	56.256s	1m 51.652s	103.098mph
16	Ellison	Yamaha	43m 52.997s	1m 13.387s	1m 52.224s	102.427mph
	Cardoso	Ducati	42m 45.597s	1 lap	1m 55.273s	100.548mph
	Stoner	Honda	14m 52.930s	15 laps	1m 50.363s	105.053mph
	Hofmann	Ducati	15m 13.323s	15 laps	1m 52.751s	102.708mph

CHAMPIONSHIP

	Rider	Team	Points
1	Capirossi	Ducati Marlboro Team	99
2	Hayden	Repsol Honda Team	99
3	Melandri	Fortuna Honda	89
4	Pedrosa	Repsol Honda Team	86
5	Rossi	Camel Yamaha Team	65
6	Stoner	Honda LCR	65
7	Elias	Fortuna Honda	53
8	Edwards	Camel Yamaha Team	49
9	Gibernau	Ducati Marlboro Team	44
10	Tamada	Konica Minolta Honda	40
11	Nakano	Kawasaki Racing Team	37
12	Roberts	Team Roberts	28
13	Hopkins	Rizla Suzuki MotoGP	27
14	Vermeulen	Rizla Suzuki MotoGP	21
15	Checa	Tech 3 Yamaha	16
16	De Puniet	Kawasaki Racing Team	11
17	Hofmann	Pramac d'Antin MotoGP	6
18	Ellison	Tech 3 Yamaha	5

7 TONI ELIAS Redeemed a troubled qualifying session with a hard-fought race that saw him come out on top of a spectacular five-man dice.

8 KENNY ROBERTS Only lost out to Elias on the last lap after his best race of the year. HRC offered Team KR some advice on chassis rigidity and Kenny was able to say that, for the first time, he felt he was riding a real race bike.

9 MAKOTO TAMADA Caught out by the increase in track temperature, his race tyre lacked grip from the start and couldn't do anything about the two bikes in front of him. Did get the better of Hopkins, though.

10 JOHN HOPKINS A bad start saw him involved with the second group for most of the race, but the Suzuki still had a slight top-end disadvantage and there was no way Hopper could move forward.

11 SHINYA NAKANO Superb qualifying and a great start followed by a dispiriting race. The ZX-RR's lack of top-end power was cruelly exposed on Mugello's long straight – even the Suzuki was able to drive past.

12 COLIN EDWARDS Gambled on using Rossi's settings after a disastrous qualifying only to be run wide by Tamada at the first corner of lap two and sent through the gravel trap. Rejoined dead last and treated the rest of the race as a test session for the new chassis.

13 RANDY DE PUNIET Terrible qualifying followed by a tentative start (probably remembering Turn 1 at Le Mans) meant he lost too much time to get on terms with the pack. Suffered back pain, another legacy of Le Mans, in the closing stages.

14 CHRIS VERMEULEN Had to treat his first visit to Mugello as a learning experience. 'Eaten alive' in the first corner, but ran good lap times mid-race.

15 CARLOS CHECA Great qualifying but his Dunlops let him down severely after fewer than ten laps. Doubly disappointing after the progress of the preceding two races.

16 JAMES ELLISON Great first lap in which he overtook de Puniet and Vermeulen, then Hofmann on the second. Hit the same tyre problems as his team-mate and finished 17 seconds behind Carlos.

17 JOSE LUIS CARDOSO Nursed his tyres to the finish but a lap behind the leaders.

NON-FINISHERS

CASEY STONER Crashed spectacularly at Arrabbiata 2 on lap nine while lying third, having already made up for his third-row start. Lucky to walk away with nothing worse than a sore neck.

ALEX HOFMANN Crashed at Correntaio, having slid backwards after a good start. Said he lost the front because his tyres weren't up to temperature.

CATALAN GP
CATALUNYA
ROUND 7

COLLATERAL DAMAGE

Rossi may have won and Hayden extended his championship lead, but it was a first-corner, multi-bike accident that dominated the weekend and overshadowed even the renaissance of Team Roberts

It is very easy to forget just how dangerous motorcycle racing can be. Modern circuits and hugely improved protective equipment have made serious injury much rarer than it was even a few years ago, but nothing can ever mitigate the consequences of the pack being skittled at the first corner.

The accident happened at over 120mph as the field accelerated from the grid towards the right-hander that makes up the first part of Turn 1, and it was instigated by the two Marlboro Ducatis touching – Gibernau was moving towards the inside of the track as Capirossi edged the other way. Sete's front brake lever hit the back of his team-mate's bike, slamming the carbon brakes on, pivoting the Desmosedici around its front-tyre contact patch and body-slamming its rider into the tarmac. Loris veered to his right and collected Marco Melandri, and both men were thrown straight down the track. By great good luck neither Ducati rider was hit by another bike, but Melandri was not so fortunate: he slid into Pedrosa's bike, pushing the Spaniard into Hopkins

and then, caught up with the Honda, was dragged along by his arm. Pedrosa toppled over as soon as the entangled bikes hit the gravel trap but Hopkins carried on, only baling out just before the Suzuki centre-punched the tyre wall. The other victim was Randy de Puniet who was on the outside of the track and had to dodge Gibernau's flying Ducati before tumbling into the gravel.

Melandri and Capirossi lay motionless as the dust cleared. Pedrosa waved his arms and remounted, and de Puniet helped Gibernau (who never lost consciousness but was concussed) to remove his gloves.

The race was stopped before the end of the lap, nearly spoiling Casey Stoner's day. The young Aussie had made a lightning start from the third row and was leading when the red flag came out. Nakano had done nearly as well but was then a victim of circumstances at the restart. Vermeulen's Suzuki stalled on the grid and he pushed the bike away. A mechanic arrived with a starter but the grid was held and the start finally aborted. Chris escaped sanction – most people thought he should have been sent to the back of the grid for further delaying the start – but poor Shinya Nakano didn't. While waiting for the Suzuki's problem to be sorted out his Kawasaki overheated and he went to pit lane to collect his spare bike. He should then have started from the back of the grid but instead went to his qualifying place. When he didn't see the board calling him in for a penalty he was black-flagged.

The restart didn't signal the end of the crashing. The tarmac at the Circuit de Catalunya undergoes extreme temperature variations very quickly, and by the time the race began track temperatures were much higher than they'd been all weekend. Temperature swings like this cause a matching change in grip levels, catching out quite a few riders. No fewer than four went down when they lost the front end, with Elias, de Puniet, Pedrosa and Stoner all succumbing to the slick track. The crashes looked like the sort usually seen in a 250cc race – and all of the crashers were 250 men not that long ago!

Stoner's exit came after his second bullet start of the day and when he'd led for one-third of the race distance. Rossi was working his way up from fifth, taking Roberts on lap four, Hopkins on lap six and Hayden two laps later. It only took another lap for him to get past Casey and half a lap later the Aussie slid

Above Stoner gets his second holeshot of the day to lead the restarted race

Opposite The nastiest crash MotoGP has seen in a while: the Ducatis tumble into the gravel as Melandri is dragged there by Pedrosa's bike

Below Dani Pedrosa tries to pick his bike up after losing the front in the restarted race

Above Carlos Checa celebrates his best result of the year in front of his home fans

Below Hayden finished second but came away with a bigger advantage at the top of the table

off at the slow left-hander before the stadium section. He claimed he was comfortable and would have been happy to follow Rossi, but it looked as if he'd simply tried to use too much bank angle and the bike slipped out from under him. De Puniet had already gone down in a similar fashion and a couple of laps later Elias did the same thing; next time round Pedrosa lost the front in Turn 1, forfeiting what looked like a good chance of third place in the process.

All this left Rossi with a clear lead, with Hayden in touch in second and performing way above the pace he'd shown any time previously in the weekend – he'd been tenth in warm-up. Valentino and Nicky were stretching their lead away from the fight for third place which now involved two men turning their teams' fortunes round: John Hopkins on the Suzuki and Kenny Roberts on his dad's Honda-engined KR machine. Twelve months previously Bridgestone tyres had had a nightmare at Catalunya but now, just as they'd done in Qatar, they put in a competitive performance and enabled Hopper to equal his best finishing position in a MotoGP race. That was fourth, because Roberts had enough in hand to let the Suzuki through so he could inspect Hopkins's strengths and weaknesses before repassing him. Roberts's third place was the first rostrum for the KR team since they started racing with their own machine in 1997, and while the big crash had removed three potential podium finishers Kenny had been as fast, if not faster, than anyone from the first session on Friday and he started from the front row.

Rossi hit the front with ten laps to go and was content to maintain his lead at around or just over a second. On lap 17 Hayden pressed and reduced the advantage to under half a second. It looked for a moment as if he could challenge Valentino but the World Champion had a bit in reserve and pulled away over the closing stages. Not a bad day for Nicky, though, despite his practice and qualifying troubles, because he went 20 points clear at the top of the table. The ramifications of the big crash would be felt for some time, and not just because this was the first of a run of three races on three consecutive weekends so any lingering injuries would seriously affect a rider's season. It was also horribly obvious that Ducati's hopes in the rider, constructor and team championships had all ended in the dust at Turn 1.

RETURN OF THE KING

Kenny Roberts Senior's model for the future of racing has always been based on F1 practice: source an engine from a specialist and build your own racer round it. However, from 1997, when he started building and racing his own bike, he'd tried to construct not just the bike but his own motor as well. With the advent of MotoGP he built his own V5, while last year there was an ultimately unsuccessful co-operation with KTM.

Finally, for 2006, Team KR had Honda motors – the first time that Kenny Snr, one of Yamaha's greatest-ever riders, has had anything to do with HRC. 'It's kinda weird,' he said early in the season. The improvement has been astonishing and considerably aided by a few words of advice from HRC in China (where, incidentally, Honda President Takeo Fukui was present). Team KR incorporated half of the suggestions in their chassis for the French GP, another 25 per cent for Mugello, and the complete package for a test on the Monday after the Italian race. The modifications concerned chassis stiffness and, say the team, confirmed that the direction in which they were moving was correct.

After the test Kenny Jnr parked the bike and told the team not to touch it before Catalunya. Even then he professed himself surprised by the team's qualifying performance, saying he thought the third or fourth row would have been pretty good. Nor was he bullish about his chances before the race: 'I'll be happy if I can see Valentino when I come down the home straight.' Afterwards he said he didn't start fast 'because I didn't want to bump into anyone important' which is Roberts' code for 'I didn't want to push as hard as those young kids early on.' His dad wasn't inclined to say much afterwards, but a tear was detected escaping from behind the shades.

HRC takes an active interest in Team KR's work, especially as the Roberts bike uses a very different air intake system from the Hondas and their chassis design is reverting to what they know from the old days with the 500s, with one end of the rear shock absorber mounted directly to the frame, unlike Honda's Unit Pro-Link design.

CATALAN GP

CATALUNYA

ROUND 7

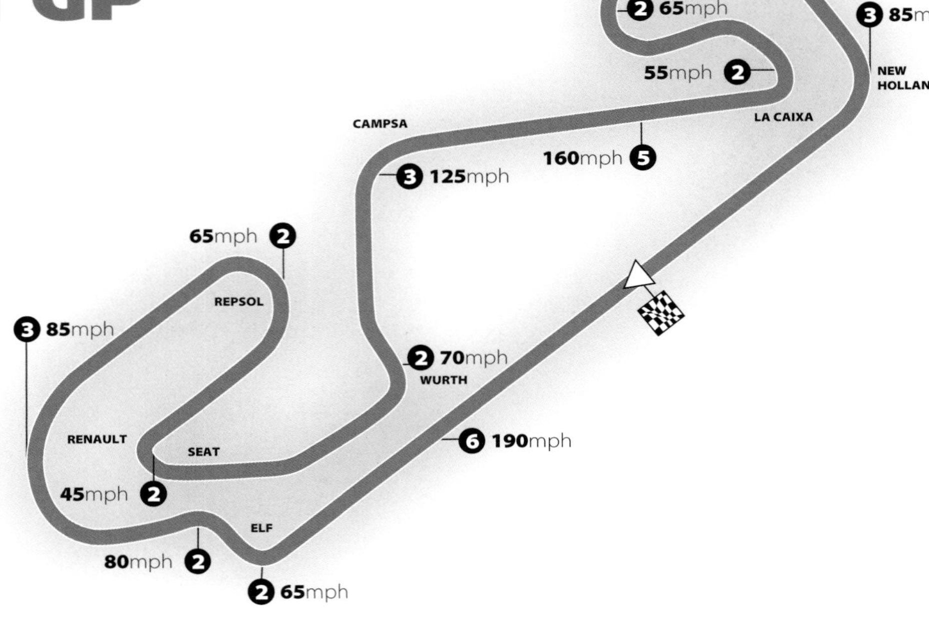

RACE RESULTS

RACE DATE June 18th
CIRCUIT LENGTH 2.937 miles
NO. OF LAPS 24
RACE DISTANCE 70.488miles
WEATHER Dry, 27°C
TRACK TEMPERATURE 47°C
WINNER Valentino Rossi
FASTEST LAP 1m 43.048s, 102.617mph, Nicky Hayden (record)
PREVIOUS LAP RECORD 1m 43.195s, 102.240mph, Valentino Rossi, 2005

QUALIFYING

	Rider	Nationality	Team	Qualifying	Pole +	Gap
1	Rossi	ITA	Camel Yamaha Team	1m 41.855s		
2	Hopkins	USA	Rizla Suzuki MotoGP	1m 41.984s	0.129s	0.129s
3	Roberts	USA	Team Roberts	1m 42.055s	0.200s	0.071s
4	Vermeulen	AUS	Rizla Suzuki MotoGP	1m 42.211s	0.356s	0.156s
5	Nakano	JPN	Kawasaki Racing Team	1m 42.216s	0.361s	0.005s
6	Capirossi	ITA	Ducati Marlboro Team	1m 42.247s	0.392s	0.031s
7	Hayden	USA	Repsol Honda Team	1m 42.305s	0.450s	0.058s
8	Stoner	AUS	Honda LCR	1m 42.344s	0.489s	0.039s
9	Melandri	ITA	Fortuna Honda	1m 42.492s	0.637s	0.148s
10	De Puniet	FRA	Kawasaki Racing Team	1m 42.620s	0.765s	0.128s
11	Pedrosa	SPA	Repsol Honda Team	1m 42.648s	0.793s	0.028s
12	Edwards	USA	Camel Yamaha Team	1m 42.655s	0.800s	0.007s
13	Gibernau	SPA	Ducati Marlboro Team	1m 42.712s	0.857s	0.057s
14	Elias	SPA	Fortuna Honda	1m 42.853s	0.998s	0.141s
15	Tamada	JPN	Konica Minolta Honda	1m 42.869s	1.014s	0.016s
16	Checa	SPA	Tech 3 Yamaha	1m 43.606s	1.751s	0.737s
17	Hofmann	GER	Pramac d'Antin MotoGP	1m 44.626s	2.771s	1.020s
18	Ellison	GBR	Tech 3 Yamaha	1m 44.727s	2.872s	0.101s
19	Cardoso	SPA	Pramac d'Antin MotoGP	1m 45.562s	3.707s	0.835s

FINISHERS

1 VALENTINO ROSSI The start was his only problem all weekend – he made a mess of it and was fifth at the end of the first lap. Then it was business as usual (or, rather, as it was in previous seasons): steady progress to the front, the lead before half-distance and controlling the one challenge that materialised.

2 NICKY HAYDEN Rossi called the American's race 'a small miracle': he qualified seventh, was tenth in morning warm-up, and then set fastest race lap! Nicky was honest enough to say he knew Valentino had plenty in hand so he had to be content with retaking the championship lead.

3 KENNY ROBERTS A fabulous weekend for the whole team, with Kenny Junior's first rostrum on the Team Roberts bike backing up an excellent front-row start. On qualifying evidence he'd have been on the rostrum even without the legion of crashers.

4 JOHN HOPKINS Caught up in the first-turn crash, then had to use his spare bike for the restart. Suffered from back pain where he'd been hit by Pedrosa's bike and never looked likely to hold off Roberts in the battle for third. Still equalled his best MotoGP finish.

5 COLIN EDWARDS An anonymous weekend; the disappointment of finishing over 20 seconds behind his team-mate outweighed the handy haul of points. Caught out by the rise in track temperature and had problems losing the front during the race.

6 CHRIS VERMEULEN Didn't back up his excellent qualifying, mainly due to a duff start. Coped with the slick surface well and was happy with his best MotoGP finish so far.

7 MAKOTO TAMADA Got a good start, then ran into serious problems with rear grip and had to back off the throttle to avoid 'useless spinning'. The second of only two Hondas to finish; just managed to hold off Checa.

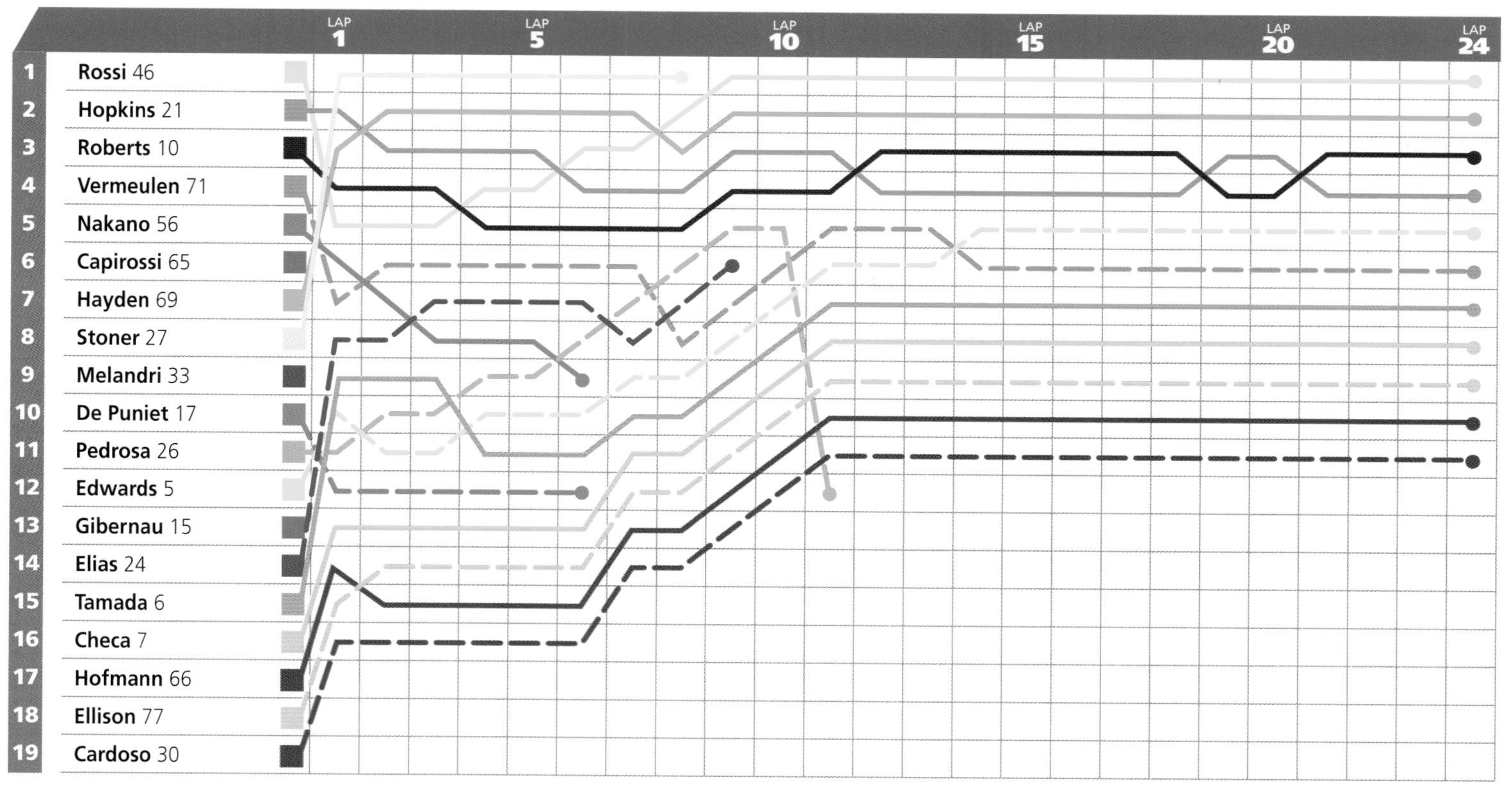

RACE

	Rider	Motorcycle	Race Time	Time +	Fastest Lap	Average Speed
1	Rossi	Yamaha	41m 31.237s		1m 43.200s	101.806mph
2	Hayden	Honda	41m 35.746s	4.509s	1m 43.048s	101.622mph
3	Roberts	KR211V	41m 40.411s	9.174s	1m 43.355s	101.433mph
4	Hopkins	Suzuki	41m 44.702s	13.465s	1m 43.275s	101.259mph
5	Edwards	Yamaha	41m 53.785s	22.548s	1m 43.808s	100.893mph
6	Vermeulen	Suzuki	41m 56.435s	25.198s	1m 43.562s	100.787mph
7	Tamada	Honda	42m 01.859s	30.622s	1m 44.164s	100.570mph
8	Checa	Yamaha	42m 02.514s	31.277s	1m 44.171s	100.544mph
9	Ellison	Yamaha	42m 30.440s	59.203s	1m 45.108s	99.443mph
10	Hofmann	Ducati	42m 45.299s	1m 14.062	1m 45.679s	98.867mph
11	Cardoso	Ducati	43m 18.052s	1m 46.815	1m 45.893s	97.620mph
	Pedrosa	Honda	20m 32.779s	13 laps	1m 43.183s	94.294mph
	Elias	Honda	15m 40.239s	15 laps	1m 43.545s	101.154mph
	Stoner	Honda	13m 52.838s	16 laps	1m 43.318s	101.510mph
	De Puniet	Kawasaki	10m 32.763s	18 laps	1m 44.171s	100.204mph
	Gibernau	Ducati				
	Melandri	Honda				
	Capirossi	Ducati				
	Nakano	Kawasaki	–	–	1m 43.835s	

CHAMPIONSHIP

	Rider	Team	Points
1	Hayden	Repsol Honda Team	119
2	Capirossi	Ducati Marlboro Team	99
3	Rossi	Camel Yamaha Team	90
4	Melandri	Fortuna Honda	89
5	Pedrosa	Repsol Honda Team	86
6	Stoner	Honda LCR	65
7	Edwards	Camel Yamaha Team	60
8	Elias	Fortuna Honda	53
9	Tamada	Konica Minolta Honda	49
10	Roberts	Team Roberts	44
11	Gibernau	Ducati Marlboro Team	44
12	Hopkins	Rizla Suzuki MotoGP	40
13	Nakano	Kawasaki Racing Team	37
14	Vermeulen	Rizla Suzuki MotoGP	31
15	Checa	Tech 3 Yamaha	24
16	Ellison	Tech 3 Yamaha	12
17	Hofmann	Pramac d'Antin MotoGP	12
18	De Puniet	Kawasaki Racing Team	11
19	Cardoso	Pramac d'Antin MotoGP	5

8 CARLOS CHECA As happy as he'd been all year, not so much with his finishing position as with the performance: consistent lap times (17 laps in the 1m 44s bracket) all very close to those of Edwards, and the ability to fight with Tamada all the way to the flag.

9 JAMES ELLISON Almost happy with himself but definitely 'chuffed' for the team and Dunlop. Disappointed at being unable to run his warm-up times in the race but encouraged by progress both in bike set-up and with the tyres.

10 ALEX HOFMANN Reckoned it was the most boring race of his life. Tried to go with Ellison but found he couldn't press at all without hitting serious problems. His depression lifted by the news that he would ride Gibernau's bike while the Spaniard recovered.

11 JOSE LUIS CARDOSO Never found a tyre or a set-up he could work with and ended up over 30 seconds adrift of his team-mate.

NON-FINISHERS

SHINYA NAKANO Black-flagged after failing to come in for a ride-through penalty. His bike overheated on the (second) grid so he ran to pit lane for his other machine but unfortunately started from his qualifying slot rather than the back, hence the penalty.

DANI PEDRODSA Used his second bike for the restart and admitted to being nervous in front of his home crowd. Made a bad start, then crashed coming onto the straight while fighting his way towards the front of the field.

TONI ELIAS A home race to forget: looked to be making up for a dreadful practice and qualifying when he lost the front.

CASEY STONER Two brilliant starts and eight laps in the lead followed by a front-end crash. Until then it was a brilliant debut at the Catalan circuit.

RANDY DE PUNIET Another ex-250 rider who lost the front end: he was trying to catch Tamada at the time. Also one of the victims of that first-corner horror show, although he simply toppled over in the gravel having taken avoiding action.

NON-STARTERS

SETE GIBERNAU The most badly injured of the six men who crashed at the first corner: he was body-slammed into the tarmac when his front brake caught on Capirossi's bike and his own Ducati locked the front wheel and looped. Suffered a re-break of his left collarbone.

MARCO MELANDRI Tangled first with his own and then with Pedrosa's bike, resulting in a dislocation of the top of his collarbone. Also suffered serious whiplash and concussion. Looked to be unconscious for a while after the crash.

LORIS CAPIROSSI Amazingly, walked into the Clinica Mobile despite, like Melandri, looking to be unconscious after the crash. The first diagnosis was pessimistic, with worries about internal bleeding. Given that he suffered internal injuries when crashing in Australia in 2005, the subsequent clean bill of health was a relief.

DUTCH TT
ASSEN

ROUND 8

LAST MAN STANDING

The injury list grew and Nicky Hayden took a big step towards the title, but only after the most dramatic last-corner shoot-out with Colin Edwards

The Dutch TT took place less than a week after that Catalunya crash, so its effects were still being felt. Capirossi's severe bruising meant he could barely ride, Melandri's shoulder was hurting and he looked like he'd been beaten up, while Sete Gibernau was at home in Barcelona after a lengthy operation to repair his collarbone. Sete's misfortune was Alex Hofmann's opportunity: the German was promoted from the satellite d'Antin team to the factory Marlboro Ducati squad. Despite the change from Dunlop to Bridgestone tyres he was optimistic; at last he had the chance to find out how good he could be given top machinery. Alex's ride was taken by double Spanish champion Ivan Silva, already a d'Antin employee for the team in the Spanish Formula Extreme Championship.

After the first practice session the list of casualties lengthened by two when a new Michelin tyre and the cool track surface caught out both Toni Elias and Valentino Rossi. The Spaniard went home with a

PlayStation
Honda Racing
MICHELIN
Spain's Nº1
Spain's Nº1
V28
LITHIUM-ION
HONDA
PlayStation

cracked bone in his shoulder while Rossi, who crashed on the high-speed run back to the final chicane, was taken to a local hospital. A precautionary scan revealed no damage to his abdomen, but he had bones broken in both his left foot and right wrist.

There was considerable doubt as to whether any of the injured riders would actually race, with rumours flying around that the local medical officer would rule against Melandri competing. In the end everybody went out for every session, although Rossi and, to a lesser extent, Capirossi only made token appearances in the third practice session to save themselves for qualifying. Valentino did qualify, but 18th and last; he was obviously hurting a lot.

Yamaha didn't suffer too badly, with the other Camel rider going well once he'd got rid of that Michelin tyre. Colin Edwards realised there was a problem after a couple of moments and toured in to change it, soon making up for the time lost by being fastest in the second and third sessions. To add to Yamaha's joy Carlos Checa was second fastest on the Dunlop-shod Tech 3 M1 in second practice. After recording an impressive, if not dominant, set of long runs on race tyres it looked as if Colin was a shoo-in for pole position but he was baulked on his last flying lap and had to settle for third spot on the front row. Nevertheless, he looked an odds-on favourite for the race, although Nicky Hayden beat him by a significant margin in morning warm-up on race day.

All of which deflected attention from John Hopkins's career-first MotoGP pole position, further proof of just how far the Rizla Suzuki team had come since the debacle of Qatar. After Edwards got the holeshot in the race everyone made it safely round the new, ultra-tight De Strubben corner, with Hopkins and Nakano leading the chase. The warm race-day weather decided the fate of the two Bridgestone riders. After warm-up Kawasaki had opted for harder tyres to cope with the predicted temperature rise so Nakano was able to stay competitive in the second half of the race; the Suzuki team hadn't and Hopkins didn't.

Nakano's tyre generated some chatter early on and he was unable to prevent Hayden getting up to third. Then he had to watch the men in front of him pull away. A quarter of the way into the race Hayden took second with a spectacular round-the-outside line at the right-

Above John Hopkins started from pole position for the first time in his career

Opposite Scars from the Barcelona crash are still fresh on Marco Melandri six days after the event

Below Colin Edwards using all the Assen track and a little bit more

Above Dani Pedrosa won the battle for the final rostrum position

Below Alex Hofmann replaced Gibernau on the factory Ducati

handed entry to the chicane, a move that would play a vital part in the dramatic denouement. As Hopkins faded with tyre problems, Nakano was able to up his pace and keep clear of the frantic fight for fourth between Pedrosa, Stoner and Roberts. Meanwhile Rossi was starting to enjoy himself, making stealthy progress through the field; by half-distance he was 12th and lapping at the same pace as the leader.

The two Americans pulled clear of the field in the second half of the race, with the gap only once creeping above a second. In the closing laps Hayden piled on the pressure: from laps 20 to 23 of the 26 the gap was a tenth of a second. With four and three laps to go Nicky showed Colin a wheel at the final chicane – but on the inside. The real attack came at the hardest braking effort of the lap, Ruskenhoek, on the penultimate lap. This is the section of track that had been modified the previous year to produce a 90-degree right-hander. Hayden went up the inside on the brakes and took Edwards's line, sending the Yamaha man across the tarmac on the outside of the track. Colin rejoined the circuit over a second adrift. It looked all over. It wasn't.

Colin Edwards rode a last lap that was perfection right up until that chicane. Half way round he had demolished Hayden's lead, and two corners from the chicane he hit the front on the way into the ultra-fast

Ramshoek corner where Rossi had crashed in practice. Then came the chicane. Colin shaped to take the defensive inside line on the right while Nicky looked to repeat the manoeuvre he'd put on Hopkins earlier by taking a wide line into the right-hand entry, thus putting himself where Colin wouldn't want to see him at the point where they flicked left. Neither of them got it right. Nicky found a false neutral and wobbled, Colin got in hot, ran wide, couldn't make the left flick and ran across the kerbing. With the Yamaha upright he touched the throttle while he was on the Astroturf on th eoutside of the track, the rear spun up and he was thrown off. His first MotoGP win disappeared – and with it, some said, went the prospect of renewing his Yamaha contract. He got going again to salvage a few points but punched his screen to pieces after he crossed the line. Amazingly he was able to make a joke out of it, but only after his little daughter Gracie had kissed his bruises better. 'Every lap it was "brake, turn, gas!" But that time it was "brake, turn, dumbass!" ' He still had time for a dig at Hayden, though. In an echo of Mick Doohan's tow-truck jibe at Alex Criville, Colin voiced the opinion that Nicky could follow but couldn't lead. If Nicky was bothered he didn't show it. His first win away from the USA was much more important, as was his significantly improved points lead.

Right Valentino Rossi takes a few deep breaths and assesses the damage following his crash in the first free practice session

Below Yee-hah! Nicky Hayden celebrates his first win outside the United States

THE BOYS ON THE BLACK STUFF

*The much-discussed new Assen layout met with an almost universal thumbs down. Pole-position man John Hopkins put it best, saying that if this were a brand-new track everyone would have been heaping praise on it but if you'd known the old layout you wouldn't be so enthusiastic. Rather touchingly, he added that he was delighted to have taken his first pole position but would rather it had been on the track his boyhood heroes raced on. As usual, Colin Edwards had an opinion. Despite being far and away the fastest man for the most laps, he described the new track as ****. Ex-125 champ Arnaud Vincent said simply, 'Assen is dead.' The only MotoGP riders to view the new track positively were the Japanese pairing of Makoto Tamada and Shinya Nakano.*

The Northern Loop that formed the first part of the old lap from the first corner round to the steeply banked De Strubben left-hand hairpin that led on to the old back 'straight' has been replaced by a set of decreasing-radius rights and a new De Strubben, much tighter than before and surrounded by a gravel trap of Qatar-like proportions. De Strubben used to be a prime passing place as well as a spectacular and unique corner; now it's just another slow bend, and it caused a first-lap pile-up in the 250 race.

Assen never used to have straight lines or right-angled bends yet it was the fastest track on the calendar. Not any more.

Local journalist Willhelm Lute had a good idea for using up the pile of surplus tarmac. Small portions were sandwiched between plates of glass and edged with aluminium strip. The resulting framed 'pictures' then had an outline trace of the old circuit enamelled on one side. They were then auctioned to benefit Riders for Health.

DUTCH TT
ASSEN

ROUND 8

RACE RESULTS

RACE DATE June 24th
CIRCUIT LENGTH 2.830miles
NO. OF LAPS 26
RACE DISTANCE 73.592 miles
WEATHER Dry, 23°C
TRACK TEMPERATURE 29°C
WINNER Nicky Hayden
FASTEST LAP 1m 37.106s, 104.934mph, Nicky Hayden (record)
PREVIOUS LAP RECORD Circuit Length Changed

QUALIFYING

	Rider	Nationality	Team	Qualifying	Pole +	Gap
1	Hopkins	USA	Rizla Suzuki MotoGP	1m 36.411s		
2	Nakano	JPN	Kawasaki Racing Team	1m 36.424s	0.013s	0.013s
3	Edwards	USA	Camel Racing Team	1m 36.755s	0.344s	0.331s
4	Hayden	USA	Repsol Honda Team	1m 36.758s	0.347s	0.003s
5	Pedrosa	SPA	Repsol Honda Team	1m 36.993s	0.582s	0.235s
6	Vermeulen	AUS	Rizla Suzuki MotoGP	1m 37.077s	0.666s	0.084s
7	Melandri	ITA	Fortuna Honda	1m 37.332s	0.921s	0.255s
8	Checa	SPA	Tech 3 Yamaha	1m 37.378s	0.967s	0.046s
9	Hofmann	GER	Ducati Marlboro Team	1m 37.399s	0.988s	0.021s
10	Roberts	USA	Team Roberts	1m 37.528s	1.117s	0.129s
11	De Puniet	FRA	Kawasaki Racing Team	1m 37.556s	1.145s	0.028s
12	Stoner	AUS	Honda LCR	1m 37.660s	1.249s	0.104s
13	Tamada	JPN	Konica Minolta Honda	1m 37.676s	1.265s	0.016s
14	Ellison	GBR	Tech 3 Yamaha	1m 38.055s	1.644s	0.379s
15	Capirossi	ITA	Ducati Marlboro Team	1m 38.060s	1.649s	0.005s
16	Cardoso	SPA	Pramac d'Antin MotoGP	1m 39.406s	2.995s	1.346s
17	Silva	SPA	Pramac d'Antin MotoGP	1m 39.496s	3.085s	0.090s
18	Rossi	ITA	Camel Yamaha Team	1m 40.298s	3.887s	0.802s

FINISHERS

1 NICKY HAYDEN His second win of the season, the first away from home and Honda's 200th in the top class. An epic battle with Edwards was concluded at the final chicane: both riders made mistakes; Nicky's was the less serious. The win, and others' misfortunes, boosted his championship lead to 42 points.

2 SHINYA NAKANO His career-best finish in MotoGP and Kawasaki's best dry-weather result. Good start from the front row but couldn't run at the leaders' early pace due to chatter from a hard front tyre. At half-distance passed Hopkins for third which, up to the last corner, Shinya thought would be his final position.

3 DANI PEDROSA Lost time at the start on a full tank and also fighting with Melandri, then had a battle with Stoner that was resolved on the last lap. Surprised to be directed to parc fermé and what he admitted was a lucky rostrum.

4 CASEY STONER A fine race after set-up problems put him back on the fourth row. His usual great start, but then boxed in at the first turn and was fifth when Pedrosa came past. Lost grip in left-handers and made a mistake on the last lap, which let Dani off the hook. A good comeback from crashes in the two previous races.

5 KENNY ROBERTS Shadowed the Pedrosa/Stoner dice but couldn't find a way past. Honest enough to say he was faster than them but didn't want to do anything stupid trying to get ahead – the duo were side by side anywhere there was a possibility of overtaking.

6 JOHN HOPKINS Started from his first pole position in MotoGP and shadowed leader Edwards for the first third of the race before dropping off the pace with grip problems. Unlike Nakano, Hopper did not choose the harder front Bridgestone for the race.

7 MARCO MELANDRI Seventh on the grid and in the race despite looking like he'd been beaten up (which he was six days previously, at the first turn of the Catalan GP). Didn't do too many laps in practice because of neck and shoulder pain, yet still managed the whole race and limited the damage to his points standing.

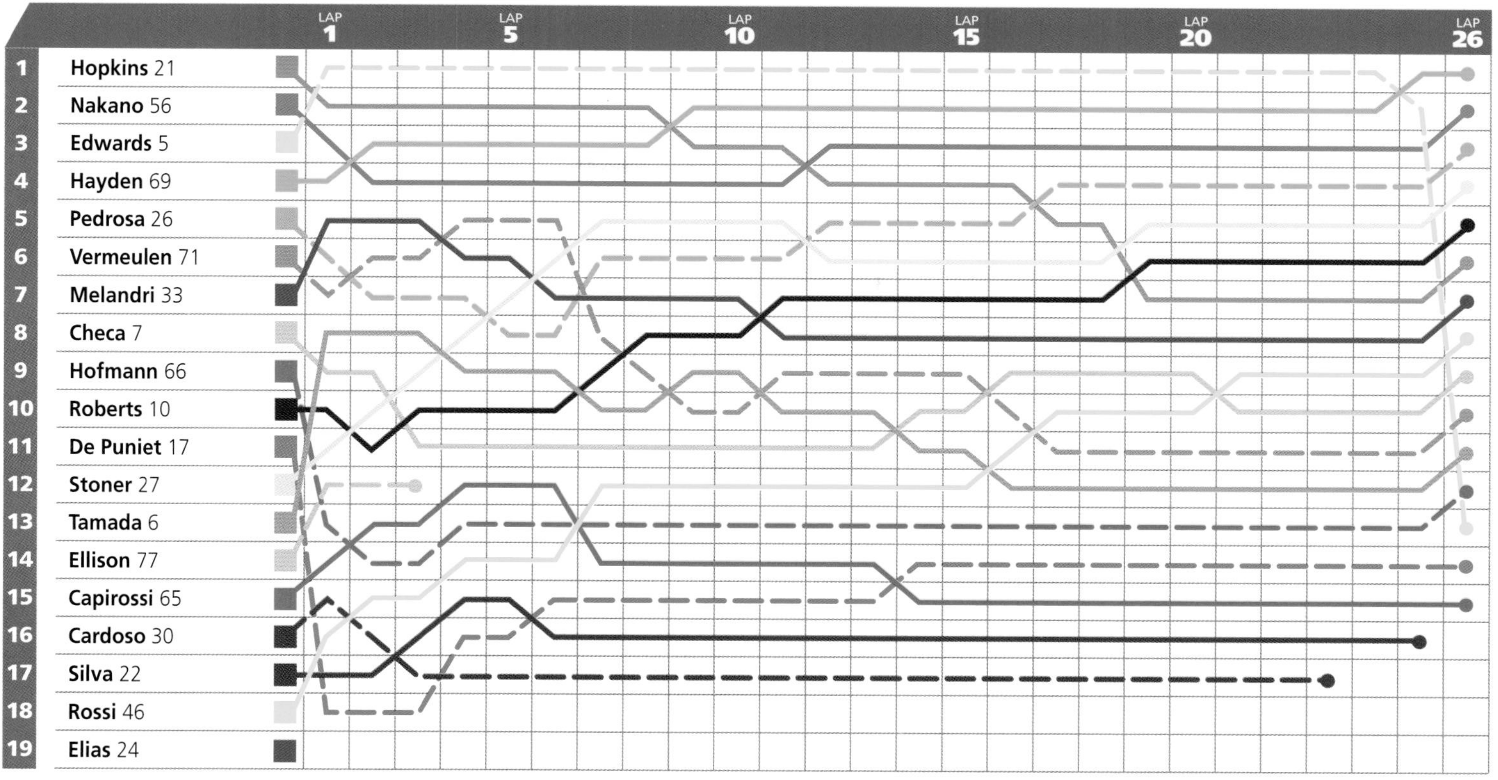

RACE

	Rider	Motorcycle	Race Time	Time +	Fastest Lap	Average Speed
1	Hayden	Honda	42m 27.404s		1m 37.106s	103.934mph
2	Nakano	Kawasaki	42m 32.288s	4.884s	1m 37.453s	103.735mph
3	Pedrosa	Honda	42m 34.929s	7.525s	1m 37.451s	103.627mph
4	Stoner	Honda	42m 34.959s	7.555s	1m 37.232s	103.626mph
5	Roberts	KR211V	42m 35.482s	8.078s	1m 37.432s	103.605mph
6	Hopkins	Suzuki	42m 44.469s	17.065s	1m 37.406s	103.242mph
7	Melandri	Honda	42m 45.494s	18.090s	1m 38.000s	103.201mph
8	Rossi	Yamaha	42m 51.355s	23.951s	1m 37.777s	102.965mph
9	Checa	Yamaha	42m 56.431s	29.027s	1m 38.119s	102.763mph
10	Vermeulen	Suzuki	42m 59.031s	31.627s	1m 37.925s	102.654mph
11	Tamada	Honda	43m 00.245s	32.841s	1m 38.003s	102.611mph
12	Hofmann	Ducati	43m 01.547s	34.143s	1m 38.397s	102.559mph
13	Edwards	Yamaha	43m 07.816s	40.412s	1m 37.324s	102.311mph
14	De Puniet	Kawasaki	43m 31.052s	1m 03.648s	1m 38.709s	101.400mph
15	Capirossi	Ducati	43m 44.707s	1m 17.303s	1m 38.962s	100.873mph
16	Silva	Ducati	43m 14.455s	1 lap	1m 40.662s	98.124mph
17	Cardoso	Ducati	42m 30.046s	3 laps	1m 40.791s	91.846mph
	Ellison	Yamaha	5m 04.700s	23 laps	1m 39.022s	100.260mph

CHAMPIONSHIP

	Rider	Team	Points
1	Hayden	Repsol Honda Team	144
2	Pedrosa	Repsol Honda Team	102
3	Capirossi	Ducati Marlboro Team	100
4	Rossi	Camel Yamaha Team	98
5	Melandri	Fortuna Honda	98
6	Stoner	Honda LCR	78
7	Edwards	Camel Yamaha Team	63
8	Nakano	Kawasaki Racing Team	57
9	Roberts	Team Roberts	55
10	Tamada	Konica Minolta Honda	54
11	Elias	Fortuna Honda	53
12	Hopkins	Rizla Suzuki MotoGP	50
13	Gibernau	Ducati Marlboro Team	44
14	Vermeulen	Rizla Suzuki MotoGP	37
15	Checa	Tech 3 Yamaha	31
16	Hofmann	Pramac d'Antin MotoGP	16
17	De Puniet	Kawasaki Racing Team	13
18	Ellison	Tech 3 Yamaha	12
19	Cardoso	Pramac d'Antin MotoGP	5

8 VALENTINO ROSSI A remarkable result, under the circumstances: broke bones in his right wrist and left foot on Thursday and qualified last on Friday. Started slowly but once the adrenaline began flowing started enjoying himself and passing people. It could all have been a lot worse.

9 CARLOS CHECA Seriously pleased to be fighting with some very good riders (he passed Tamada and Vermeulen) and satisfied with the performance of his tyres at this and the previous race. By the time Rossi got to him the front was chattering so decided to bring it home for the points.

10 CHRIS VERMEULEN Up front in the opening laps but ran into front-tyre problems as early as lap ten. Had a difficult race from then on and was grateful to get a top-ten finish.

11 MAKOTO TAMADA Thought he'd found a magic new front tyre and wasn't too worried about qualifying 13th, but after a confident start lost all feeling from it. Admitted he didn't do any long runs on the tyre as the suspension had to be sorted before working on the rubber.

12 ALEX HOFMANN A difficult first race on the factory Ducati as deputy for the injured Gibernau. Qualified well but made a mess of the first few corners, deferred to Capirossi but had to repass him, and by then too far behind the Vermeulen/Tamada group to make an impression.

13 COLIN EDWARDS The hard-luck story of the season. More fast laps through practice than anyone else, only the third front-row start of his MotoGP career, led every lap bar the final two, and rode one of the best last laps one could hope to see. Then it all went wrong at the last corner.

14 RANDY DE PUNIET A problem on the warm-up lap meant swapping to his spare bike and starting from pit lane. Took a while to get his brand-new tyres up to temperature but then ran well. Frustrated because he'd been fast in morning warm-up and thought he'd have a good race.

15 LORIS CAPIROSSI Never has a racer suffered so much for a single point. His chest was one enormous bruise, a legacy of the Catalunya crash, and he was seen during practice taking deep breaths and propping himself up with his fist on the tank. If Loris said it was 'almost unbearable' then it must have been the sort of pain that would send a normal human being to intensive care.

16 IVAN SILVA An impressive debut as a replacement for Hofmann, who was promoted to the factory Ducati team. Delighted to finish in his first MotoGP event and said he learnt a lot, especially about how a bike behaves when the tyres are worn.

17 JOSE LUIS CARDOSO Came into the pits after a half-dozen laps to replace a defective tyre, so never got a chance to race new team-mate Silva or grab a point or two.

NON-FINISHERS

JAMES ELLISON Right on his team-mate's tail when he lost the front end on the fourth lap. Nevertheless, happy with progress made through the meeting.

NON-STARTERS

TONI ELIAS Hurt in the same session as Rossi, returning home to Barcelona with a cracked bone in his left shoulder.

SETE GIBERNAU Ended a run of 112 starts thanks to the collarbone that was re-broken in Catalunya. Operation to replace a 13-year old plate was much more complicated than the usual surgery.

BRITISH GP
DONINGTON

ROUND 9

ONE-MAN SHOW

Pedrosa made everyone else look slow, Rossi won the battle of the walking wounded, and championship leader Hayden had a bad day at the office and lost ground to all his serious competitors

It was painfully obvious to the rest of the grid what was about to happen when the lights went out on Sunday afternoon. Barring an act of God, Dani Pedrosa would clear off into the distance, leaving the rest to sort out who was going to be second. The Spaniard had been fastest in both Friday practice sessions, had to give best to Casey Stoner on Saturday morning, but then set his third pole position of the year. As no-one else had yet set more than one pole, the rookie's achievement was astounding – and this time he beat the field by almost half a second, an unheard-of margin when one second usually covers the top ten riders, or even more.

Dani reacted by expressing mild surprise: 'I am not an expert with qualifying tyres.' Factor in that Capirossi was still hurting badly enough to sit out one practice session, Rossi was

Above The fight for second featured a lot of good riders a long way behind Dani Pedrosa

Opposite As ever, John Hopkins did his best to keep the crowd entertained

Below James Ellison doing a bit of flag-waving on the grid with his brother Dean

nursing a week-old fracture of his wrist, Melandri's shoulder was giving him hell and Hayden wasted Friday testing new parts, and it was unlikely the odds would be against a Pedrosa victory.

As this is motorcycle racing, though, it didn't pan out quite as simply as that; or, rather, it took a little bit longer than expected to pan out like that. The ever-heroic Marco Melandri was the early race leader, dutifully followed by an increasingly frustrated Pedrosa. On the fifth lap Dani made a big lunge up the inside at that favourite Donington passing place, the Melbourne Loop. He was sideways before he got level with Melandri, who thankfully saw him coming, then tried to highside himself when he got back on the gas while way off-line. It was a big enough double moment to let Hopkins through into second and lose Pedrosa over 1.5 seconds to the leader. Within three laps Dani was back in front of the Suzuki, and four laps later he was in the lead with the sort of move on the way into McLeans that's just not seen at this level, a measure of how much he had in hand. To prove the point Pedrosa was 0.8 seconds faster than Marco that time round, and next time, his first with empty tarmac in front of him, he set the best lap of the race and had a lead of over 1.5 seconds. The lead grew to over 7.5 seconds before Dani eased the pace slightly.

Thankfully both TV viewers and the crowd had a spectacular race for second to keep them entertained. It didn't involve Nicky Hayden – he'd tried a new swinging arm and revised exhaust on Friday but then decided not to race the new bike. He spent the rest of the weekend ruing the time he'd lost and wrestling a machine that looked seriously unstable in corners; electrics were blamed, although the lightweight clutch that had given problems before could have been at least partially culpable. Rossi decided it was time to have a dig at the championship leader, saying he'd followed the American for a few laps and noticed him making quite a few mistakes so the pressure must be getting to him. As Valentino never wastes effort on no-hopers who are no threat to him, that could be construed as a compliment. Nicky looked to be making up for his Friday and Saturday troubles, but then he ran straight on at the Esses, having just passed Capirossi, after which there was no way he could get to the dice for second place.

It didn't look as if Valentino Rossi would get there

Arai
Red Bull
MOTUL
CRESCENT
BRIDGESTONE
RIZLA+
SUZUKI
NGK
21
RIZLA+
SUZUKI
MOTUL
RIZLA+
SUZUKI
RIZLA+
CRESCENT
GSV-R
RIZLA+
SUZUKI
MOTUL
BRIDGESTONE
MITSUBISHI
KOKUSAN DENKI
NGK
RK
AFAM

seconds behind – and one lap later he was right on Roberts' rear wheel at the back of the group.

As soon as Rossi joined them the group was nearly skittled as Melandri clipped the inside kerb at McLeans and all but crashed: his left boot was way off the footrest and the tyres left black lines while the bike was at full lean. That let Rossi through to third, behind Stoner, and held up Roberts, who later said how impressed (and not a little relieved) he was by Marco's save.

Nothing daunted, Melandri took two laps to get back to second, a position he only held for a lap before Rossi came past. The group never really split up, but it was the two Italians who spent the rest of the race disputing second place. Almost inevitably it came down to the Melbourne Loop last time round after Melandri had finally found a way past Rossi at Foggy's. Both men went deep but Marco went deeper, and Rossi took him on the inside to make sure there was no room for a comeback on the last corner.

After the now traditional track invasion, Rossi celebrated in parc fermé with a smoking, rolling burnout that enveloped Pedrosa and his quietly celebrating Repsol crew in rubber smoke. Dani looked mildly irked. Given Rossi's physical condition and his problems in qualifying it's understandable that Valentino claimed the result was as good as a win, and that it was more important he improved his position in the championship than won the race. The crowd agreed and celebrated with Rossi as if he had taken the victory. Did any of the attention lavished on the runner-up bother the winner? Highly unlikely, especially as he too had significantly improved his second-place position in the World Championship.

Above Pedrosa ran away from the field

Opposite Casey Stoner chases Roberts and Melandri through Foggy's

Right That damaged wrist was still up to a little light exercise after the race

either. Whenever he has started from the third or, as in this case, the fourth row of the grid, he has blitzed the first lap to get with the front men as soon as possible. Not this time. As is their habit, his team had rescued what looked like a lost cause with some inspired work, despite effectively losing the 20-minute warm-up to rain. However, it took Valentino eight laps 'to understand how good my pace could be'. Once he understood he dropped his pace into the 1m 29s bracket, only lowering it once to 1m 30s. At mid-race that was the same pace as the dice in front of him, consisting of Melandri, Roberts and Stoner once Hopkins had faded with tyre worries. The gap stuck at around two seconds for the third quarter of the race, then suddenly, at two-thirds' distance, he was 1.6

THE ROYAL MARCH

The Spanish national anthem, the Marca Real, is probably unique in that it has no words. It was heard three times at Donington Park to mark a very special occasion, for there were three Spanish winners: Alvaro Bautista in the 125s, Jorge Lorenzo in the 250s and the all-conquering Dani Pedrosa in MotoGP. This was not a unique occurrence in itself, but the fact that all three of them had won from pole position certainly was because it's never happened before in the 57-year history of Grand Prix racing. Spaniards did achieve a hat-trick of wins at Le Mans in 2003, thanks to Pedrosa, Elias and Gibernau, and at Rijeka in the old Yugoslavia in 1988 when Sito Pons won the 250s and Aspar Martinez did the 80 and 125cc double. At the final race of 2005, in Valencia, Spanish riders took all three poles: Gadea in the 125s, Pedrosa in the 250s and Gibernau in MotoGP. However, the 2006 British GP demonstrated a new level of domination and reflected the position of motorcycle racing nationally in Spanish sport. Of the 27 races in the three classes so far in 2006, Spanish riders had won 13 of them, the next most successful nation being Italy, with eight victories.

Pedrosa's second win in only his ninth race in the top class meant he had more wins, more podiums, more pole positions and scored more points than Valentino Rossi had in his first nine races in what was then the 500cc class in 2000.

BRITISH GP
DONINGTON

ROUND 9

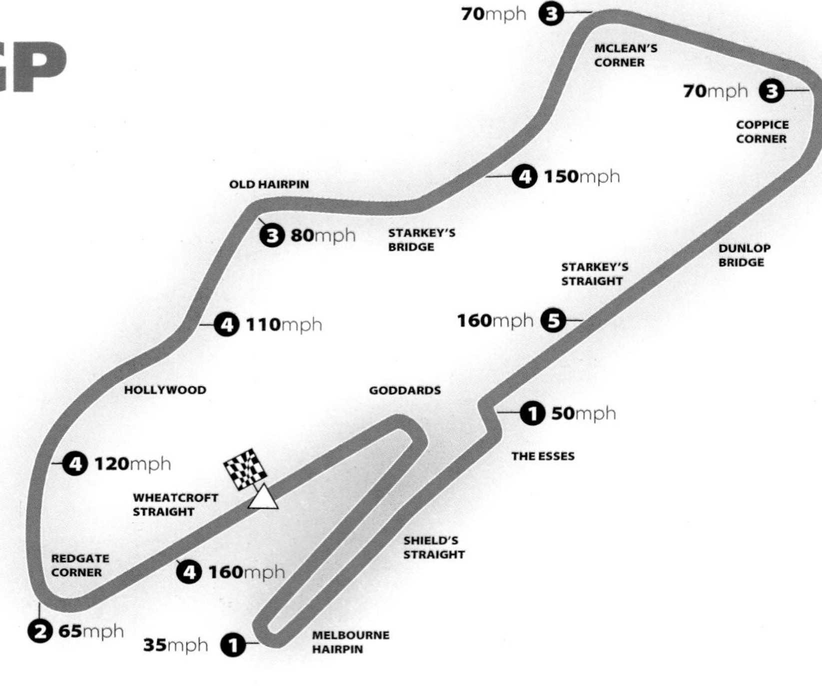

RACE RESULTS

RACE DATE July 2nd
CIRCUIT LENGTH 2.500 miles
NO. OF LAPS 30
RACE DISTANCE 74.993 miles
WEATHER Dry, 27°C
TRACK TEMPERATURE 45°C
WINNER Dani Pedrosa
FASTEST LAP 1m27.714s, 101.440kph, Dani Pdrosa (Record)
PREVIOUS LAP RECORD 1m29.973s, 100.026mph, Colin Edwards, 2004

QUALIFYING

	Rider	Nationality	Team	Qualifying	Pole +	Gap
1	Pedrosa	SPA	Repsol Honda Team	1m 27.676s		
2	Vermeulen	AUS	Rizla Suzuki MotoGP	1m 28.158s	0.482s	0.482s
3	Melandri	ITA	Fortuna Honda	1m 28.205s	0.529s	0.047s
4	Hopkins	USA	Rizla Suzuki MotoGP	1m 28.252s	0.576s	0.047s
5	Capirossi	ITA	Ducati Marlboro Team	1m 28.394s	0.718s	0.142s
6	De Puniet	FRA	Kawasaki Racing Team	1m 28.428s	0.752s	0.034s
7	Nakano	JPN	Kawasaki Racing Team	1m 28.431s	0.755s	0.003s
8	Stoner	AUS	Honda LCR	1m 28.447s	0.771s	0.016s
9	Roberts	USA	Team Roberts	1m 28.473s	0.797s	0.026s
10	Edwards	USA	Camel Yamaha Team	1m 28.481s	0.805s	0.008s
11	Hayden	USA	Repsol Honda Team	1m 28.509s	0.833s	0.028s
12	Rossi	ITA	Camel Yamaha Team	1m 28.808s	1.132s	0.299s
13	Checa	SPA	Tech 3 Yamaha	1m 29.294s	1.618s	0.486s
14	Tamada	JPN	Konica Minolta Honda	1m 29.362s	1.686s	0.068s
15	Hofmann	GER	Ducati Marlboro Team	1m 29.479s	1.803s	0.117s
16	Ellison	GBR	Tech 3 Yamaha	1m 30.382s	2.706s	0.903s
17	Silva	SPA	Pramac d'Antin MotoGP	1m 31.838s	4.162s	1.456s
18	Cardoso	SPA	Pramac d'Antin MotoGP	1m 32.252s	4.576s	0.414s
19	Fabrizio	ITA	Fortuna Honda			

FINISHERS

1 DANI PEDROSA Pole position, fastest lap and a runaway win: it was as close to a perfect weekend as racing can get. The only blemish was trying to get past Melandri early in the race and nearly outbraking himself at the Melbourne Loop. As his team-mate had a bad day, Dani also closed the gap at the top of the points table by a significant amount.

2 VALENTINO ROSSI Despite the broken bone in his wrist and having severe set-up problems on Friday, the Doctor managed another minor miracle, the highlight of which was the dice for second place with Melandri that enlivened the closing stages of the race. His team made educated guesses for race day and it took Rossi eight laps to understand what he could do, which explains the slow start.

3 MARCO MELANDRI Another triumph for the Clinica Mobile! Marco was still hurting but also fast and difficult to beat. Found the physical effort needed for the fast part of the circuit difficult early on, but survived one mammoth moment at Coppice and carried the fight to Rossi right up to the penultimate corner.

4 CASEY STONER Found the perfect set-up in practice but couldn't make it work in qualifying or the race. Got up to second, then his rear tyre began spinning not driving, so had to settle for fourth after his fitness level stopped him braking as hard as he could early on.

5 KENNY ROBERTS Another competitive race, though faded slightly towards the end. Found it hard on the flowing section and good on the brakes early on, but the other way round late in the race. Said he really wanted a good result as the bike was capable of getting on the rostrum but 'didn't quite get there'.

6 COLIN EDWARDS Never happy with his set-up – 'It just hasn't clicked for us ... we never really found our way' – but did improve on his qualifying by four places. Found useful pace on race day but not enough to allow him to pass on the brakes. 'The race was a struggle from start to finish.'

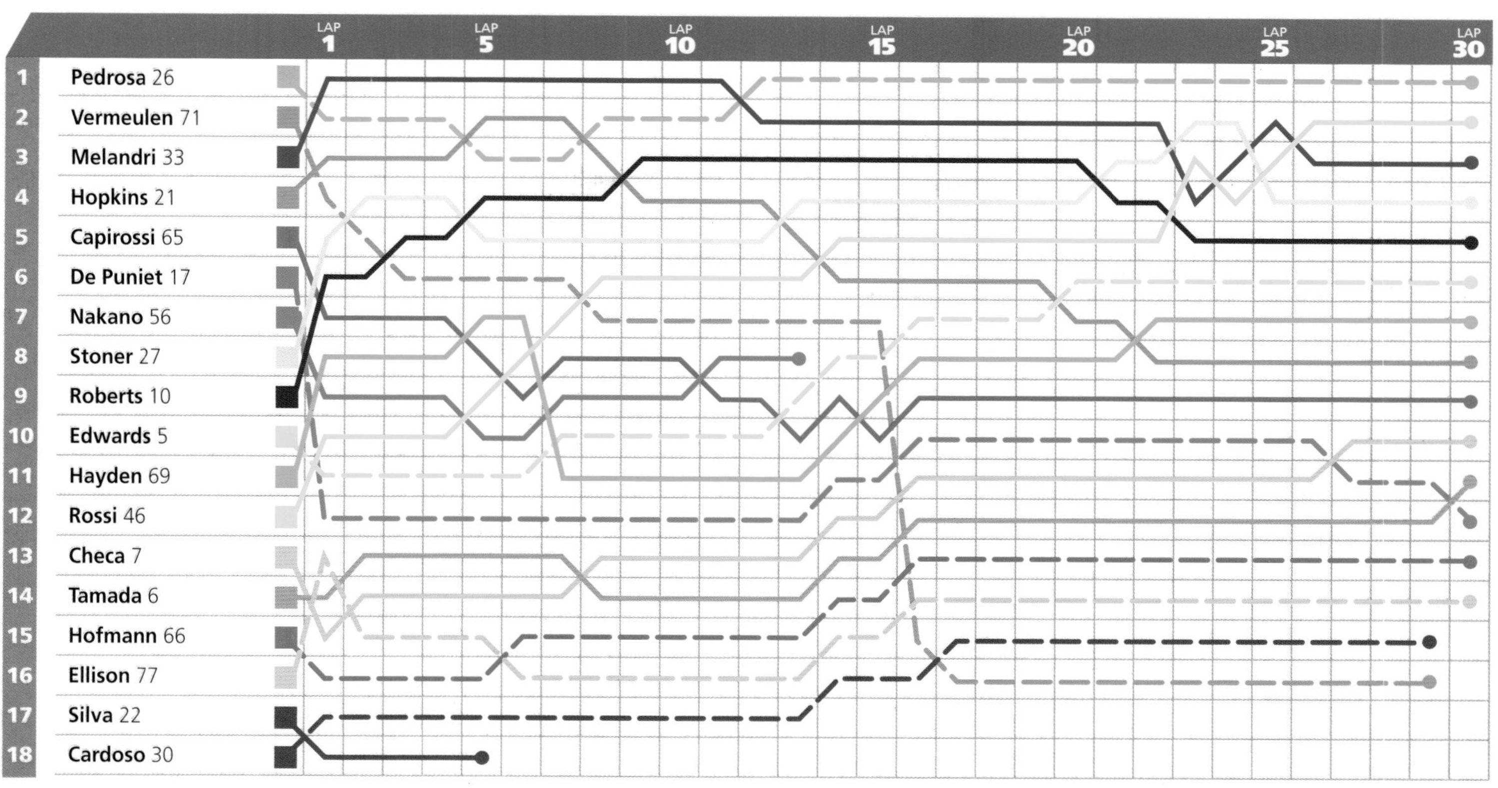

RACE

	Rider	Motorcycle	Race Time	Time +	Fastest Lap	Average Speed
1	Pedrosa	Honda	44m 54.878s		1m 28.714s	100.121mph
2	Rossi	Yamaha	44m 58.742s	3.864s	1m 29.196s	99.978mph
3	Melandri	Honda	44m 58.894s	4.016s	1m 29.164s	99.972mph
4	Stoner	Honda	45m 00.654s	5.776s	1m 29.372s	99.907mph
5	Roberts	KR211V	45m 04.474s	9.596s	1m 29.351s	99.765mph
6	Edwards	Yamaha	45m 16.588s	21.710s	1m 29.729s	99.321mph
7	Hayden	Honda	45m 20.642s	25.764s	1m 29.721s	99.173mph
8	Hopkins	Suzuki	45m 23.912s	29.034s	1m 29.578s	99.054mph
9	Capirossi	Ducati	45m 30.484s	35.606s	1m 30.079s	98.815mph
10	Checa	Yamaha	45m 35.320s	40.442s	1m 30.496s	98.641mph
11	Tamada	Honda	45m 35.940s	41.062s	1m 30.260s	98.618mph
12	De Puniet	Kawasaki	45m 37.075s	42.197s	1m 30.093s	98.577mph
13	Hofmann	Ducati	45m 46.332s	51.454s	1m 30.467s	98.245mph
14	Ellison	Yamaha	46m 12.682s	1m 17.804s	1m 31.402s	97.311mph
15	Cardoso	Ducati	45m 13.279s	1 lap	1m 31.811s	96.127mph
16	Vermeulen	Suzuki	45m 43.130s	1 lap	1m 30.062s	95.081mph
	Nakano	Kawasaki	19m 39.618s	17 laps	1m 30.084s	99.116mph
	Silva	Ducati	7m 58.157s	25 laps	1m 33.585s	94.046mph

CHAMPIONSHIP

	Rider	Team	Points
1	Hayden	Repsol Honda Team	153
2	Pedrosa	Repsol Honda Team	127
3	Rossi	Camel Yamaha Team	118
4	Melandri	Fortuna Honda	114
5	Capirossi	Ducati Marlboro Team	107
6	Stoner	Honda LCR	91
7	Edwards	Camel Yamaha Team	73
8	Roberts	Team Roberts	66
9	Tamada	Konica Minolta Honda	59
10	Hopkins	Rizla Suzuki MotoGP	58
11	Nakano	Kawasaki Racing Team	57
12	Elias	Fortuna Honda	53
13	Gibernau	Ducati Marlboro Team	44
14	Vermeulen	Rizla Suzuki MotoGP	37
15	Checa	Tech 3 Yamaha	37
16	Hofmann	Pramac d'Antin MotoGP	19
17	De Puniet	Kawasaki Racing Team	17
18	Ellison	Tech 3 Yamaha	14
19	Cardoso	Pramac d'Antin MotoGP	6

7 NICKY HAYDEN The only bright spot of his weekend was being fastest in the wet warm-up. Tested new parts on Friday (later saying this was a mistake), then suffered electrical problems that made the bike look very unsettled. Was making good progress from lowly qualifying when he went straight on at Foggy's and dropped to 11th, a mistake from which he never really recovered.

8 JOHN HOPKINS Very good qualifying and a competitive opening few laps until, as at Assen, his tyres reacted badly to the high track temperature and he slipped back. The points were enough to move him into the top ten of the championship, though.

9 LORIS CAPIROSSI Still hurting enough to sit out Friday afternoon's free practice session and unable to ride the bike as he would have liked. The pain kicked in as his tyres started sliding, around ten laps in, and he finished the race exhausted.

10 CARLOS CHECA Another good race despite tough qualifying. Overtook Tamada (Honda-Michelin) and de Puniet (Kawasaki-Bridgestone) in the race and was quicker than Hopkins and Capirossi over the last ten laps but had given them too much of a start.

11 MAKOTO TAMADA After another frustrating practice decided on a radical change of plan for the race: stopped looking for a setting to match his riding style and reverted to Honda's standard settings. Was not expecting a magic cure for his form; hoped this new approach would pay dividends over the second half of the season.

12 RANDY DE PUNIET Fitted a soft race tyre to try and hang with the leading group, but a bad start put paid to that plan. Ran into tyre problems after half-distance and could do nothing to hold off Checa and Tamada.

13 ALEX HOFMANN Depressed because he thought this would be his last ride for the Reds and he hadn't been able to do himself justice. Hit grip problems in the race, like the other Bridgestone runners, despite choosing a hard rear tyre.

14 JAMES ELLISON Led his team-mate early on but rapidly ran out of edge grip. Unable to test some radical chassis changes due to the wet weather on Sunday morning, which contributed to the problems. Happy with the points but had hoped to do better at home.

15 JOSE LUIS CARDOSO Used new-spec Dunlops but was still lapped. However, did score points for the second time in the season.

16 CHRIS VERMEULEN Had a coming-together with Edwards at the Melbourne Loop, which resulted in Chris crashing. Had to go into the pits to replace a handlebar, but went out again without a brake balance adjuster and with his left footrest rubbing on the chain.

NON-FINISHERS

SHINYA NAKANO The first problem was with the gearbox, which he got round by using the clutch on down changes. Was pushing hard to catch the group ahead when he felt the engine suddenly lose power: the only thing to do was retire.

IVAN SILVA Hurting after a practice crash, Hofmann's replacement retired early to give himself a chance of being fully fit for an upcoming Spanish Championship race.

NON-STARTERS

TONI ELIAS At home in Barcelona recovering from his Assen shoulder injury.

MICHEL FABRIZIO Elias's replacement broke a collarbone when he highsided at Goddard's on Saturday morning. He was on the same rear Michelin that had caught out both Elias and Rossi in Assen.

SETE GIBERNAU Still recuperating from the collarbone operation he needed after the big crash at the start of the Catalan GP.

GERMAN GP

SACHSENRING

ROUND 10

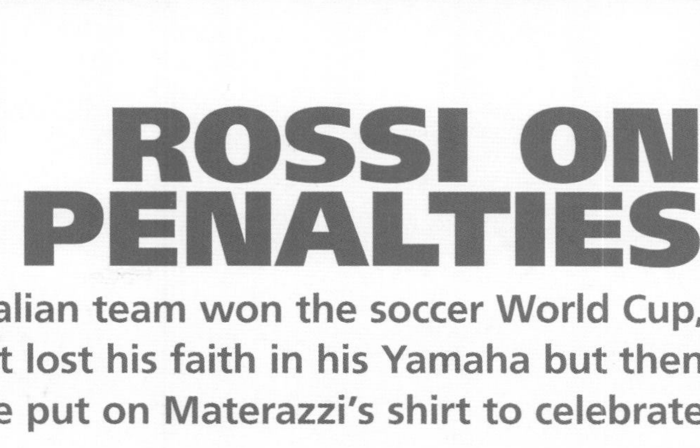

ROSSI ON PENALTIES

A week after the Italian team won the soccer World Cup, Valentino Rossi almost lost his faith in his Yamaha but then regained it. He put on Materazzi's shirt to celebrate

It did not look good for the reigning World Champion. Another terrible qualifying as his crew struggled to match his Yamaha's chassis to the new Michelins, another fourth-row start, and for the first time Rossi admitted in public that he had doubts about his ability to retain the title. That was on Saturday afternoon, before the race. Afterwards he made an even bigger admission – that he had actually begun to doubt his M1. This was more confession than admission for he had just won another stunning victory, and to atone for his misapprehensions he hugged the windscreen of his Yamaha on the slow-down lap, then apologised in front of the world's media: 'For the first time in two-and-a-half years I start to have some doubts about my M1, and I need to say sorry because it's not real.'

Valentino's penance was to work hard for his win. First he had to fight his way to the front of a six-man group, then he had to deal with another storming ride from the still-injured Melandri. The previous week Marco's doctors had discovered a previously undiagnosed crack in his right collarbone to accompany the damage his left one had suffered at Catalunya. For

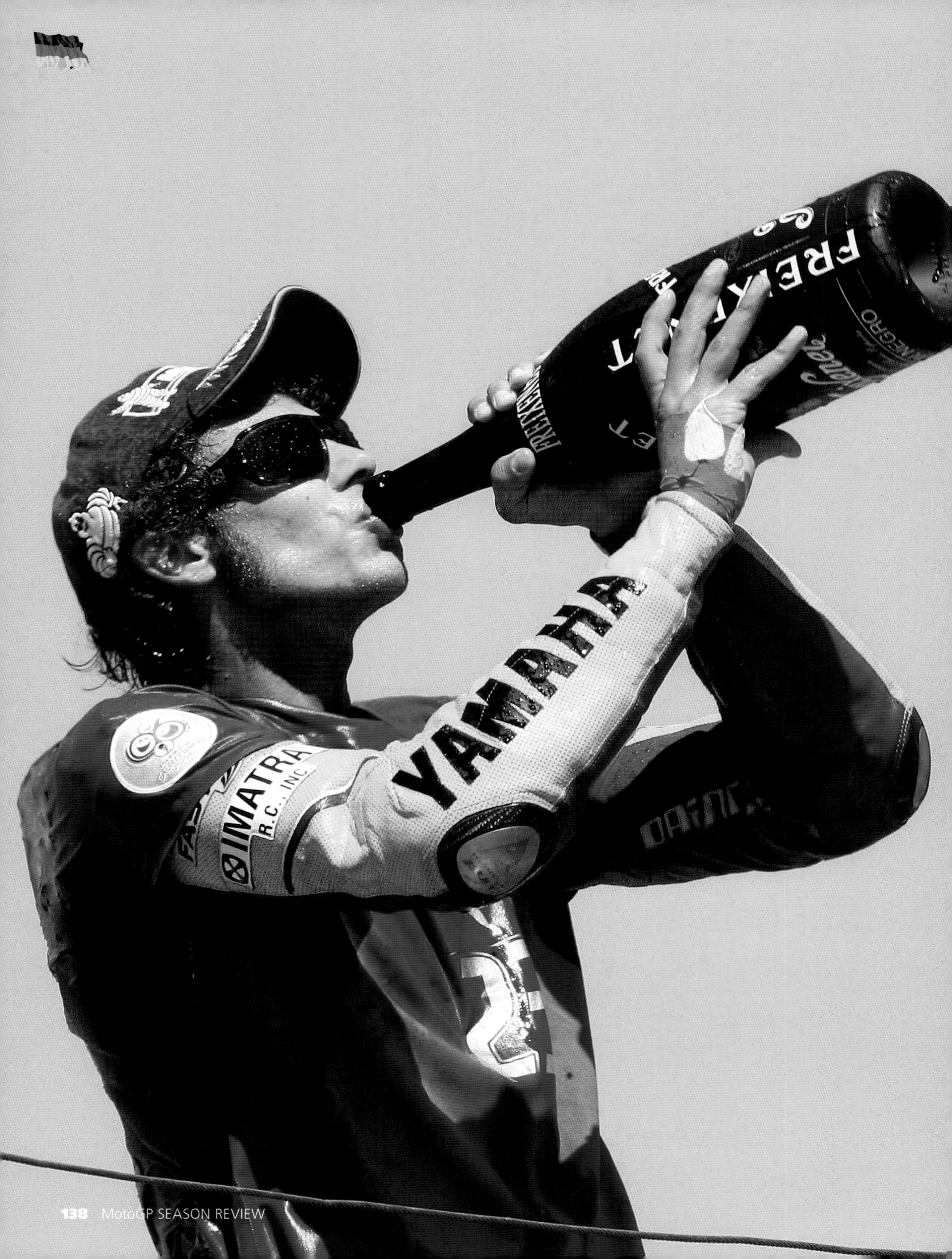
FREIXENET
YAMAHA
IMATRA
R.C. INC.
DAINESE

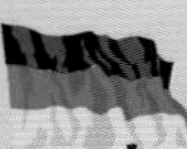

most people this would be cause for concern, but for the Honda rider it was a blessed relief; now he knew why it had hurt so much. Relieved of his burden of worry, Melandri was always in the action and was the last man to mount an attack on Rossi: a brave, probably ill-advised, ultimately futile but definitely heart-stopping run round the outside on the last corner of the last lap. That was the final move of a race which concentrated more overtakes with a closely bunched group of riders on a tight and twisty track than anyone had a right to expect. At the flag the first four were covered by less than one-third of a second, and if two men hadn't crashed out of the original six-rider dogfight it could have been even tighter.

The two crashers were the surprises of the weekend: Kenny Roberts and Makoto Tamada. Roberts was only deprived of pole position by a last-gasp effort from Dani Pedrosa, who took his fourth pole of the year while no-one else had managed more than one. Roberts looked good in the race, too, right up to the moment he tried an inside move on Tamada at the penultimate corner at the bottom of the long downhill, the Sachsenring's favourite passing place. He had to hang on to the brake for longer than he wanted, lost the front and slid off, collecting the luckless Japanese who surfed the Team Roberts bike into the gravel. To add insult to injury, Kenny rushed over to Makoto and asked if he was okay in fractured Japanese – which at least made him forget the pain in his left leg. It was the first time in a complete season that Tamada had looked anything like as confident on his Michelins, and being the innocent victim of Kenny's crash just proves that when luck is out it really is out.

The departure of Roberts and Tamada left a group of four at the front: long-time leader Hayden, Melandri, Pedrosa and Rossi. Capirossi had hung on to them until half-distance but his Bridgestones, while an improvement on the disastrous Donington situation, weren't up to fighting for the win. Uncharacteristically it was Valentino who did most of the leading as the four pulled away from Loris, who was being closed down by a very fast Shinya Nakano. Despite his pole, and setting the fastest lap early in the race, Pedrosa seemed the weakest of the quartet at the Sachsenring's preferred spot for overtaking, on the brakes at the bottom of the hill where Tamada and Roberts had come to grief. Dani did manage to get past a couple of times at the next-best option, Turn 1, and even found places in the ultra-tight Omega where he could take advantage of any gap

Above The traffic's always a bit heavy in the Omega on the first lap

Opposite Rossi celebrates his – and Italy's – victory

Below Vermeulen beat his Suzuki team-mate Hopkins for the first time in a race

DOCTOR'S ORDERS

The name Casey Stoner did not figure in the results because of a crash in Sunday morning warm-up. The young Australian was taken to hospital for a precautionary scan, which found no problem. Nevertheless, the circuit's chief medical officer decided that Casey wasn't fit enough to race and it is he, not any member of the race authorities or the doctors of the Clinica Mobile, who has the final say.

There was a rumour that Stoner had suffered concussion in the crash, but this was denied by both the rider and his team. Next to the injuries suffered by the men involved in the first-turn crash in Catalunya, Casey seems to have suffered very minor damage, yet both Melandri and Capirossi raced less than a week after that incident, in which Marco had been knocked unconscious. No-one would wish to prevent someone riding while hurt if he's capable of doing so, but concussion is a very different issue, as Sete Gibernau was first to point out on his return from the Catalunya crash – and he, by the way, had never lost consciousness. His collarbone injury, he said, was neither here nor there, but a serious concussion was quite another matter: he was much more concerned about being sure he was over the effects of that bang on the head than the pain in his shoulder.

Many other sports, from Formula 1 to rugby, have mandatory bans for any competitor who suffers concussion, yet the decision-making process for who is and isn't fit to race in a motorcycle Grand Prix is confused to say the least.

on the inside. It was his uncertainty at that vital corner, though, that found out the young Spanish rider. Four laps from home he was second going in and fourth coming out as both Melandri and Hayden came past. Just over a lap later he tried to force down the inside of his team-mate on the descent from Turn 1 after Hayden had gone marginally wide on the brakes, only to find the American leaning all over his front wheel. Nicky finished the race with rubber from Dani's front Michelin adorning the right side of his leathers.

That intra-team dispute left the two Italians fighting for the win. Marco did get to the front three laps from the flag but he always looked the more ragged. On the penultimate lap Rossi carried more speed out of the blind right before the downhill and was able to position himself perfectly on the inside for the left. The pass was over and done with before they hit the brakes. Hayden had been hoping that Melandri would be able to try an inside move and push Rossi wide, so he had positioned himself well to the left on the last lap – only to be presented with a good view of Rossi's rear tyre. All that was left was Marco's heroic final charge and Rossi's rolling embrace of his Yamaha.

How good a win was it? By Rossi's standards, a victory from way back on the grid is nothing new. Neither is his team turning what was an unrideable bike on Saturday into a winning machine on Sunday. Even his post-race celebration was well-judged in the country that had just hosted a very successful World Cup. Colin Edwards summed it up best from his 12th position, nearly 30 seconds behind his team-mate: 'Valentino accomplished what seems like his 700th miracle and you can only take your hat off to a great champion.'

Opposite Carlos Checa's ninth place showed that Dunlop were making progress

Right Nicky Hayden rode with enough aggression to collect some rubber from his team-mate's front tyre on his AlpineStars

GERMAN GP

SACHSENRING

ROUND 10

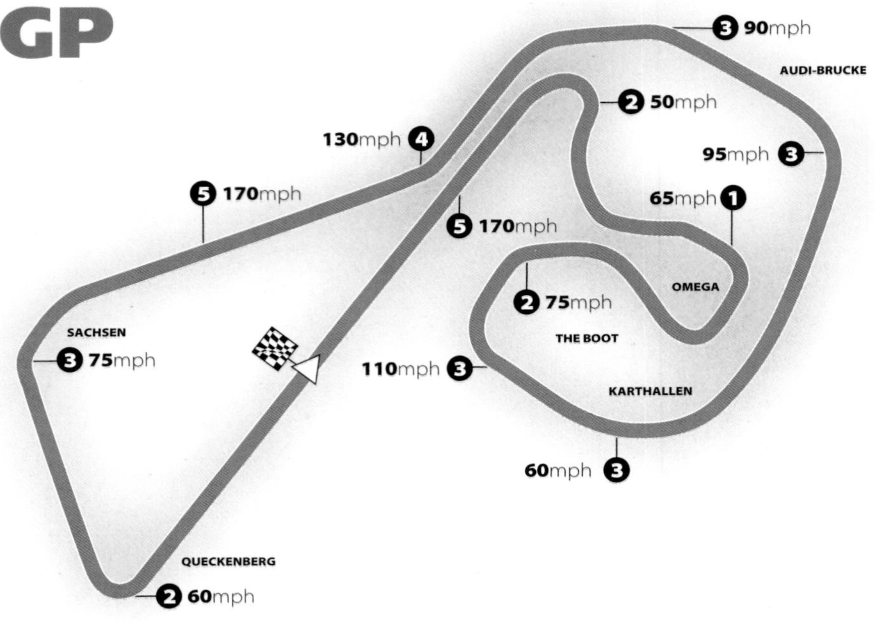

RACE RESULTS

RACE DATE July 16th
CIRCUIT LENGTH 2.281miles
NO. OF LAPS 30
RACE DISTANCE 68.43miles
WEATHER Dry, 20°C
TRACK TEMPERATURE 38°C
WINNER Valentino Rossi
FASTEST LAP 1m 23.355s, 98.456mph, Dani Pedrosa (record)
PREVIOUS LAP RECORD 1m 23.705s, 97.887mph, Sete Gibernau, 2005

QUALIFYING

	Rider	Nationality	Team	Qualifying	Pole +	Gap
1	Pedrosa	SPA	Repsol Honda Team	1m 21.815s		
2	Roberts	USA	Team Roberts	1m 21.907s	0.092s	0.092s
3	Hayden	USA	Repsol Honda Team	1m 22.083s	0.268s	0.176s
4	Nakano	JPN	Kawasaki Racing Team	1m 22.273s	0.458s	0.190s
5	Capirossi	ITA	Ducati Marlboro Team	1m 22.329s	0.514s	0.056s
6	Melandri	ITA	Fortuna Honda	1m 22.420s	0.605s	0.091s
7	Gibernau	SPA	Ducati Marlboro Team	1m 22.469s	0.654s	0.049s
8	Stoner	AUS	Honda LCR	1m 22.577s	0.762s	0.108s
9	Hopkins	USA	Rizla Suzuki MotoGP	1m 22.701s	0.886s	0.124s
10	Tamada	JPN	Konica Minolta Honda	1m 22.866s	1.051s	0.165s
11	Rossi	ITA	Camel Yamaha Team	1m 22.868s	1.053s	0.002s
12	Checa	SPA	Tec 3 Yamaha	1m 22.964s	1.149s	0.096s
13	De Puniet	FRA	Kawasaki Racing Team	1m 22.974s	1.159s	0.010s
14	Vermeulen	AUS	Rizla Suzuki MotoGP	1m 23.050s	1.235s	0.076s
15	Edwards	USA	Camel Yamaha Team	1m 23.087s	1.272s	0.037s
16	Elias	SPA	Fortuna Honda	1m 23.660s	1.845s	0.573s
17	Hofmann	GER	Pramac d'Antin MotoGP	1m 24.115s	2.300s	0.455s
18	Ellison	GBR	Tech 3 Yamaha	1m 24.464s	2.649s	0.349s
19	Cardoso	SPA	Pramac d'Antin MotoGP	1m 24.651s	2.836s	0.187s

FINISHERS

1 VALENTINO ROSSI A win from 11th on the grid after another dismal qualifying now seems like a normal day at the office for the Doctor. His fourth win of the season promoted him to second in the championship, but it was hard work: he had to pass all the leading group and, when he got to the front, never escaped the attentions of Melandri and the Repsol Honda men.

2 MARCO MELANDRI Claimed he was back to full fitness despite a newly diagnosed fracture to his collarbone. Got the better of Pedrosa but couldn't find a way past Rossi on a spectacular final lap, despite an extremely hopeful round-the-outside move at the last turn.

3 NICKY HAYDEN Always in the leading group, but couldn't find an opening at the bottom of the hill on the last lap. Claimed to be unhappy with third but didn't mention his obvious satisfaction at beating his team-mate. Still having trouble getting the development RCV out of corners.

4 DANI PEDROSA Pole position, the holeshot and fastest lap of the race but, crucially, couldn't get to the front of the leading group because he was unable to use the prime overtaking spot at Turn 13, at the bottom of the hill.

5 LORIS CAPIROSSI Still not fully fit, but shadowed the leading group until his rear tyre started to lose grip. Ended up having to fight off Nakano. First Bridgestone finisher on a weekend that wasn't kind to the Japanese tyre brand.

6 SHINYA NAKANO Got hung out to dry at the first turn, negating a good qualifying performance, so spent the rest of the race trying to close the gap to Capirossi. Didn't set his best time of the race until lap 13. Expected better, but at least the points put him into the top ten of the championship.

7 CHRIS VERMEULEN Pretty happy with his performance on this first visit to the Sachsenring, a track he said was difficult to learn. A tough weekend for the Suzuki team, but Chris won the dice with team-mate Hopkins, Checa and Gibernau.

8 SETE GIBERNAU Back after missing the last two races because of the collarbone he broke in Catalunya. No pain, but unfortunately no strength either, which

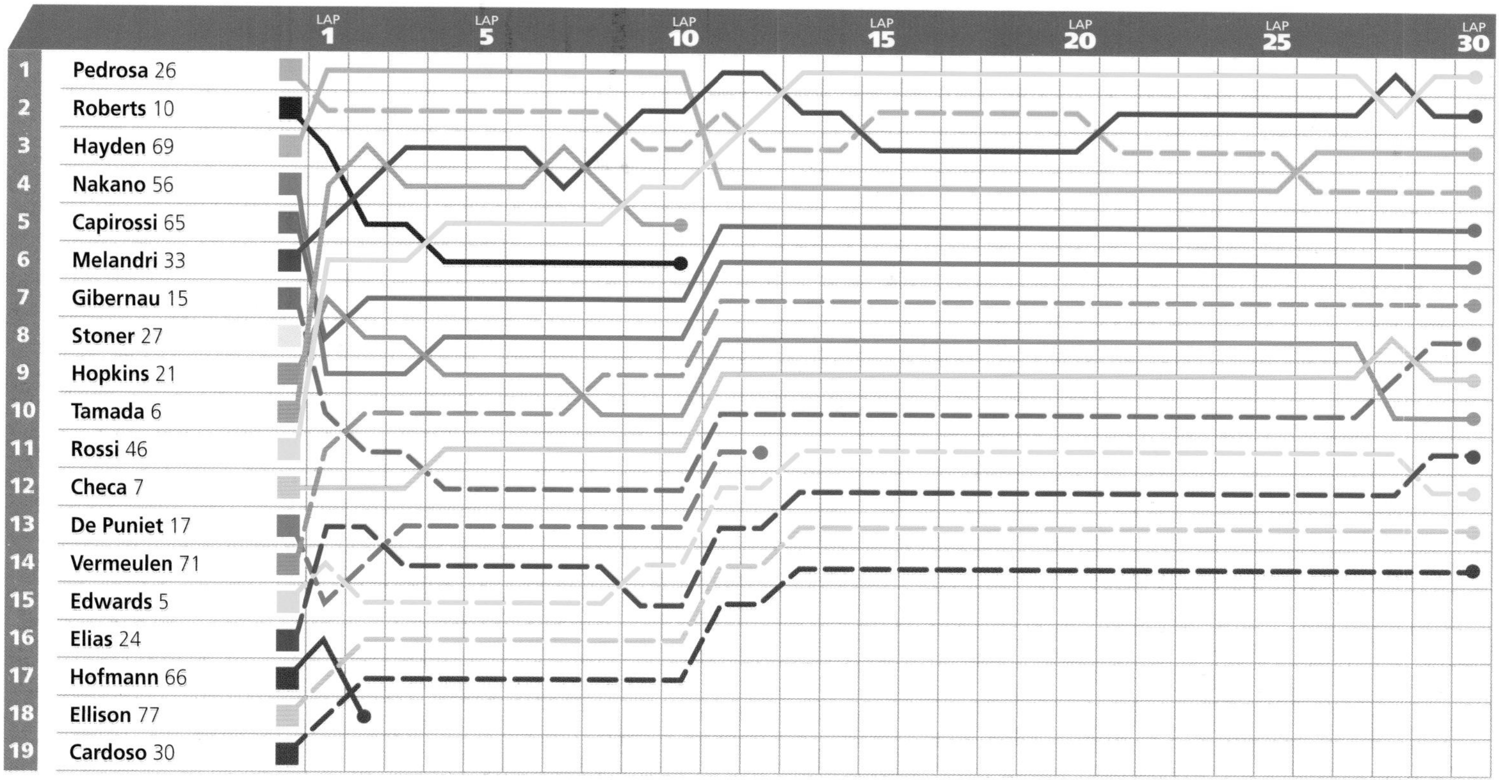

RACE

	Rider	Motorcycle	Race Time	Time +	Fastest Lap	Average Speed
1	Rossi	Yamaha	41m 59.248s		1m 23.449s	97.730mph
2	Melandri	Honda	41m 59.393s	0.145s	1m 23.450s	97.724mph
3	Hayden	Honda	41m 59.514s	0.266s	1m 23.533s	97.719mph
4	Pedrosa	Honda	41m 59.555s	0.307s	1m 23.355s	97.718mph
5	Caprossi	Ducati	42m 08.012s	8.764s	1m 23.428s	97.391mph
6	Nakano	Kawasaki	42m 08.395s	9.147s	1m 23.712s	97.376mph
7	Vermeulen	Suzuki	42m 15.856s	16.608s	1m 23.940s	97.090mph
8	Gibernau	Ducati	42m 15.896s	16.648s	1m 23.979s	97.088mph
9	Checa	Yamaha	42m 16.345s	17.097s	1m 23.779s	97.071mph
10	Hopkins	Suzuki	42m 17.034s	17.786s	1m 23.904s	97.045mph
11	Elias	Honda	42m 26.673s	27.425s	1m 24.163s	96.677mph
12	Edwards	Yamaha	42m 28.556s	29.308s	1m 24.138s	96.606mph
13	Ellison	Yamaha	43m 01.277s	1m 02.029s	1m 23.196s	95.381mph
14	Cardoso	Ducati	43m 19.245s	1m 19.997s	1m 25.634s	94.722mph
	De Puniet	Kawasaki	16m 56.506s	18 laps	1m 23.690s	96.883mph
	Tamada	Honda	14m 01.468s	20 laps	1m 23.480s	97.530mph
	Roberts	KR211V	14m 01.753s	20 laps	1m 23.526s	97.497mph
	Hofmann	Ducati	3m 04.603s	28 laps	1m 29.488s	88.913mph

CHAMPIONSHIP

	Rider	Team	Points
1	Hayden	Repsol Honda Team	169
2	Rossi	Camel Yamaha Team	143
3	Pedrosa	Repsol Honda Team	140
4	Melandri	Fortuna Honda	134
5	Capirossi	Ducati Marlboro Team	118
6	Stoner	Honda LCR	91
7	Edwards	Camel Yamaha Team	77
8	Nakano	Kawasaki Racing Team	67
9	Roberts	Team Roberts	66
10	Hopkins	Rizla Suzuki MotoGP	64
11	Tamada	Konica Minolta Honda	59
12	Elias	Fortuna Honda	58
13	Gibernau	Ducati Marlboro Team	52
14	Vermeulen	Rizla Suzuki MotoGP	46
15	Checa	Tech 3 Yamaha	44
16	Hofmann	Pramac d'Antin MotoGP	19
17	Ellison	Tech 3 Yamaha	17
18	De Puniet	Kawasalo Racing Team	17
19	Cardoso	Pramac d'Antin MotoGP	8

made braking problematic. Still managed to pass both Hopkins and Checa in the closing stages; a brave ride.

9 CARLOS CHECA Another impressive race – second Yamaha, only 17 seconds behind the winner at the flag and 12 seconds in front of Edwards – and all after an engine problem kicked in just after the half-way mark. Team-manager Hervé Poncharal described it as Tech 3's best race of the year so far.

10 JOHN HOPKINS With the front men in the early laps but dropped back through the field as his tyres lost grip at maximum lean. Hopper refused to make excuses, but with his home GP the following week was grateful to get away unscathed from the track where he'd had two big crashes in 2005.

11 TONI ELIAS Returning after the injury he suffered at Assen but not yet fully fit. Felt a lot of pain from lap eight onwards, but managed it by riding hard in short bursts. Nevertheless, overtook Edwards two laps from the flag.

12 COLIN EDWARDS 'I guess I'm just slow round here,' was Colin's analysis, after a thoroughly dispiriting weekend. 'We simply couldn't get the bike working and I never had the pace.' Chased the settings round the clock without ever finding a direction to work in, then got caught behind Elias early in the race.

13 JAMES ELLISON Scored points again, but increasingly frustrated at being the only Yamaha rider still on an unmodified '06 chassis and having to cope with the chatter to which it is prone.

14 JOSE LUIS CARDOSO Points for the second race in a row, improved his pace from qualifying and didn't get lapped around a comparatively short circuit. The team regarded the improvement in tyre performance as a small but useful step forward.

NON-FINISHERS

RANDY DE PUNIET Looking good after a bad start, then his motor stopped with a top-ten finish on the cards. On the positive side, reckoned to have gained a lot of confidence in his Kawasaki over the weekend.

MAKOTO TAMADA Running as high as third in the early laps and looking like his old self as he diced with the leading group, then became the innocent victim of Roberts's crash at the bottom of the big hill. Took a bang on his left leg as the Team KR bike hit him and surfed into the gravel trap.

KENNY ROBERTS Another front-row start and another race where the 2000 World Champion looked comfortable running with the leaders. It all ended on lap 11 when Hayden came across his nose as he was trying to make his own move: slid out and took Tamada with him.

ALEX HOFMANN Back on the d'Antin Ducati after his stint on the works bike, but his luck didn't improve at his home GP – an electrical fault saw him in the pits after two laps. At least it was better than the hundred metres he'd managed the previous year.

NON-STARTERS

CASEY STONER Given a new chassis, which he promptly crashed in practice. Controversially ruled out of the race by the circuit's medical officer after another crash in Sunday morning warm-up.

LAGUNA SECA

ROUND 11

HOME RUN

Nicky Hayden made it two out of two at home as Valentino Rossi suffered yet another mechanical failure in the hottest conditions anyone could remember

Twelve months previously, the first American GP in more than a decade had not been without its problems. Chief among them was the issue of track safety and that, at least, had now been addressed to everyone's satisfaction. This year there was some very welcome run-off at the high-speed Turn 1, and the run up to the Corkscrew had been opened out and the crest flattened to prevent the MotoGP bikes becoming airborne. This had the effect of making life easier for both newcomers and non-Americans by simplifying a previously mysterious section of the circuit. Welcome as the improvements were, there were two factors that once more made life difficult – one in the control of the organisers, the other very much not.

The first was the resurfacing of the track. Carried out in the previous six weeks, this had left the tarmac even

Above Casey Stoner didn't have a trouble-free weekend

Opposite Kenny Roberts flies the flag at the Corkscrew

Below It was hot, it was dry, it was a sell-out

bumpier than it had been beforehand. The high-speed descent from the Corkscrew was particularly affected, and it was possible to see space under both wheels of a bike on its way through Rainey Curve. The second factor was blistering heat in the central California region, with the nearby towns of Hollister and Gilroy breaking their records by ten whole degrees Fahrenheit. The scorching weather may well have exacerbated the track problem, for the new surface soon began to break up in several places, notably on the inside of the fast right after the Corkscrew. As air temperatures climbed to a nearly unbearable 40° Centigrade, the track temperature also reached a new high of 64°, hotter by eight degrees than Qatar's previous record.

The heat's effects were felt all through race day. Overnight the offending patches of tarmac had been treated with sealant and carbon black; the price of a bottle of water at the concession stands had been dropped from $4 to $1; and Race Direction, fearful of the track breaking up before the main event, rescheduled two AMA support race practice sessions and the race itself to start after, not before, the MotoGP race. This entailed the patient crowd having to endure a very long wait between morning warm-up and the first race.

There was plenty to look forward to, though, with two Americans – Edwards and Roberts – on the front row, and Chris Vermeulen's first dry-weather pole confirming that the form he'd displayed when winning a World Superbike double here in 2004 had carried over to MotoGP. The same could not be said of fellow Bridgestone users Ducati, for the team had a disastrous weekend. Gibernau was still injured and even Capirossi was down in 13th and telling his team manager, Livio Suppo, that if Vermeulen could go faster than him on Ducati number 65 he could have all his money.

The Suzuki rider led away from the start and looked comfortable at the front for half the race. Neither of his fellow front-row men was happy: Edwards was sick and Roberts hadn't got the grip he'd had in qualifying. The challenge would come from Hayden, who had yet again suffered in qualifying. The contrast between this year and 2005, when no-one could touch Nicky in any session, let alone in the race, was striking. Now he worked his way past Roberts, then gradually closed down on Vermeulen, with his team-mate again over-achieving just behind him. Dani Pedrosa had never seen America before, and he liked it. Efficient as ever, he

Arai
PARTS UNLIMITED
Roberts
riders
PHANTOM ENERGY DRINK
10
VENTURE
PHANTOM

worked up from a slow start to lead the second row in qualifying, never lost touch with the group chasing Hayden and took advantage of the misfortunes of others. He finished the race in second place, just three seconds behind Nicky Hayden.

The unluckiest of the leading riders was Chris Vermeulen: he'd looked a cast-iron certainty for a rostrum when he was struck by fuelling problems, probably due to the extreme heat, just three laps from the flag. That let a delighted Marco Melandri into third place. After the previous year, when he'd openly spoken of a boycott of Laguna, Marco changed his attitude, came to the US early to acclimatise and painted stars and stripes on his helmet. And it worked.

If anyone had a worse afternoon than Vermeulen, it was Rossi. He made very little progress from his tenth place on the grid in the first third of the race ('This place is even more difficult to pass at than the Sachsenring'), but his usual mastery of worn tyres did look as though it would give him the final rostrum place. Valentino had got up to fourth after passing Melandri on lap 20 out of 32 and was closing on Vermeulen when his troubles began. Like many of the Michelin runners, Rossi suffered serious problems on the left side of his rear tyre. He lost a big chunk of tread, which forced him to ease the pace, and then the engine's cooling system malfunctioned, putting him out of the race almost in sight of the flag. Afterwards Valentino looked seriously down. The championship, he said, had gone. Now it was just a matter of racing for fun, for race wins.

All of which left Nicky Hayden with an extended lead at the top of the table. This win, he said, felt even better than his first victory last year (although he later recanted that opinion). In truth, it had been much tougher because his rear tyre was missing small chunks of rubber at 6-inch intervals all round its circumference, and he had started from sixth on the grid as opposed to taking pole in 2005. No-one had ever won the US GP from anywhere other than the front row before. He was asked about a well-publicised opinion of Wayne Rainey's, that Hayden was good and fast but had to win a lot more races. Nicky said he was right, but then took a swipe at the 'trash talking' about him, a reference to Colin Edwards' opinion post-Assen that Hayden could follow but couldn't lead. Typically, though, he didn't go any further, preferring to thank his elder brother, Tommy, whom he rather endearingly referred to as 'T-Baby'. Tommy had been out on track, watching as Nicky struggled in practice and qualifying. He'd asked why Nicky was doing certain things, why he wasn't doing others, making his brother think about things from a different angle. With the Haydens, it's always a family affair.

Opposite top Camel Yamaha had a disastrous day: Rossi went out with a sick motor, Edwards was just sick

Opposite bottom If ever a rider deserved more from a race it was Chris Vermeulen at Laguna Seca

Right Two out of two on home soil for Nicky Hayden

STRANGE CUSTOMS

What use is a redundant MotoGP engine? The Japanese factories tend to scrap all but one, which they put in a museum. Kenny Roberts, on the other hand, does things rather differently: he gave one of his old V5 motors to Roland Sands, who then built a custom bike around it.

Sands was also a racer, but he's better known now as one of the bike builders to feature on TV programmes like 'Biker Build Off', in which top customisers compete against each other, riding their bikes to a show where the paying public decides the winner. Sands isn't just into the clichéd bling of some chopper builders, though, because he likes his machines to be fast as well – and his father, Perry, was one of the founders of the Performance Machine tuning company. Roland decided that a unique motor like the Roberts V5 needed some special treatment so he harked back to the barnstorming days of the board-track racers, when big Harley and Indian V-twins roared around banked ovals made of wood and a big crash meant death by splinters.

Working with Kenny Roberts had been a long-time dream of Roland's, and he took design inspiration from a 1914 board-tracker. The job, he said, was to marry modern technology to an iconic American style. Roberts' view was that 'Roland sees a bike in a very different way from me, as a form of art. It's a different discipline but I find it very interesting.' Kenny's old rider, Jeremy McWilliams, at

*Laguna to ride in an AMA race, had an interesting take: 'I want to see the old ******** ride that bike, no front brake and all!'*

UNITED STATES GP

LAGUNA SECA

ROUND 11

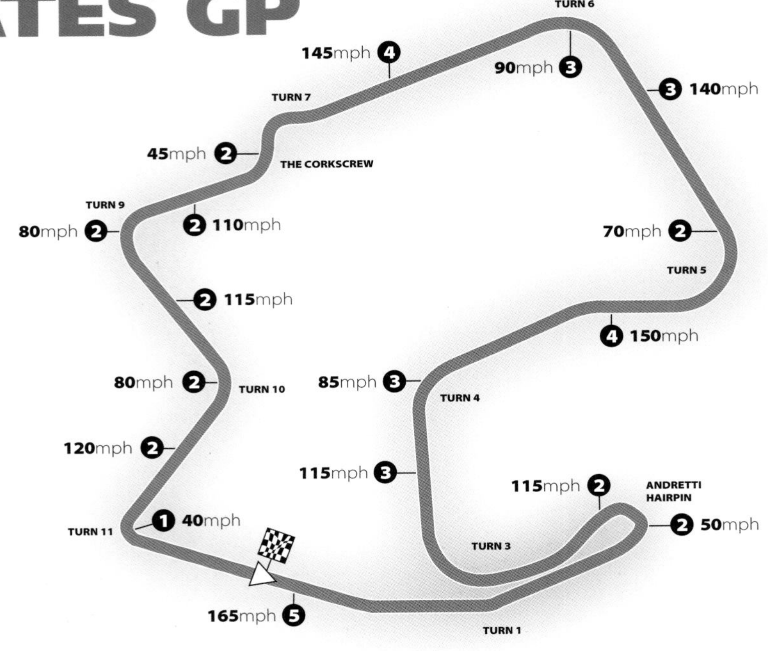

RACE RESULTS

RACE DATE July 23rd
CIRCUIT LENGTH 2.243 miles
NO. OF LAPS 32
RACE DISTANCE 71.776 miles
WEATHER Dry, 39°C
TRACK TEMPERATURE 56°C
WINNER Nicky Hayden
FASTEST LAP 1m 23.333s, 96.846mph, Dani Pedrosa (record)
PREVIOUS LAP RECORD 1m 23.915s, 96.020mph, Colin Edwards, 2005

QUALIFYING

	Rider	Nationality	Team	Qualifying	Pole +	Gap
1	Vermeulen	AUS	Rizla Suzuki MotoGP	1m 23.168s		
2	Edwards	USA	Camel Yamaha Team	1m 23.321s	0.153s	0.153s
3	Roberts	USA	Team Roberts	1m 23.420s	0.252s	0.099s
4	Pedrosa	SPA	Repsol Honda Team	1m 23.490s	0.322s	0.070s
5	Hopkins	USA	Rizla Suzuki MotoGP	1m 23.498s	0.330s	0.008s
6	Hayden	USA	Repsol Honda Team	1m 23.536s	0.368s	0.038s
7	Stoner	AUS	Honda LCR	1m 23.651s	0.483s	0.115s
8	Nakano	JPN	Kawasaki Racing Team	1m 23.656s	0.488s	0.005s
9	Melandri	ITA	Fortuna Honda	1m 23.750s	0.582s	0.094s
10	Rossi	ITA	Camel Yamaha Team	1m 24.047s	0.879s	0.297s
11	Checa	SPA	Tech 3 Yamaha	1m 24.153s	0.985s	0.106s
12	Elias	SPA	Fortuna Honda	1m 24.230s	1.062s	0.077s
13	Capirossi	ITA	Ducati Marlboro Team	1m 24.268s	1.100s	0.038s
14	Tamada	JPN	Konica Minolta Honda	1m 24.578s	1.410s	0.310s
15	De Puniet	FRA	Kawasaki Racing Team	1m 24.592s	1.424s	0.014s
16	Gibernau	SPA	Ducati Marlboro Team	1m 24.634s	1.466s	0.042s
17	Hofmann	GER	Pramac d'Antin MotoGP	1m 25.420s	2.252s	0.786s
18	Ellison	GBR	Tech 3 Yamaha	1m 25.763s	2.595s	0.343s
19	Cardoso	SPA	Pramac d'Antin MotoGP	1m 26.567s	3.399s	0.804s

FINISHERS

1 NICKY HAYDEN Another victory at home, but totally different from last year's absolute domination. He had to work hard for his third MotoGP win after qualifying in sixth: got away in third, stalked Roberts for eight laps, steadily closed down a fast-starting Vermeulen and finished with a shredded rear tyre.

2 DANI PEDROSA Thoroughly enjoyed his first experience of Laguna Seca, particularly the politeness of the local fans – all very different from the Latin frenzy of a Spanish track. Set the fastest lap at the notoriously difficult-to-learn circuit on his way to the rostrum, a remarkable achievement for a rookie.

3 MARCO MELANDRI The man who wanted to boycott Laguna Seca 12 months previously turned up with the stars and stripes on his helmet and moved up to third in the points table. Also the first time he'd finished on the rostrum in three consecutive MotoGP races: not bad for a man who was still not fully fit.

4 KENNY ROBERTS Didn't have the grip on race day he had when setting fastest time on Friday and third on Saturday. Kenny Senior reckoned the bike was still a quarter-second a lap away from where it needed to be. Pushed back into sixth for most of the second half but fought back to within a second of a podium finish, setting the third-best lap time of the day.

5 CHRIS VERMEULEN If ever a rider deserved a podium it was the Aussie. After his first dry-weather pole he led the first half of the race but, just after Hayden came past, his engine started hesitating in corners and his lap times slowed. The cause was vaporisation in the fuel line, probably exacerbated by the extreme temperatures.

6 JOHN HOPKINS Made a mess of the start, got stuck behind Edwards and then made a mistake when Rossi came past. Fifth and sixth positions for the Rizla Suzuki team would usually be considered a good weekend, but this time they didn't know whether to laugh or cry.

7 CARLOS CHECA First Yamaha home and his best finish of the year. Despite

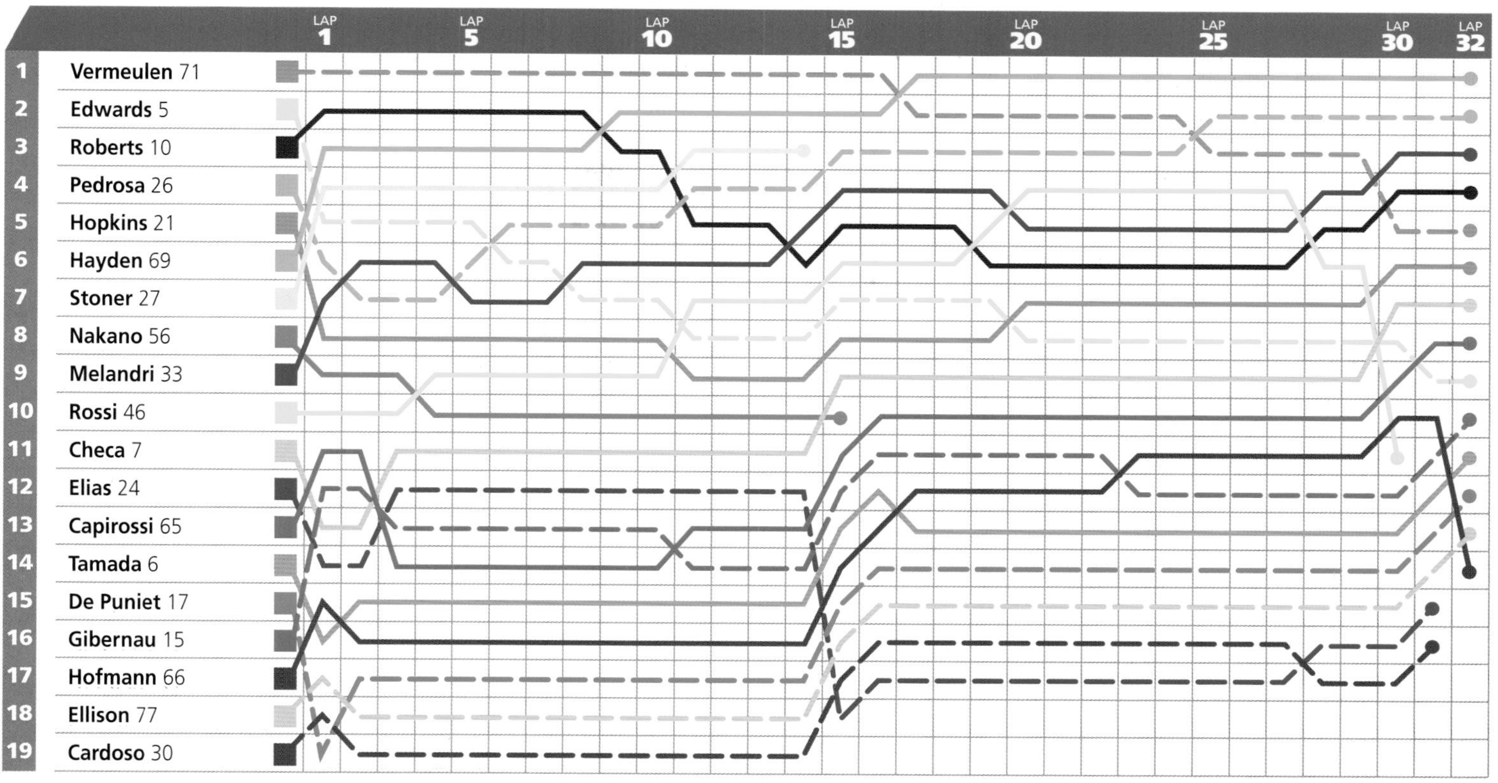

RACE

	Rider	Motorcycle	Race Time	Time +	Fastest Lap	Average Speed
1	Hayden	Honda	45m 04.867s		1m 23.495s	95.478mph
2	Pedrosa	Honda	45m 08.053s	3.186s	1m 23.333s	95.366mph
3	Melandri	Honda	45m 15.796s	10.929s	1m 23.899s	95.094mph
4	Roberts	KR211V	45m 16.808s	11.941s	1m 23.591s	95.058mph
5	Vermeulen	Suzuki	45m 32.306s	27.439s	1m 23.606s	94.519mph
6	Hopkins	Suzuki	45m 43.687s	38.820s	1m 24.002s	94.127mph
7	Checa	Yamaha	45m 49.692s	44.825s	1m 24.463s	93.922mph
8	Capirossi	Ducati	45m 53.393s	48.526s	1m 25.142s	93.795mph
9	Edwards	Yamaha	45m 58.095s	53.228s	1m 24.191s	93.636mph
10	Gibernau	Ducati	46m 11.146s	1m 06.279s	1m 25.226s	93.195mph
11	Tamada	Honda	46m 16.808s	1m 11.941s	1m 25.518s	93.005mph
12	De Puniet	Kawasaki	46m 19.274s	1m 14.407s	1m 25.438s	92.922mph
13	Ellison	Yamaha	46m 24.150s	1m 19.283s	1m 26.089s	92.759mph
14	Hofmann	Ducati	46m 46.144s	1m 41.277s	1m 24.960s	92.032mph
15	Elias	Honda	45m 30.873s	1 lap	1m 24.845s	91.614mph
16	Cardoso	Ducati	45m 38.744s	1 lap	1m 26.098s	91.350mph
	Rossi	Yamaha	43m 14.667s	2 laps	1m 23.809s	93.313mph
	Nakano	Kawasaki	21m 29.242s	17 laps	1m 24.247s	93.898mph
	Stoner	Honda	19m 44.864s	18 laps	1m 23.798s	95.358mph

CHAMPIONSHIP

	Rider	Team	Points
1	Hayden	Repsol Honda Team	194
2	Pedrosa	Repsol Honda Team	160
3	Melandri	Fortuna Honda	150
4	Rossi	Camel Yamaha Team	143
5	Capirossi	Ducati Marlboro Team	126
6	Stoner	Honda LCR	91
7	Edwards	Camel Yamaha Team	84
8	Roberts	Team Roberts	79
9	Hopkins	Rizla Suzuki MotoGP	74
10	Nakano	Kawasaki Racing Team	67
11	Tamada	Konica Minolta Honda	64
12	Elias	Fortuna Honda	59
13	Gibernau	Ducati Marlboro Team	58
14	Vermeulen	Rizla Suzuki MotoGP	57
15	Checa	Tech 3 Yamaha	53
16	Hofmann	Pramac d'Antin MotoGP	21
17	De Puniet	Kawasaki Racing Team	21
18	Ellison	Tech 3 Yamaha	20
19	Cardoso	Pramac d'Antin MotoGP	8

being further behind the leaders than the previous couple of races, this was more proof of the improvement in his Dunlop tyres and the quality of his development work.

8 LORIS CAPIROSSI A disastrous weekend for the factory Ducati team: neither rider got near a useable set-up and both suffered badly in qualifying. Put on untried hard tyres and rode what he said was a very good race 'considering what we had at our disposal', to salvage some points.

9 COLIN EDWARDS Suffering from a nasty bout of 'flu which, added to race-day temperatures, robbed him of any strength after a few laps – felt so bad he seriously considered pulling in. Ran into the same tyre problems as Rossi in the final ten laps.

10 SETE GIBERNAU No fitter than he was in Germany. More concerned with making sure his lack of strength on the brakes didn't interfere with someone else's race rather than pushing for an extra point or two. Later discovered that the plate on his broken collarbone had fatigued and he'd require further surgery.

11 MAKOTO TAMADA Aggravated his German leg injury (Roberts' bike had slid into him) when he lost the front in practice and pushed up the bike with his knee. From mid-race distance was in considerable pain on the left-handers and couldn't push hard.

12 RANDY DE PUNIET Described this as the hardest race of his life. Problems with the Kawasaki moving around on corner entry were compounded by a start that saw him at the back of the field by the end of the first lap. Put his head down, persevered and profited from several other people's misfortune.

13 JAMES ELLISON A good start and a good finish, but slowed when his front tyre started moving around mid-race. Found that he could push through the problem and was closing on de Puniet at the flag.

14 ALEX HOFMANN An excellent ride, on tyres he was happier with, looked like being rewarded with a top-ten finish, then he crashed at the final corner. Ducati team-manager Livio Suppo went to the d'Antin pit to congratulate him after the race.

15 TONI ELIAS Fell at the Corkscrew while lying 12th, rejoined at the back of the field and caught Cardoso seven laps from home. Still handicapped by his Assen injury.

16 JOSE LUIS CARDOSO The final finisher, and lapped.

NON-FINISHERS

VALENTINO ROSS In fourth place when tyre failure slowed him, then a fault in the cooling system caused overheating. Tried to cruise round for a point or two but parked it on the penultimate lap as the black flag was being prepared.

SHINYA NAKANO Did a great job in qualifying but stopped by motor failure on the 16th lap. Made his feelings known in a very non-stereotypically Japanese way when he got back to the pits.

CASEY STONER Crashed out of third place before half-distance when he lost the front after getting into Turn 5 a little too fast. Shadowing Pedrosa when he fell.

CZECH REPUBLIC GP
BRNO

ROUND 12

SWEET AND SOUR

Capirossi won the race but the championship contenders had very different days. Rossi looked to have his Yamaha behaving as he wanted, but the same couldn't be said of Hayden and the Honda

Yamaha must have worked very hard over the summer break to get their previously unruly M1 behaving so well at Brno. Right from the word go Rossi and Edwards were fast, and although the American couldn't get to grips with his qualifying tyre Rossi took his second pole of the year. It was only Valentino's third front-row start of the season but he was nearly 1.5 seconds quicker than last year's pole and an astonishing 2.5 seconds under his own lap-record time (lap records have to be set during races). What had Yamaha done? The rider, as

touch 4..
MRA
MOTORCYCLE WINDSHIELDS
Kawasaki
Arai
BRIDGESTONE

usual, praised both his team and Michelin for their hard work, but Ohlins got a good mention too. Rumour had it that a new rear-suspension linkage had contributed significantly to the M1 chassis's new-found useability. Jerry Burgess reckoned it was merely the consequence of the good work they'd done in the first half of the season: 'One of the mechanics just asked me what was going on, because we haven't done anything.'

Whatever the Camel team had or hadn't done over summer, they certainly adopted different tactics here, putting a qualifying tyre on the bike on Friday to make sure they understood what could happen on Saturday afternoon. After the disaster of Laguna Seca, Rossi had said that all he could do now was race for wins. A month of reflection, though, had persuaded him not to give up hope of the championship; Valentino's new mantra was to put pressure on Nicky Hayden – and to do that he had to start from the first or second row of the grid. 'If I start 11th or 12th, there is no pressure.'

Superficially it looked as if Nicky was standing up to this quite well: he was only just squeezed off the front row. However, his starting position disguised some serious set-up problems and ever-increasing worries about his clutch. The man who definitely wasn't worrying come Sunday morning was Loris Capirossi. He'd dominated most of practice in 2005 but started this year with a disastrous Friday, after which he later confessed to wanting to fly home. A major overnight rethink saw him looking a certainty for pole position until Rossi's last-moment miracle lap.

Loris may have been a little disgruntled by losing pole, but he didn't let it get to him for the race. He hit the first corner in the lead, finished the first lap nearly a second clear of Valentino, set a new lap record third time round, and by lap four had a lead of well over two seconds. Before he eased off, in the final few laps, Capirossi had stretched his lead to over eight seconds, a margin not seen in MotoGP since Rossi came home alone in Jerez last season, after he'd punted Gibernau into the gravel at the final turn, or, more relevantly, since Rossi's win at Phillip Island in '03 after he received a 10-second penalty for a yellow-flag offence and still came home with a winning margin of more than five seconds. The Ducati/Bridgestone combination was perfect and Loris was visibly enjoying himself. Never has the question 'Who's going to come second?' been asked so early in a MotoGP race.

As usual, the Brno track provided great entertainment all the way down the field. In the first half of the race the Repsol Honda team-mates scrapped over third place behind Rossi before Pedrosa eventually found a way past Hayden, on the brakes at the first corner. That propelled Nicky backwards and into a fearsome fight for fourth involving Stoner, Nakano, Melandri and Roberts – the latter two were doing a good job of swapping positions on every corner. Initially, Edwards had looked set to play a part in this fight but he faded. John Hopkins did quite the reverse, grimly hanging on to the bunch for most of the race before mounting a fearsome attack in the last three laps. At a different track Hayden would have slipped back to a lonely fourth place, but here he wouldn't be that lucky. Although Nicky got a good start, he'd damaged his clutch getting off the line and was having problems going into corners. Add in a hard rear tyre that he'd had no time to test and which spun up on the

Opposite For the first time the Kawasakis worked well at Brno

Below Rossi leads the chase of the fast-disappearing Capirossi

LIVE LONG AND PROSPER

Loris Capirossi's win at Brno made his the longest winning career in Grand Prix history. His first victory, in the 125cc race at the 1990 British Grand Prix, came 16 years and 15 days before this one, breaking the record of 13-times World Champion Angel Nieto, whose winning career in the smaller-capacity classes started with the 50cc East German GP in 1969 and ended with the 80cc race at the French GP of 1985. The gap between those victories is exactly a week shorter than between Loris's first win and this one.

However, if Loris wants to have the longest winning career in the top class, he's going to have to keep going for a while. His first 500cc win, at the Australian GP in 1996, was nine years and 304 days before the triumph at Brno. Giacomo Agostini, Phil Read and Alex Barros all have longer time spans between their first and last 500cc/MotoGP wins, with the Brazilian having a record 11 years and 204 days between his (admittedly rare) victories at Jarama in 1993 and Estoril in 2005.

Loris was genuinely pleased to have passed his milestone, and he was still smiling on the Monday after the race when he tested the 2007-spec 800cc Ducati for the first time. His grin became even broader after he passed Toni Elias's Fortuna Honda on the straight, and put in lap times that would have been very competitive against the 990s on Sunday. He reported that the 800 seemed noticeably easier to manoeuvre than the 990 through the many fast changes of direction around Brno. Looks like Loris isn't finished with winning yet...

exit of corners almost from the start and it was obvious he wasn't having an easy time.

In between the runaway Capirossi and the fight for fourth, Pedrosa was closing on Rossi. The Spaniard was content to shadow the Doctor until lap 15, when he tried an inside move going into the first of the high-speed Esses, only to have Rossi shut the door in the firmest possible manner. Undeterred, Dani attacked again, this time in the second part of the first of the two uphill Esses that end the lap. Valentino immediately repassed going into the final Ess but Dani was on the inside for the final right and led over the line – and was passed once more on the brakes at the first corner. Dani got by again, going into the first Ess, but was then put firmly in his place in the double right which follows. It was the first proper on-track confrontation between the two since Le Mans, and for a second time Rossi came out on top. It was very noticeable that Valentino didn't let Dani lead him for even one corner, and at least one repass was very tough indeed. In his first English-language post-race interview (with Randy Mamola, for British Eurosport), Pedrosa complained that both Rossi and Hayden had been unnecessarily tough closing the door on him. He didn't repeat the remarks, but when Rossi heard of them his response was dismissive: 'I haven't raced in 250 for a long time, but this is our racing.'

If anyone had cause for complaint it was Hayden. Having struggled with his clutch problem he then lost two places in the final two corners. First Hopkins took both Hayden and Nakano in one move, then Shinya rode round the outside of the American coming out of the last right-hander. Nicky had the Honda sideways and the rear tyre spinning but the Kawasaki motored round him. It was a major improvement for the green team at their bogey circuit, but the worst result of the season so far for Nicky.

Over at Ducati there were a few mixed feelings. Loris's win had been even more impressive than his victory at the opening race of the year, in Jerez, but it also generated thoughts about what might have been but for the Barcelona crash which had put him out of one race and severely limited his scoring potential in two others. Adding in even a pessimistic number of points for those three races would have put Capirossi right up there in the fight for the title.

Opposite Kenny Roberts won the dogfight for fourth place

Above John Hopkins overtook Hayden and Nakano on the last lap

Below Hofmann was back on a red Ducati – here he chases Checa

CZECH REPUBLIC GP

BRNO

ROUND 12

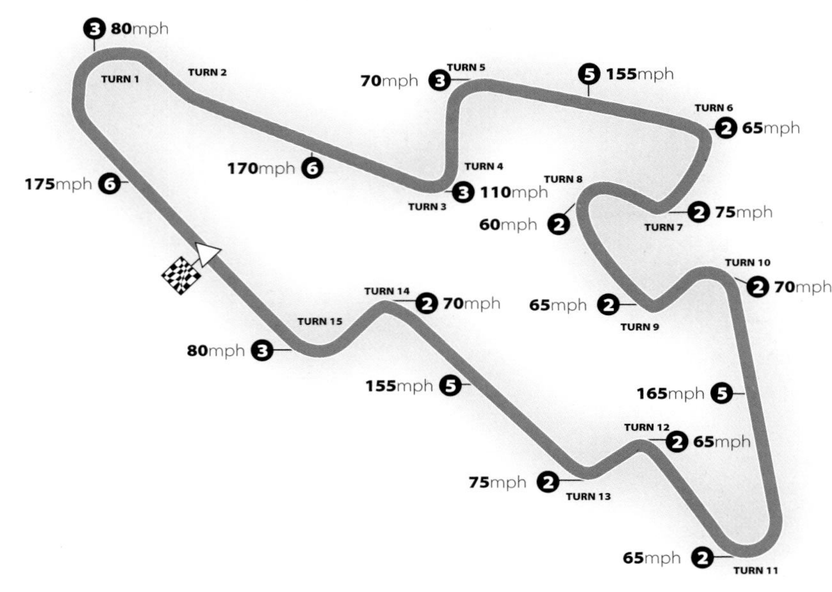

RACE RESULTS

RACE DATE August 20th
CIRCUIT LENGTH 3.357 miles
NO. OF LAPS 22
RACE DISTANCE 73.854 miles
WEATHER Dry, 24°C
TRACK TEMPERATURE 36°C
WINNER Loris Capirossi
FASTEST LAP 1m 58.157s, 102.228mph, Loris Capirossi (record)
PREVIOUS LAP RECORD 1m 58.787s, 101.522mph, Valentino Rossi, 2005

QUALIFYING

	Rider	Nationality	Team	Qualifying	Pole +	Gap
1	Rossi	ITA	Camel Yamaha Team	1m 56.191s		
2	Capirossi	ITA	Ducati Marlboro Team	1m 56.441s	0.250s	0.250s
3	Roberts	USA	Team Roberts	1m 56.603s	0.412s	0.162s
4	Hayden	USA	Honda Repsol Team	1m 56.694s	0.503s	0.091s
5	Nakano	JPN	Kawasaki Racing Team	1m 56.770s	0.579s	0.076s
6	Elias	SPA	Fortuna Honda	1m 56.875s	0.684s	0.105s
7	Hopkins	USA	Rizla Suzuki MotoGP	1m 56.913s	0.722s	0.038s
8	Edwards	USA	Camel Yamaha Team	1m 56.967s	0.776s	0.054s
9	Pedrosa	SPA	Repsol Honda Team	1m 57.139s	0.948s	0.172s
10	De Puniet	FRA	Kawasaki Racing Team	1m 57.185s	0.994s	0.046s
11	Melandri	ITA	Fortuna Honda	1m 57.221s	1.030s	0.036s
12	Stoner	AUS	Honda LCR	1m 57.679s	1.488s	0.458s
13	Vermeulen	AUS	Rizla Suzuki MotoGP	1m 57.894s	1.703s	0.215s
14	Hofmann	GER	Ducati Marlboro Team	1m 57.906s	1.715s	0.012s
15	Tamada	JPN	Konica Minolta Honda	1m 58.239s	2.048s	0.333s
16	Ellison	GBR	Tech 3 Yamaha	1m 59.011s	2.820s	0.772s
17	Checa	SPA	Tech 3 Yamaha	1m 59.289s	3.098s	0.278s
18	Cardoso	SPA	Pramac d'Antin MotoGP	2m 00.971s	4.780s	1.682s
19	Silva	SPA	Pramac d'Antin MotoGP	2m 01.433s	5.242s	0.462s

FINISHERS

1 LORIS CAPIROSSI Total domination on race day after a worrying start on Friday. Led from lights to flag without looking remotely troubled, and in the process became the rider with the longest winning career in GP history. Ducati's first win at Brno reinstated Loris as a major player in the championship, if not a genuine contender.

2 VALENTINO ROSSI Couldn't lay a glove on Capirossi but decisively won his first serious on-track encounter with Pedrosa. Took points off all those ahead of him in the title chase but seemed most pleased about his second pole of the year. Not a bad way to celebrate the tenth anniversary of his first GP win, the 1996 125cc race here at Brno.

3 DANI PEDROSA Difficult practice and qualifying but comfortably outpaced all the other Hondas in the race, riding past Stoner and Hayden. Sat behind Rossi before launching his ultimately unsuccessful attack, but made Valentino work for his points. Not too happy with Rossi or Hayden after the race but soon calmed down.

4 KENNY ROBERTS Another front-row start – his third in a row and the fourth in six races – and another great race. Tried a new fuel tank in practice, designed to help him early in the race, but didn't use it on Sunday, so lost out in the early laps before winning the best fight of the day, the scrap for fourth. 'I just tried to keep it tidy and we made it,' was his laconic comment.

5 MARCO MELANDRI Not very happy with his finishing position, but it was probably better than he expected after qualifying in 11th. Couldn't go with Rossi and Pedrosa early on, then found he couldn't attack in the closing stages either. Had to be content with taking four points out of his deficit to Hayden.

6 CASEY STONER After no-scores in Germany and the USA, misjudged the timing of his final run on qualifiers and finished on the back of the fourth row. The race went much better, although he'd used up his rear tyre before the crucial closing laps.

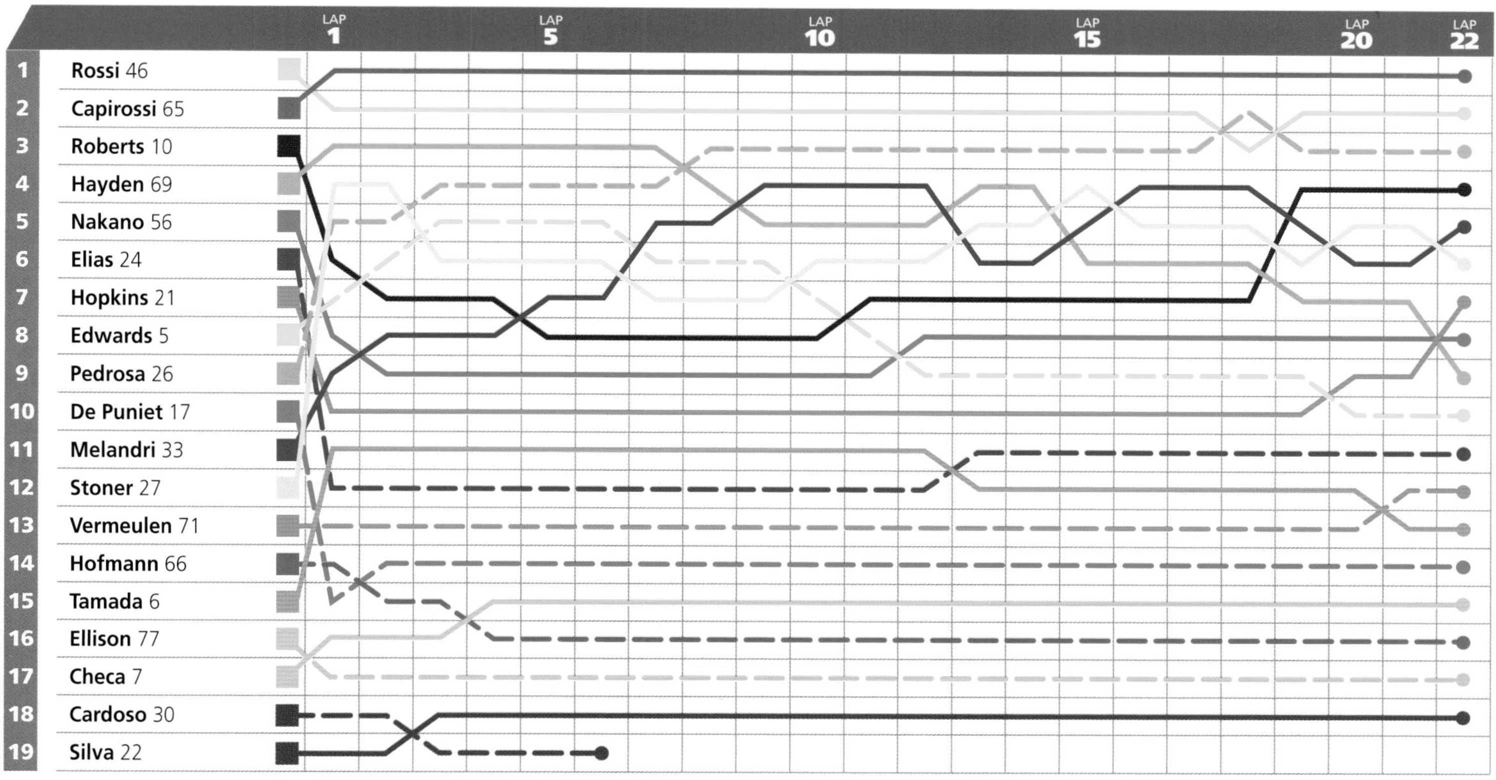

RACE

	Rider	Motorcycle	Race Time	Time +	Fastest Lap	Average Speed
1	Capirossi	Ducati	43m 40.145s		1m 58.157	101.420mph
2	Rossi	Yamaha	43m 45.047s	4.902s	1m 58.575	101.231mph
3	Pedrosa	Honda	43m 48.157s	8.012s	1m 58.630	101.111mph
4	Roberts	KR211V	43m 54.945s	14.800s	1m 58.793	100.850mph
5	Melandri	Honda	43m 55.170s	15.025s	1m 58.684	100.842mph
6	Stoner	Honda	43m 55.844s	15.699s	1m 58.794	100.816mph
7	Hopkins	Suzuki	43m 56.920s	16.775s	1m 58.951	100.775mph
8	Nakano	Kawasaki	43m 57.087s	16.942s	1m 58.831	100.769mph
9	Hayden	Honda	43m 57.206s	17.061s	1m 58.885	100.764mph
10	Edwards	Yamaha	43m 59.580s	19.435s	1m 58.585	100.673mph
11	Elias	Honda	44m 02.360s	22.215s	1m 59.298	100.568mph
12	Vermeulen	Suzuki	44m 04.123s	23.978s	1m 59.439	100.501mph
13	Tamada	Honda	44m 05.112s	24.967s	1m 59.157	100.463mph
14	De Puniet	Kawasaki	44m 09.106s	28.961s	1m 59.339	100.311mph
15	Checa	Yamaha	44m 09.441s	29.296s	1m 59.630	100.299mph
16	Hofmann	Ducati	44m 09.946s	29.801s	1m 59.856	100.280mph
17	Ellison	Yamaha	44m 43.127s	1m 02.982s	2m 00.608	99.039mph
18	Silva	Ducati	45m 24.920s	1m 44.775s	2m 02.397	97.520mph
	Cardoso	Ducati	12m 36.505s	16 laps	2m 03.007	95.800mph

CHAMPIONSHIP

	Rider	Team	Points
1	Hayden	Repsol Honda Team	201
2	Pedrosa	Repsol Honda Team	176
3	Rossi	Camel Yamaha Team	163
4	Melandri	Fortuna Honda	161
5	Capirossi	Ducati Marlboro Team	151
6	Stoner	Honda LCR	101
7	Roberts	Team Roberts	92
8	Edwards	Camel Yamaha Team	90
9	Hopkins	Rizla Suzuki MotoGP	83
10	Nakano	Kawasaki Racing Team	75
11	Tamada	Konica Minolta Honda	67
12	Elias	Fortuna Honda	64
13	Vermeulen	Rizla Suzuki MotoGP	61
14	Gibernau	Ducati Racing Team	58
15	Checa	Tech 3 Yamaha	54
16	De Puniet	Kawasaki Racing Team	23
17	Hofmann	Ducati Marlboro Team	21
18	Ellison	Tech 3 Yamaha	20
19	Cardoso	Pramac d'Antin MotoGP	8

7 JOHN HOPKINS Put a demon pass on Nakano and Hayden on the last lap to top off what John called his best race of the season so far. The team worked brilliantly to control the chatter afflicting the bike at the start of the weekend and produced a machine that came good towards the end of the race.

8 SHINYA NAKANO On paper not that good a result, but a second-row start and a top-ten finish were just dreams for Kawasaki after previous outings at Brno. If Shinya hadn't been pushed to the back of his group at the first corner, it might have been even better.

9 NICKY HAYDEN The development Honda has always had traction problems coming out of corners, and the Czech GP took them to extremes. Nicky even chose a hard race tyre that hadn't done any long runs in practice to try to alleviate this, but it spun from the start. A very bad afternoon that reduced his championship lead to just 25 points.

10 COLIN EDWARDS Looked very competitive early on, making several aggressive overtakes, but the lack of a good set-up took its toll on his tyres and he faded badly in the second half of the race.

11 TONI ELIAS A superb performance in qualifying ruined by a terrible start. It then took him a dozen laps to find his rhythm, by which time a top-ten finish was out of the question.

12 CHRIS VERMEULEN A weekend of hard work with precious little reward: battled with Elias and Tamada but discovered that Hondas are always difficult to get past at a circuit where a strong engine is vital.

13 MAKOTO TAMADA Over his Sachsenring injury but still in serious trouble with set-up. Reported he was losing all his time coming out of the corner, so the team tried everything – long and short swingarms, hard and soft suspension – but never improved the situation.

14 RANDY DE PUNIET Used up his rear tyre after a mistake at Turn 1: he braked early and ended the first lap in 15th, five places down on his qualifying. Tried to get back to the group in front but ran out of rear grip eight laps from the flag.

15 CARLOS CHECA An improvement on qualifying but overall a difficult weekend. Couldn't use the tyres with which he'd been so impressive in the previous two races and had to deal with a lot of chatter.

16 ALEX HOFMANN Back on the factory bike as Gibernau was unfit after another operation on his collarbone. Raced on tyres he'd not done too many laps on in practice and then 'ran into a wall' in the race.

17 JAMES ELLISON A repeat of the Donington race, with no rear grip after a handful of laps. Had to be content with outqualifying his team-mate for the first time this season.

18 IVAN SILVA A third MotoGP ride for the d'Antin Spanish Formula Xtreme Champion, deputising for Hofmann.

NON-FINISHERS

JOSE LUIS CARDOSO Pulled in after a half-dozen laps citing tyre problems.

NON-STARTERS

SETE GIBERNAU The plate fixing his collarbone had fatigued and the bone wasn't healing, so had to go back under the surgeon's knife. Was advised to miss Brno to ensure full fitness for the run of three back-to-back races that were next on the calendar.

MALAYSIAN GP
SEPANG

ROUND 13

THE BATTLE OF WOUNDED KNEE

Rossi and Capirossi fought out another epic, race-long battle but it was third-place finisher Dani Pedrosa who was the biggest hero of the weekend

The one thing a rider really doesn't need at the start of a run of three races in three weekends is a bad injury. Capirossi, Gibernau and Melandri had all suffered in Barcelona; Pedrosa was a victim at Sepang. During the second free practice session Dani appeared to lose the front coming out of a fast right-hander, causing the bike suddenly to increase its bank angle which shoved his knee into the kerb with some force. The impact on the serrated concrete was enough to slice through his leathers and cause the bike to highside. He landed painfully on his knees and, although he was up and walking immediately, he was hurting. Pedrosa was convinced the original contact had caused the injury to his right knee, a gash under the kneecap with the complication, as his race engineer Mike Leitner put it, of someone then inserting a spoon and removing a lump of flesh. As there's precious little flesh around anyone's kneecap, let alone the diminutive Honda rider's, stitching the wound proved problematical, as did bending his knee afterwards without pulling the

REPSOL
HONDA
69
GAS
Red Bull
Arai

Above Rossi leads Capirossi and the Repsol Hondas early on

Opposite Nicky Hayden at speed on Sepang's front straight

stitches. Moving around on the bike was going to be a serious problem; add in a broken big toe on his left foot and Dani was a serious doubt for the race.

The other Repsol Honda man also had problems. Nicky Hayden had tested a new chassis after Brno, where it proved to be a significant step forward. In Sepang, however, he found the improvement in side grip and traction involved a trade-off against feeling for what the front tyre was doing. The only consolation, he may have thought, was that his team-mate wouldn't be posing a threat. Capirossi, carrying his form over from the Czech Republic, and Rossi on his reformed M1 would surely show no mercy. The Ducati man, in particular, was exuding confidence. Loris is a rider who carries the weight of expectation lightly; when things are going well he's relaxed and smiling, with no doubt in his mind about who's going to stand on top of the rostrum. This time his positive attitude crossed the line into over-confidence.

Pedrosa was not at all confident. His race engineer, the HRC personnel and all the Repsol staff were doubtful about his ability to race. To keep his knee mobile he was getting up every couple of hours through the night to do exercises: 'You don't need an alarm clock,' said Dani, dry as ever. In the paddock he was pushed around in a wheelchair. Anyone who thought the effects of the injury were being exaggerated was disabused of that notion as soon as they talked to someone, like James Ellison, who'd been in the Clinica Mobile with the Spaniard.

Dani made his decision at the last moment, deciding during the 250cc race to have a painkilling injection for the first time since his crash. Whatever they gave him, it worked. Despite only being faster than one other rider in Sunday warm-up, Pedrosa led at the first corner, was second at the end of the first lap and was only passed during the race by Rossi and Capirossi. Hayden was pleased to get to the first turn in fourth after 'babying the clutch off the line', but he never managed to move forward. His bike looked unstable going into corners, but Nicky later said he just didn't have the speed and was trying to make up time on the brakes. The championship leader could hardly have had a more dispiriting weekend. There was plenty of excellent work being done further down the field, though. Gibernau looked good on his return from injury, although he claimed to need the race to get back on the pace, while Hopkins managed to recover from an incident-packed first lap to claim a useful sixth place.

At the front Rossi and Capirossi fought out an epic duel – never more than three-quarters of a second apart until the very final act of the drama. There were plenty of overtaking moves, four in one lap alone, but the pivotal moment came, as everyone knew it would, on the last lap. Capirossi had opened up what looked like a decisive lead – all of 0.6 seconds – and he'd been fiendishly quick in the final section of the lap all weekend. Ducati team manager Livio Suppo had noticed, however, that his rider was anything but fast in the third sector, the comparatively twisty section leading up to the right-hander on to the back straight. Loris had dismissed these concerns, saying that it was impossible to overtake there and emphasising his speed in the final sector, which included the last passing opportunity, the

heavy braking for the left-hand hairpin at the end of the back straight which concludes the lap.

Rossi had also been paying attention to Capirossi's strengths and weaknesses. By the time the pair got to the left/right Esses, Valentino had demolished Loris's lead. The Doctor got alongside the Ducati in the first part of the linked corners and was in the right place to lead out of the second part. Who said you couldn't pass in the third sector? Rossi had also noticed that the Ducati was spinning a lot coming on to the back straight – where the Yamaha was driving perfectly – and, sure enough, he took sufficient advantage there to ensure he was out of range of Capirossi's final desperate lunge on the brakes.

It was a fitting finale to a fabulous race, although there was one curious footnote. On his way to the rostrum Rossi picked up a chair, took it out to the front of the podium and sat on it – Capirossi even sat on his knee. As rostrum celebrations go it was about as undignified as possible. Was Valentino really poking fun at Dani's use of a wheelchair? Rossi later claimed he was simply tired because of the heat, but most people took it as a dig at Pedrosa, a suggestion that the Honda man had been exaggerating the effects of his injury. In fact Dani's painkilling injection had worked miracles. During the race his broken toe had given him more trouble than his gashed knee, although he could feel the stitches pulling and rubbing on his leathers. Unsurprisingly, he missed the rostrum to have the wound re-stitched, which meant he didn't witness the Italians' performance. But his team and the Spanish press had seen it – and they didn't like it.

WASH OUT

After a tropical storm washed out Saturday's qualifying session, Race Direction had to find a way of forming the grid. There were two obvious choices: use the current championship standings or, despite the fact that it's forbidden by the rulebook, use the times from free practice. They chose the latter. As most riders had tried a qualifier in the third session the grid had a familiar look to it; only Casey Stoner felt the decision to be unfair as his tenth place was lower than he'd finished in any session and he hadn't used a qualifier.

The man who benefited most was Pedrosa, so for once the rain was kind to him. If the qualifying session had been run as normal he would surely have been struggling at the back of the grid, just as Rossi did at Assen after injuring himself in practice. The downpour meant Dani would start from the second row thanks to a time he'd put in just before he crashed.

Conspiracy theorists were quick to seize upon this as evidence of some sort of plot to help out the Spaniard. Of course if that were really true then Race Direction would have used the points standing for the grid, which would have put Dani on the front row.

Race Director Paul Butler agreed that the rulebook didn't cover this particular situation and he promised the omission would be rectified over winter.

Opposite top Rossi stalks Capirossi in the closing stages

Opposite bottom Dani Pedrosa broke toes on his left foot as well as gashing his right knee in a qualifying crash; didn't slow him down though

Below Casey Stoner getting his weight over the front end as he powers out of a corner

MALAYSIAN GP

SEPANG

ROUND 13

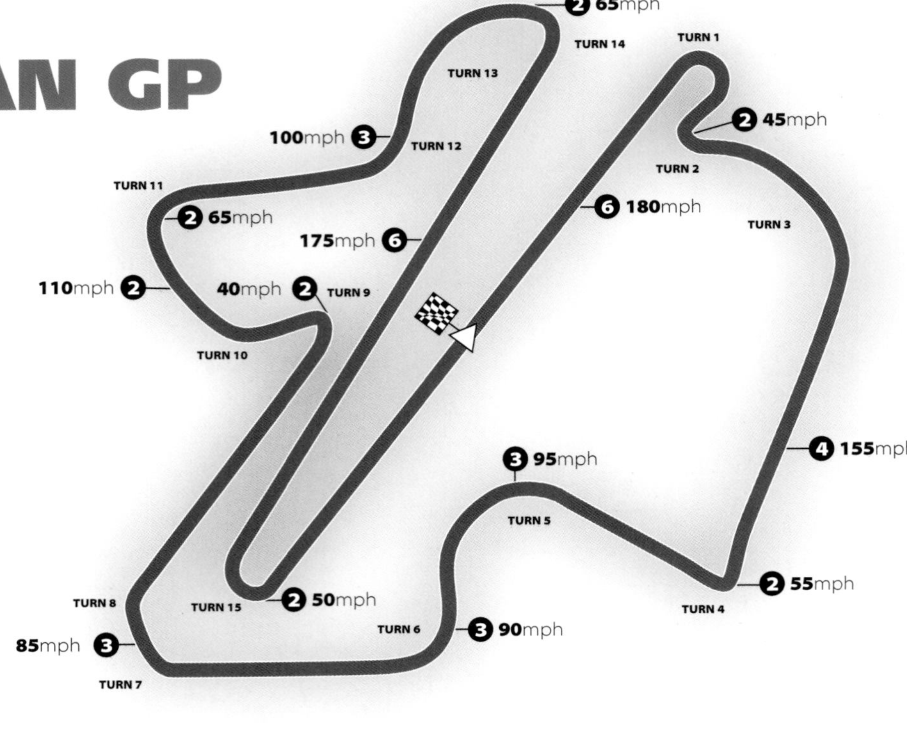

RACE RESULTS

RACE DATE September 10th
CIRCUIT LENGTH 3.447 miles
NO. OF LAPS 21
RACE DISTANCE 72.387 miles
WEATHER Dry, 33°C
TRACK TEMPERATURE 46°C
WINNER Valentino Rossi
FASTEST LAP 2m 02.127s, 101.559mph, Loris Capirossi
PREVIOUS LAP RECORD 2m 01.731s, 101.696mph, Valentino Rossi, 2005

QUALIFYING

	Rider	Nationality	Team	Qualifying	Pole +	Gap
1	Rossi	ITA	Camel Yamaha Team	2m 00.605s		
2	Hayden	USA	Repsol Honda Team	2m 01.043s	0.438	0.438
3	Capirossi	ITA	Ducuti Marlboro Team	2m 01.167s	0.562	0.124
4	Roberts	USA	Team Roberts	2m 01.898s	1.293	0.731
5	Pedrosa	SPA	Repsol Honda Team	2m 02.021s	1.416	0.123
6	Gibernau	SPA	Ducati Marlboro Team	2m 02.181s	1.576	0.160
7	De Puniet	FRA	Kawasaki Racing Team	2m 02.131s	1.708	0.132
8	Hopkins	USA	Rizla Suzuki MotoGP	2m 02.453s	1.848	0.140
9	Melandri	ITA	Fortuna Honda	2m 02.560s	1.955	0.107
10	Stoner	AUS	Honda LCR	2m 02.790s	2.185	0.230
11	Edwards	USA	Camel Yamaha Team	2m 02.800s	2.195	0.010
12	Nakano	JPN	Kawasaki Racing Team	2m 02.832s	2.227	0.032
13	Tamada	JPN	Konica Minolta Honda	2m 02.918s	2.313	0.086
14	Elias	SPA	Fortuna Honda	2m 03.102s	2.497	0.184
15	Checa	SPA	Tech 3 Yamaha	2m 03.123s	2.518	0.021
16	Vermeulen	AUS	Rizla Suzuki MotoGP	2m 03.285	2.680	0.162
17	Hofmann	GER	Pramac d'Antin MotoGP	2m 04.706s	4.101	1.421
18	Ellison	GBR	Tech 3 Yamaha	2m 05.023s	4.418	0.317
19	Cardoso	SPA	Pramac d'Antin MotoGP	2m 05.958s	5.353	0.935

FINISHERS

1 VALENTINO ROSSI The man himself called it 'another legendary battle', which certainly summed it up. His Yamaha M1 looked to be doing all he asked of it during the weekend, which boded well for the season's four remaining races and Valentino's now much-improved chance of retaining his title. His deficit to the leader was down to 26 points.

2 LORIS CAPIROSSI After the last GP and his Sepang victory in 2005, Loris must have thought this was another race he could win – and he very nearly did. Fulsome in his praise of Rossi, and refused to say he was disappointed after such a great dice. And at least he overtook Melandri to go fourth overall in the championship.

3 DANI PEDROSA A nasty crash in practice left him with a gashed right knee and a broken left toe, and made it doubtful he would even race. But race he did and, despite being seconds off the pace in morning warm-up, he got the holeshot, briefly led the race and never looked in danger of losing third. The whole paddock was amazed, with the possible exception of Dani himself.

4 NICKY HAYDEN A deeply frustrating weekend. Used the revised chassis tested successfully after Brno but what he gained in edge grip and rear traction he lost in front-end adhesion. Refused to make excuses, simply saying everything worked well but he didn't have the speed. Being beaten by Rossi and Capirossi may have been inevitable, but being unable to pass his injured team-mate must have hurt.

5 SETE GIBERNAU As good a return as could be expected after missing Brno because of further surgery on his Catalunya collarbone injury. Had been unable to ride or train properly for a month but said the team made his return as easy as possible. Felt he was tentative at the start and needed the race to complete the comeback.

6 JOHN HOPKINS Probably started further back than if qualifying had been run normally, then got boxed in at Turn 1

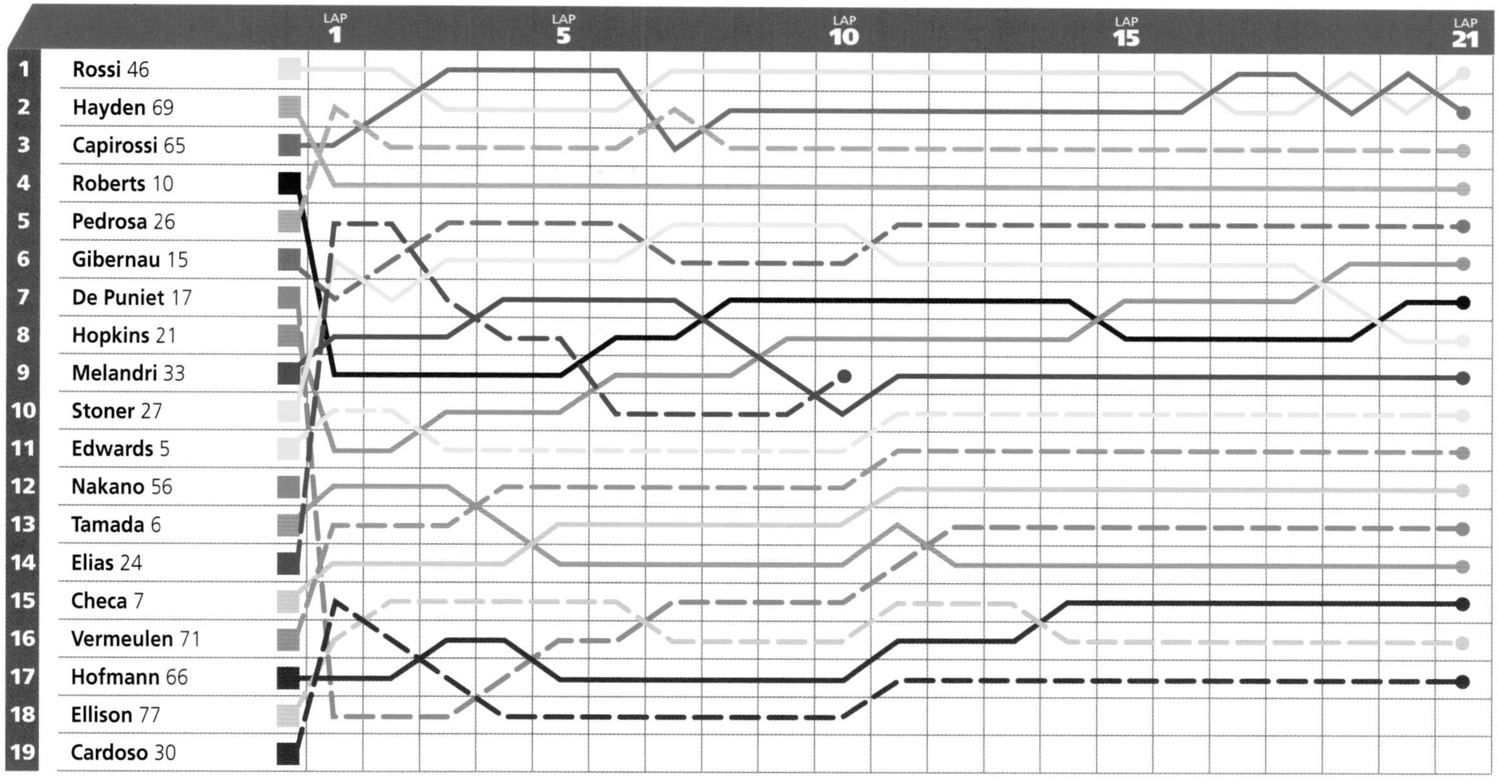

RACE

	Rider	Motorcycle	Race Time	Time +	Fastest Lap	Average Speed
1	Rossi	Yamaha	43m 07.829s		2m 02.332s	100.650mph
2	Capirossi	Ducati	43m 08.678s	0.849s	2m 02.127s	100.617mph
3	Pedrosa	Honda	43m 11.692s	3.863s	2m 02.727s	100.499mph
4	Hayden	Honda	43m 13.609s	5.780s	2m 02.749s	100.426mph
5	Gibernau	Ducati	43m 17.130s	9.301s	2m 02.581s	100.290mph
6	Hopkins	Suzuki	43m 18.910s	11.081s	2m 02.584s	100.221mph
7	Roberts	KR211V	43m 19.667s	11.838s	2m 02.753s	100.191mph
8	Stoner	Honda	43m 20.096s	12.267s	2m 02.623s	100.175mph
9	Melandri	Honda	43m 22.848s	15.019s	2m 02.780s	100.069mph
10	Edwards	Yamaha	43m 27.738s	19.909s	2m 03.107s	99.882mph
11	Vermeulen	Suzuki	43m 32.200s	24.371s	2m 02.896s	99.711mph
12	Checa	Yamaha	43m 38.713s	30.884s	2m 03.466s	99.463mph
13	De Puniet	Kawasaki	43m 44.164s	36.335s	2m 03.063s	99.256mph
14	Tamada	Honda	43m 56.606s	48.777s	2m 03.597s	98.788mph
15	Hofmann	Ducati	44m 06.910s	59.081s	2m 04.907s	98.403mph
16	Ellison	Yamaha	44m 13.616s	1m 05.787s	2m 04.692s	98.155mph
17	Cardoso	Ducati	44m 45.691s	1m 37.862s	2m 06.325s	96.982mph
	Elias	Honda	20m 39.952s	11 laps	2m 02.829s	100.029mph
	Nakano	Kawasaki				

CHAMPIONSHIP

	Rider	Team	Points
1	Hayden	Repsol Honda Team	214
2	Pedrosa	Repsol Honda Team	192
3	Rossi	Camel Yamaha Team	188
4	Capirossi	Ducati Marlboro Team	171
5	Melandri	Fortuna Honda	168
6	Stoner	Honda LCR	109
7	Roberts	Team Roberts	101
8	Edwards	Camel Yamaha Team	96
9	Hopkins	Rizla Suzuki MotoGP	93
10	Nakano	Kawasaki Racing Team	75
11	Gibernau	Ducati Marlboro Team	69
12	Tamada	Konica Minolta Honda	69
13	Vermeulen	Rizla Suzuki MotoGP	66
14	Elias	Fortuna Honda	64
15	Checa	Tech 3 Yamaha	58
16	De Puniet	Kawasaki Racing Team	26
17	Hofmann	Pramac d'Antin MotoGP	22
18	Ellison	Tech 3 Yamaha	20
19	Cardoso	Pramac d'Antin MotoGP	8

and was nearly involved in the Kawasaki accident. After finishing the first lap in 11th Hopper used Suzuki's new engine to great effect to make five passes and be in range of Gibernau when the flag came out. Delighted with the potential of his bike.

7 KENNY ROBERTS In the light of recent performances, a slightly disappointing result at a track the team has never really come to grips with. A bad start led to him overshooting the slow corners and getting wheelspin coming out of them. Still beat all the Honda satellite team riders.

8 CASEY STONER Not happy with the way the grid was selected, but got his customary lightning start. Challenging Hayden for fourth when he had a wobble on the brakes which tweaked an old injury in his back, so unable to move properly on the bike. Not surprisingly, dropped back and finished exhausted.

9 MARCO MELANDRI Never solved his problems with the front end in what looked like a flashback to his difficulties with the 2006 RCV at the beginning of the year.

10 COLIN EDWARDS Another rider revisiting old problems: Colin 'turned it upside-down' trying to find enough rear grip. Tried a near carbon copy of Rossi's settings for the race to no avail. At least extended his points-scoring run to 34 races, second only to Doohan's total of 37.

11 CHRIS VERMEULEN Suffered badly from a 'flu bug on Friday and Saturday which affected his qualifying slot. Started strongly, did his fastest-ever lap of the circuit during the race, but then faded physically towards the chequered flag.

12 CARLOS CHECA Content to have done the best he could with what he had at a track where he'd been in the top ten for the past seven years, including three podium finishes. Was a little down on power but the tyres were consistent and he made no mistakes.

13 RANDY DE PUNIET Taken off track by his team-mate on the first lap after a good start. Took four laps to catch up with Cardoso at the back of the field, then made four passes. Was tenth when the incident happened and reckons he could have made the top ten.

14 MAKOTO TAMADA Another frustrating and difficult weekend. Reported that all front grip was gone after just three laps.

15 ALEX HOFMANN A bad start and lack of grip meant Alex was happy to come away with a point. Once he got past Ellison he was lapping at the same pace as Tamada.

16 JAMES ELLISON Very disappointed: 'No matter what my hard-working team does we can't get weight on the rear to make it steer into corners.'

17 JOSE LUIS CARDOSO Tailed off at the back of the field despite an excellent start. Like his team-mate Hofmann, blamed a lack of grip for most of his problems.

NON-FINISHERS

TONI ELIAS Got his best start of the season and said he felt comfortable running at the pace of the front group. Nevertheless he had dropped back to tenth just before half-distance when he crashed going into the first turn.

SHINYA NAKANO Started from his worst grid position for almost a year and tried to make up for it on the first lap. Going into Turn 9 he was lining up de Puniet for an inside move when the riders in front of him braked earlier than expected, forcing him to the outside and into contact with his team-mate. Both went into the gravel trap; Randy was able to rejoin the race but Shinya crashed.

AUSTRALIAN GP

PHILLIP ISLAND

ROUND 14

CLIMATE CHANGE

The 'flag-to-flag' wet-weather regulations were applied for the first time – and they worked. Melandri took his third win of the season while Rossi was involved in another yellow-flag controversy

If ever the football cliché about a game of two halves could be applied to a motorcycle race, then it was here at Phillip Island. The rain came after seven laps, early enough to force the entire field into the pits to swap their slick-shod bikes for their spare machines with full rain tyres. The resulting scramble proved unlucky for some and very fortuitous indeed for others.

Chief among the losers was Shinya Nakano. He alone of the Bridgestone runners made his qualifying tyre last a lap; by only pushing hard in the final, vital part of the lap, Shinya put himself on the front row. When the lights went out the Kawasaki bolted away from the field and had a three-and-a-half second lead by the end of the second lap. He was nearly that far

Above In the dry, Shinya Nakano was untouchable

Below Carlos Checa has a little rest after crashing. This was the incident that led to the argument about Rossi passing under a yellow flag

ahead when the rain came down, but the Japanese was one of the unfortunate riders who found his wet bike was nowhere near as good as his dry one. Dani Pedrosa was fast in practice, fast in the dry but lamentably off the pace in the wet and suffered the humiliating fate of being lapped. The other big loser was Sete Gibernau. He'd started impressively in the dry and was even faster in the wet. When he took the lead

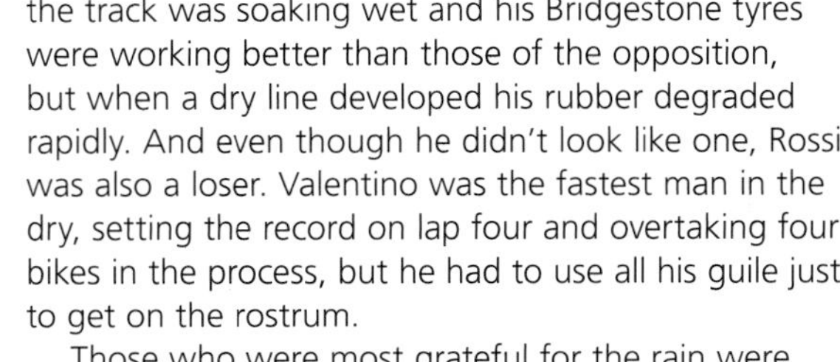

the track was soaking wet and his Bridgestone tyres were working better than those of the opposition, but when a dry line developed his rubber degraded rapidly. And even though he didn't look like one, Rossi was also a loser. Valentino was the fastest man in the dry, setting the record on lap four and overtaking four bikes in the process, but he had to use all his guile just to get on the rostrum.

Those who were most grateful for the rain were Chris Vermeulen and Nicky Hayden. By riding the laps before and after the bike change as hard as he could, Vermeulen elevated himself from 15th to fourth. It was not a risk-free strategy: 'I got to Turn 2, put my knee on the ground and hoped the tyres would grip.' Two laps later he was second. Hayden started from pole, his first for a year, but the Honda's clutch again gave trouble and Nicky only had a couple of bikes behind him going into the first corner. After the bike change he came out alongside Rossi, and the pair were never far apart until the flag. They did, however, get tangled up with Casey Stoner, and subsequently became involved in another row about passing under a yellow flag.

The incident happened after Carlos Checa had crashed at Honda Corner. Rossi appeared to pass Stoner, but the view from behind and to the inside, provided by the TV camera, suggested that Valentino had allowed the Australian to repass him – as regulations require – before instantly taking the place back. The sector marshals didn't report an offence. Since, ironically, the rule was rewritten after Rossi was penalised at Donington in 2003, there has been

ALL CHANGE

The chance to use the 'flag-to-flag' rules was deemed a success by just about everyone, if only because no-one could come up with a better idea. If the race is declared 'wet' before the start, or a white flag is shown during the race (to indicate a change of weather conditions), then riders may come in and change to a bike equipped with different types of tyre – in this case, they came in on slicks and went out on treaded rain tyres. The Yamaha Dunlop riders came in twice and therefore also used the third option: intermediates. The rule is designed to avoid the confusion of two-part races with aggregate timing that are so unsatisfactory for paying spectators and TV viewers.

The practicalities of the process went as well as could be expected, especially given that the Phillip Island pit lane is both the shortest and narrowest used by MotoGP, and that the majority of the field came in at the same time.

There was one near-miss when Hayden set off and came perilously close to side-swiping Capirossi, and a mechanic who gave his rider a helpful push found himself stranded in the middle of pit lane. If there was a problem it was overcrowding as team members not directly involved with the bike change rubber-necked along with 125 and 250cc team staff. Next time, the International Road Racing Teams Association (IRTA) who organise and police the paddock and pit lane will be finding ways of keeping people without a job to do well out of the way.

Below Chris Vermeulen got his first rostrum finish in MotoGP at his home race, which went some way to making up for his bad luck at Laguna Seca

CAMEL
YAMAHA
CAMEL
YAMAHA
MOTUL
MICHELIN
brembo
ÖHLINS
2D
NGK
D.I.D
Beta

no way to punish such an offence once a race has finished. The current regulations state that if a rider doesn't drop back a place then he'll be given a ten-second penalty, as happened to Rossi at Phillip Island in '03. He learned of the penalty from his pit board on that occasion and promptly went on to win the race by more than 15 seconds.

The problem was that a different camera angle clearly showed Rossi's guilt. HRC requested a review of the tapes, after which Race Direction admitted they'd missed the crucial move and nothing could now be done. Honda's management were incandescent with rage, but Hayden was more laid back. He'd seen the flag – Stoner, by the way, hadn't – and assumed Rossi would move over to allow the Australian to pass and had immediately tucked up behind Casey's rear wheel hoping to take advantage. It didn't happen and he was stuck behind Stoner and Nakano for three laps before getting back to Rossi. After the race Nicky refused to place too much emphasis on Rossi's luck: 'He didn't pass me under a yellow.' He did admit, though, that during the race he'd assumed Rossi would be penalised. HRC weren't so forgiving. President Suguru Kanazawa wrote to FIM President Francesco Zerbi demanding action, which was code for some sackings at Race Direction. He even made the text of the letter public at the Japanese GP the following weekend, where the Grand Prix Commission met for an emergency session and after 'full and frank discussions' promised to review procedures. They also took a pop at the Australian marshals for not pulling the flag in when told. Whatever the rights and wrongs of the situation, the subject of how to ensure that riders see flags came up for its regular debate.

Among all this chaos Melandri was having a perfect day. He was with the group chasing the runaway Nakano in the dry and his wet bike worked just as well in the changed conditions. Marco was third when the fog of confusion generated by the bike swaps cleared and he was the fastest man when the track was both properly wet and patchy. The two riders in front of him, Vermeulen and Gibernau, were running into trouble with their Bridgestones on the drying track and circulating well over a second slower than the Fortuna Honda rider. Melandri hit the front ten laps from the flag and didn't put a foot wrong, ending the race with a spectacular, smoky, one-handed slide out of the final turn. The rest were now ten seconds behind him, reduced to squabbling among themselves. Vermeulen just managed to hang on to second but Gibernau, whose bike looked seriously unstable in the closing laps, was mugged by Rossi as he came out of the last corner and denied his first rostrum as a Ducati rider. By luck or design Rossi timed his pass perfectly, for Hayden couldn't get past the Ducati and had to give up another five points to Rossi.

Vermeulen became the first Aussie to stand on the Phillip Island rostrum since Mick Doohan in 1998. Paul Denning, the Suzuki team manager, described it as a 'get out of jail' result which, given the trouble the Rizla bikes had during practice and qualifying, was probably accurate. However, since Chris had been robbed of at least a podium at Laguna Seca, no-one minded.

Opposite Valentino Rossi and flags – not a happy mixture

Above Nicky Hayden was grateful for the rain

Left Marco Melandri made it three wins in the season

AUSTRALIAN GP

PHILLIP ISLAND

ROUND 14

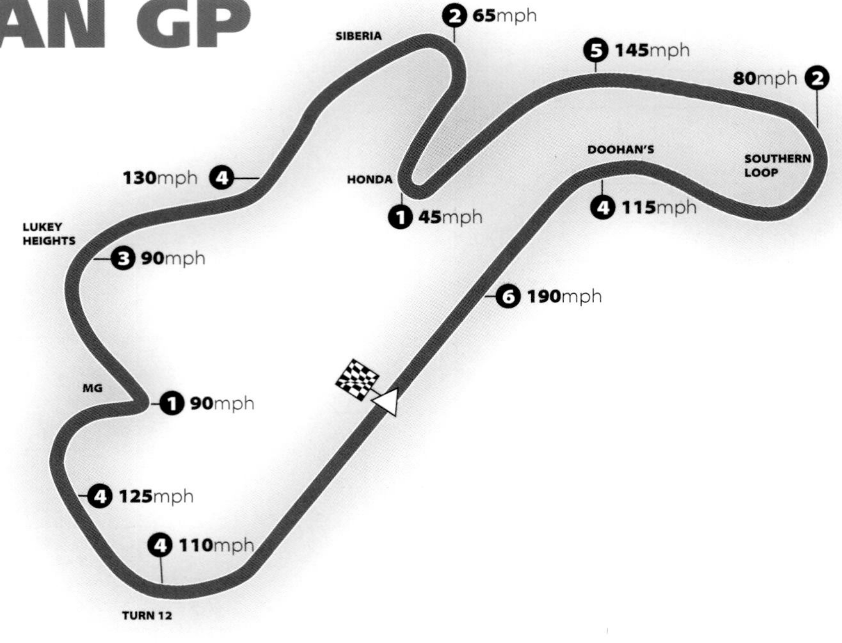

RACE RESULTS

RACE DATE September 17th
CIRCUIT LENGTH 2.764 miles
NO. OF LAPS 26
RACE DISTANCE 71.864 miles
WEATHER Wet, 23°C
TRACK TEMPERATURE 33°C
WINNER Marco Melandri
FASTEST LAP 1m 30.917s, 109.373mph, Valentino Rossi (record)
PREVIOUS LAP RECORD 1m 29.337s, 111.129mph, Nicky Hayden, 2005

QUALIFYING

	Rider	Nationality	Team	Qualifying	Pole +	Gap
1	Hayden	USA	Repsol Honda Team	1m 29.020s		
2	Nakano	JPN	Kawasaki Racing Team	1m 29.258s	0.238s	0.238s
3	Rossi	ITA	Camel Yamaha Team	1m 29.271s	0.251s	0.013s
4	Roberts	USA	Team Roberts	1m 29.662s	0.642s	0.391s
5	Edwards	USA	Camel Yamaha Team	1m 29.680s	0.660s	0.018s
6	Checa	SPA	Tech 3 Yamaha	1m 29.865s	0.845s	0.185s
7	Melandri	ITA	Fortuna Honda	1m 29.949s	0.929s	0.084s
8	Stoner	AUS	Honda LCR	1m 29.969s	0.949s	0.020s
9	De Puniet	FRA	Kawasaki Racing Team	1m 30.037s	1.017s	0.068s
10	Pedrosa	SPA	Repsol Honda Team	1m 30.081s	1.061s	0.044s
11	Tamada	JPN	Konica Minolta Honda	1m 30.132s	1.112s	0.051s
12	Gibernau	SPA	Ducati Marlboro Team	1m 30.237s	1.217s	0.105s
13	Capirossi	ITA	Ducati Marlboro Team	1m 30.393s	1.373s	0.156s
14	Elias	SPA	Fortuna Honda	1m 30.498s	1.478s	0.105s
15	Hopkins	USA	Rizla Suzuki MotoGP	1m 31.143s	2.123s	0.645s
16	Vermeulen	AUS	Rizla Suzuki MotoGP	1m 31.288s	2.268s	0.145s
17	Hofmann	GER	Pramac d'Antin MotoGP	1m 31.676s	2.656s	0.388s
18	Ellison	GBR	Tech 3 Yamaha	1m 31.998s	2.978s	0.322s
19	Cardoso	SPA	Pramac d'Antin MotoGP	1m 32.870s	3.850s	0.872s

FINISHERS

1 MARCO MELANDRI Quick in the dry, fourth before the rain came and often over a second a lap quicker than the rest in the wet. Kept it smooth after he took the lead with 11 laps to go and became the first man to win all three classes at Phillip Island.

2 CHRIS VERMEULEN Brave, aggressive riding on the laps before and after the pit stop elevated Chris from also-ran to second place. Held on bravely as his tyre degraded on the drying surface to take his first rostrum finish in MotoGP.

3 VALENTINO ROSSI Fastest in the dry and cleverest in the wet. Timed his attack on Gibernau perfectly to put the Spaniard between himself and Hayden at the flag. However, his pass on Stoner under a yellow flag started a row that threatened to rumble on beyond the end of the season.

4 SETE GIBERNAU Brilliant start from the back of the fourth row and second in the dry. Led for six laps after the pit stop before Melandri and Vermeulen came past. Only lost out on third place in the final run to the flag, missing his first rostrum for Ducati by less than one-tenth of a second.

5 NICKY HAYDEN A fabulous lap for pole followed by a truly appalling start saw him almost last into Turn 1. Carved through the field in both wet and dry conditions. Had a grandstand view of the Rossi yellow-flag incident but refused to blame that for losing five points to Valentino at the top of the table.

6 CASEY STONER Described the race as 'a disaster' despite finishing sixth. Fastest in warm-up, made steady if unspectacular progress in the dry part of the race, but stopped moving forward on his second bike due, he said, to a hard rear tyre that 'felt like a slick'.

7 LORIS CAPIROSSI Displayed by far the best pace in the dry all weekend but hampered by the Bridgestone qualifiers not working. Took a couple of laps to get used to the feel of his wet bike and then

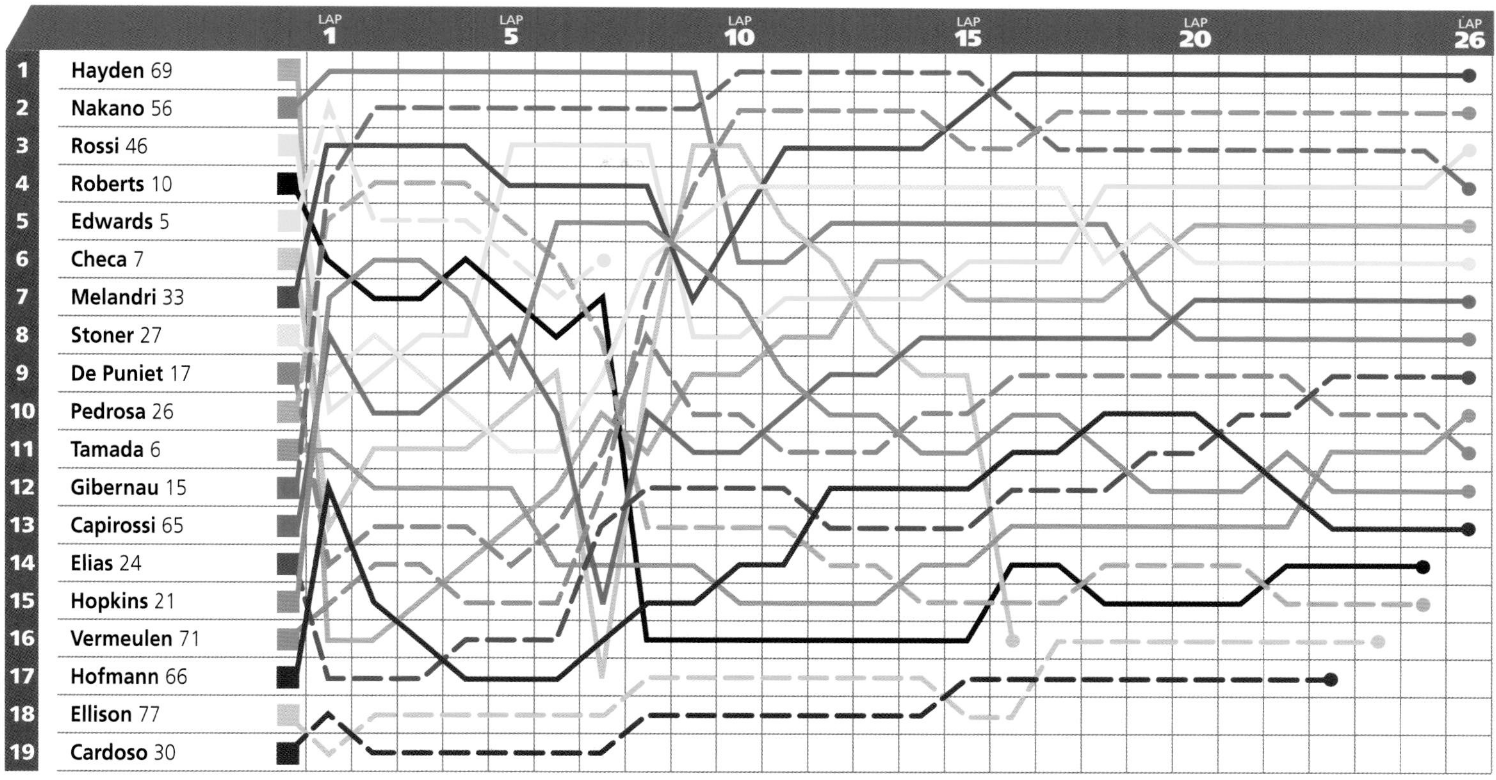

RACE

	Rider	Motorcycle	Race Time	Time +	Fastest Lap	Average Speed
1	Melandri	Honda	44m 15.621s		1m 31.363s	97.357mph
2	Vermeulen	Suzuki	44m 25.320s	9.699s	1m 32.074s	97.002mph
3	Rossi	Yamaha	44m 26.147s	10.526s	1m 30.917s	96.972mph
4	Gibernau	Ducati	44m 26.236s	10.615s	1m 31.237s	96.969mph
5	Hayden	Honda	44m 26.315s	10.694s	1m 31.428s	96.966mph
6	Stoner	Honda	44m 26.944s	11.323s	1m 31.678s	96.943mph
7	Capirossi	Ducati	44m 42.176s	26.555s	1m 31.432s	96.393mph
8	Nakano	Kawasaki	44m 42.287s	26.666s	1m 31.188s	96.388mph
9	Elias	Honda	45m 12.855s	57.234s	1m 32.629s	95.302mph
10	Tamada	Honda	45m 17.852s	1m 02.231s	1m 31.814s	95.127mph
11	De Puniet	Kawasaki	45m 18.053s	1m 02.432s	1m 31.901s	95.120mph
12	Hopkins	Suzuki	45m 34.430s	1m 18.809s	1m 31.500s	94.550mph
13	Hofmann	Ducati	46m 03.854s	1m 48.233s	1m 32.977s	93.544mph
14	Roberts	KR211V	44m 23.691s	1 lap	1m 31.499s	93.328mph
15	Pedrosa	Honda	44m 31.119s	1 lap	1m 31.433s	93.069mph
16	Ellison	Yamaha	45m 35.526s	2 laps	1m 35.287s	87.242mph
17	Cardoso	Ducati	44m 57.572s	3 laps	1m 36.194s	84.784mph
	Checa	Yamaha	28m 26.506s	10 laps	1m 31.500s	93.233mph
	Edwards	Yamaha	11m 11.818s	19 laps	1m 31.497s	103.611mph

CHAMPIONSHIP

	Rider	Team	Points
1	Hayden	Repsol Honda Team	225
2	Rossi	Camel Yamaha Team	204
3	Melandri	Fortuna Honda	193
4	Pedrosa	Repsol Honda Team	193
5	Capirossi	Ducati Marlboro Team	180
6	Stoner	Honda LCR	119
7	Roberts	Team Roberts	103
8	Hopkins	Rizla Suzuki MotoGP	97
9	Edwards	Camel Yamaha Team	96
10	Vermeulen	Rizla Suzuki MotoGP	86
11	Nakano	Kawasaki Racing Team	83
12	Gibernau	Ducati Marlboro Team	82
13	Tamada	Konica Minolta Honda	75
14	Elias	Fortuna Honda	71
15	Checa	Tech 3 Yamaha	58
16	De Puniet	Kawasaki Racing Team	31
17	Hofmann	Pramac d'Antin MotoGP	25
18	Ellison	Tech 3 Yamaha	20
19	Cardoso	Pramac d'Antin MotoGP	8

suffered when the track dried out. Not at all happy with the way his weekend turned out.

8 SHINYA NAKANO Terrifyingly fast in the opening few laps to build up a significant lead, then stayed out a lap longer than most when the rain came. Rejoined in second but never had the same feel in the wet. Another to suffer from the aversion of treaded Bridgestones to dry tarmac.

9 TONI ELIAS Not really happy in either wet or dry conditions. Didn't get a good start and was way down before the pit stops, then made a bit of progress, but he was a long way behind Nakano and only just in front of Tamada.

10 MAKOTO TAMADA For once he wasn't the last Honda finisher. Happy in the dry and quick in morning warm-up, but his wet-weather bike was set up way too stiffly for the conditions.

11 RANDY DE PUNIET Another man depressed with his race after looking very fast on both Friday and Saturday. Comfortable in the dry on race day but not in the wet, thanks to visibility problems and fast-wearing wet tyres.

12 JOHN HOPKINS Awful practice and qualifying due mainly to what his team called 'a total lack of grip'. Looked to be on much better form in the early part of the race but then went backwards with his wet bike. Gracious enough to offer fulsome congratulations to his team-mate.

13 ALEX HOFMANN Absolutely determined not to be lapped for the first time in his racing career. Finished the race with an enormous chunk missing from his rear Dunlop's tread.

14 KENNY ROBERTS With the front runners until he toppled off just before the round of pit stops. That didn't lose him a lot of time but his wet bike's throttle was loose and there was no way he could do anything but hang on for a couple of points. Not happy.

15 DANI PEDROSA Happy – and fast – in the dry, but Dani's wet-weather hoodoo struck again. Got the worst of the pit-lane traffic when changing bikes, then found his rear wet tyre was way too soft. Suffered the indignity of being lapped as his championship chances dematerialised.

16 JAMES ELLISON The first rider in the history of MotoGP to take advantage of the new regulations and come in to change bikes. Unfortunately his tyres were destroyed after a few laps and he had to come in again to change to intermediates.

17 JOSE LUIS CARDOSO Troubled by his tyres in both wet and dry conditions but managed to limp to the chequered flag .

NON-FINISHERS

CARLOS CHECA Brilliant in practice and qualifying, got out of the pits in second place when he changed to the wet bike, but then his tyres only lasted a couple of laps. Pitted again to change to intermediates but then had what he called a 'soft crash'.

COLIN EDWARDS Made some big leaps forward in practice and looked good in the opening laps. Decided to come in to change bikes so signalled his crew with a wave of his left leg as he came past the pits. Unfortunately, he highsided two corners later, coming down heavily on his bottom.

JAPANESE GP
MOTEGI

ROUND 15

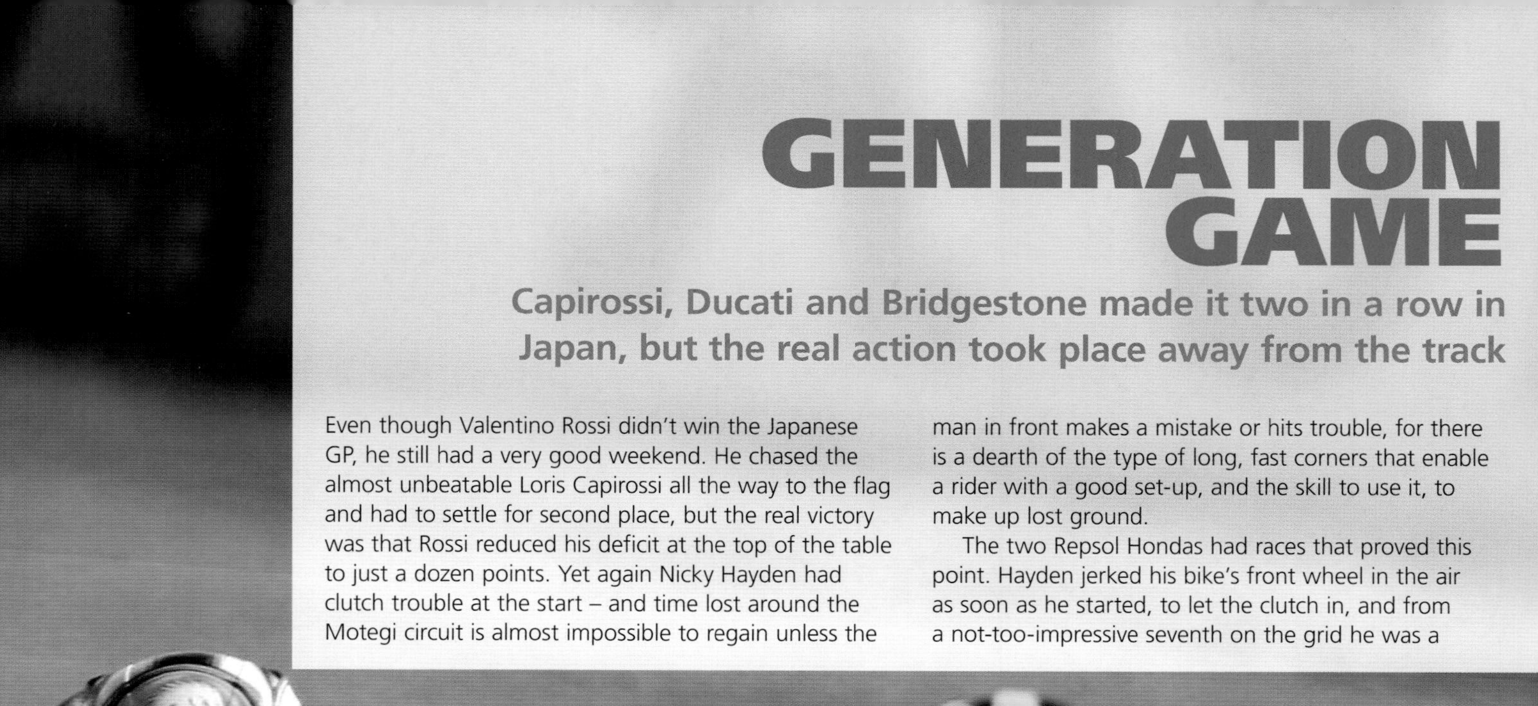

GENERATION GAME

Capirossi, Ducati and Bridgestone made it two in a row in Japan, but the real action took place away from the track

Even though Valentino Rossi didn't win the Japanese GP, he still had a very good weekend. He chased the almost unbeatable Loris Capirossi all the way to the flag and had to settle for second place, but the real victory was that Rossi reduced his deficit at the top of the table to just a dozen points. Yet again Nicky Hayden had clutch trouble at the start – and time lost around the Motegi circuit is almost impossible to regain unless the man in front makes a mistake or hits trouble, for there is a dearth of the type of long, fast corners that enable a rider with a good set-up, and the skill to use it, to make up lost ground.

The two Repsol Hondas had races that proved this point. Hayden jerked his bike's front wheel in the air as soon as he started, to let the clutch in, and from a not-too-impressive seventh on the grid he was a

Above Turn 1 and already the three Italians are looking good

Opposite Valentino Rossi in the half-light of one of the two tunnels that take Motegi's Road Course under the oval

potentially disastrous 11th into the first corner, ninth at the end of the first lap and one place higher a lap later, once the field had formed some sort of pattern. Nicky was left behind an enthusiastic Toni Elias, having his best ride since he set the fastest lap way back in April at the Turkish GP; the Spanish rider is not the easiest man to pass. Pedrosa, still suffering from his Sepang injuries, was pushed off the track early on and passed by the pack as he got things back together, but by then he was 15th and effectively out of the hunt.

Loris Capirossi, as expected, got the holeshot. The Ducati rider had dominated practice and qualifying, and he went on to dominate the race. He had to fend off Marco Melandri early on and also make sure he didn't let Rossi get within range towards the flag, but Loris never looked likely to lose. It wasn't quite the supremacy of the previous year – Valentino set the fastest lap with Michelins – but it capped a strange afternoon for the Japanese motorcycle industry at their home race, as KTM won both the 125 and 250 events. However, Honda drew considerable satisfaction from the fact that Melandri's third place clinched the Constructors' Championship for them. It was Honda's 17th title and took them past MV Agusta in the standings.

Off track, Honda were very busy indeed. There was much activity both before and after the race to try to give Hayden a clutch that would work the way he wanted. A top HRC man reported that Nicky used his clutch differently from any other Honda rider. They had tried to use a diaphragm spring to get the best possible feel but it proved too delicate, so they reverted to a conventional spring design, with extra cooling ducts apparent in the centre. And HRC had not forgotten about the perceived injustices of the yellow-flag incident the previous week. On the Friday evening they made public the text of a letter sent to the FIM by HRC President Suguru Kanazawa. Although it was couched in diplomatic terms, Honda were obviously still very angry and demanding that heads roll. Kanazawa opened HRC's press conference by showing the letter to the crowd before moving on to happier matters. First he announced that Nicky Hayden had signed to stay with Honda for 2007 and '08 – and then he referred to the inner workings of the RCV211 engine. This unprecedented outbreak of glasnost is examined in our technical analysis on page 24. It was a big hint that the 2007-specification 800cc Honda due to be seen in public for the first time on the Monday after the race wouldn't be a V5.

Once the three Italians had established their domination of race proceedings, attention focused on Hayden's attempts to limit the damage to his points lead. He was stuck behind Elias for five laps and, when he finally got past, he found himself more than four-and-a-half seconds behind the leaders. Four laps later he moved up another place when Stoner crashed out, but at the end of lap ten he was nearly seven seconds behind and with no real prospect of finishing any higher than sixth.

However, the dispute for fourth place between Sete Gibernau and Shinya Nakano handed Nicky an extra point. Motegi's favourite passing place is the nasty, downhill, off-camber right-hander at the end of the back straight. It was the scene of the infamous coming-together between Tamada and Gibernau at the 2003 Pacific GP which resulted in the Japanese rider's exclusion,

agv
TRIBÙ DEI CHIHUAHUA
46
CAMEL
THE DOCTOR
YAMAHA
MOTUL
YAMAHA
ÖHLINS

Opposite A rostrumful of Italians – Rossi, Capirossi and Melandri

Left The 800s came out to play on the Monday after the GP. From top to bottom: Akiyoshi on the Suzuki, Rossi on the Yamaha, factory tester Kamada on the V4 Honda and, below, Sete Gibernau on the GP7 Ducati

and also the site of Rossi's torpedoing of Melandri in 2005. This time it was Nakano who fell, trying a last-lap pass on the Spaniard and coming very close to taking Sete out with him. It looked as if they had touched but Gibernau reported later that he never felt a thing.

Meanwhile, on the rostrum, Capirossi was saying how good it felt to win in Japan and Rossi was saying how good it was to have 'three generations of Italians on the rostrum – and three of the fastest, too'. Loris is 33 years old, Valentino is 27 and Marco is the youngest, at 24.

For once, a large media contingent stayed on after race day to observe the 800cc Honda's first appearance. The occasion was given added spice by the fact that Ducati had brought along their 800 for the two-day test and Suzuki were also unveiling their bike for 2007. Dani Pedrosa got to ride the new Honda while Nicky Hayden was trying out some revised clutches by doing practice starts; his scheduled ride was cancelled due to rain on the Tuesday. Some very unofficial timing showed lap times well on a par with the best that the 990cc bikes had managed during race weekend, with Sete Gibernau especially rapid on the GP7 Desmosedici.

The Japanese GP usually includes a crop of fast wild-card riders, and this one was no exception. Suzuki fielded the impressive Kousuke Akiyoshi, their 31-year-old test rider and winner of the All-Japan Championship, while 250 veteran Naoki Matsudo was Kawasaki's third man. They were the only wild cards of the whole season, further proof of just how much the factories have been concentrating on their 800cc projects, but it's perhaps debatable whether all that money, research and development will translate into significantly improved lap times in 2007.

TYRE TRUCE

The much-rumoured new tyre regulation for 2007 emerged from the Grand Prix Commission meeting on the Saturday of Motegi. All three tyre companies – Michelin, Bridgestone and Dunlop – were broadly in favour of slowing the rate at which costs have been rising by imposing some sort of limit on the number of tyres a rider can use in a race weekend. Each rider will be limited to 31 slicks for the Grand Prix weekend – 14 fronts and 17 rears. These tyres must be marked by the MotoGP Technical Director the day before practice begins and they will be checked each time the bike goes on the track.

One major reason for this rule is to stop Michelin bringing in newly designed and manufactured tyres overnight at European races, and Bridgestone doing the same at Asian events. The rule will only apply to tyre manufacturers who have won two races in dry conditions since the start of the 2005 season, so Dunlop can continue to supply as many tyres as they want to their team(s). The rule will only apply to slicks. The supply of rain tyres will not be subject to restriction, and there is a provision for emergency replacement of three tyres in an allocation for safety reasons. However, any rider allowed to use that exemption will have to start from the back of the grid.

The big question is whether teams will risk using up any of their allocation on qualifying tyres...

JAPANESE GP

MOTEGI

ROUND 15

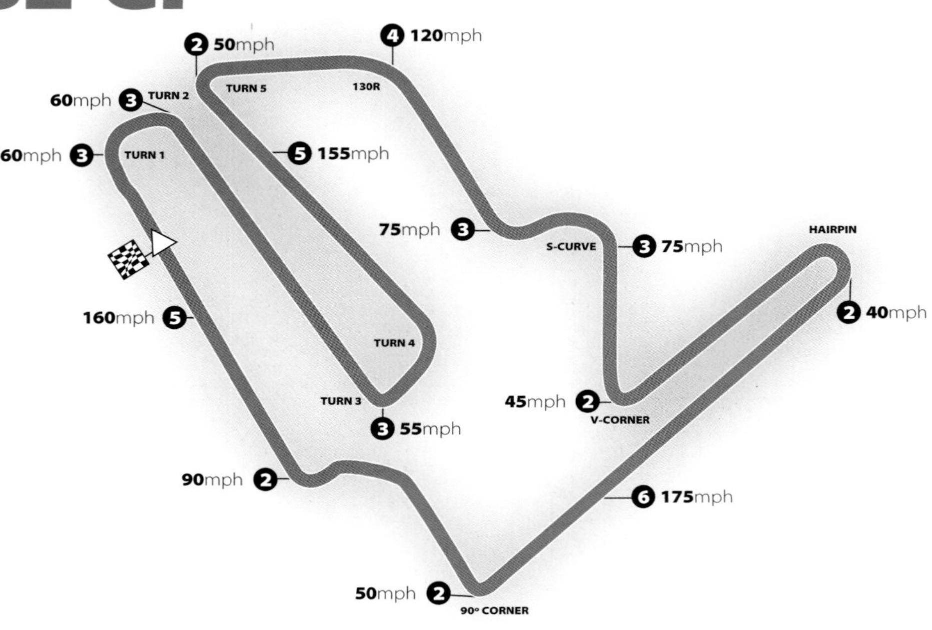

RACE RESULTS

RACE DATE September 24th
CIRCUIT LENGTH 2.983 miles
NO. OF LAPS 24
RACE DISTANCE 71.592 miles
WEATHER Dry, 27°C
TRACK TEMPERATURE 43°C
WINNER Loris Capirossi
FASTEST LAP 1m 47.288s, 100.039mph, Valentino Rossi
PREVIOUS LAP RECORD 1m 46.363s, 100.747mph, Loris Capirossi, 2005 (record)

QUALIFYING

	Rider	Nationality	Team	Qualifying	Pole +	Gap
1	Capirossi	ITA	Ducati Marlboro Team	1m 45.724s		
2	Rossi	ITA	Camel Yamaha Team	1m 45.991s	0.267s	0.267s
3	Melandri	ITA	Fortuna Honda	1m 46.250s	0.526s	0.259s
4	Nakano	JPN	Kawasaki Racing Team	1m 46.291s	0.567s	0.041s
5	Gibernau	SPA	Ducati Marlboro Team	1m 46.316s	0.592s	0.025s
6	Elias	SPA	Fortuna Honda	1m 46.326s	0.602s	0.010s
7	Hayden	USA	Repsol Honda Team	1m 46.489s	0.765s	0.163s
8	De Puniet	FRA	Kawasaki Racing Team	1m 46.512s	0.788s	0.023s
9	Pedrosa	SPA	Repsol Honda Team	1m 46.576s	0.852s	0.064s
10	Edwards	USA	Camel Yamaha Team	1m 46.726s	1.002s	0.150s
11	Stoner	AUS	Honda LCR	1m 46.847s	1.123s	0.121s
12	Akiyoshi	JPN	Team Suzuki MotoGP	1m 46.958s	1.234s	0.111s
13	Hopkins	USA	Rizla Suzuki MotoGP	1m 47.071s	1.347s	0.113s
14	Roberts	USA	Team Roberts	1m 47.310s	1.586s	0.239s
15	Vermeulen	AUS	Rizla Suzuki MotoGP	1m 47.451s	1.727s	0.141s
16	Matsudo	JPN	Kawasaki	1m 47.826s	2.102s	0.375s
17	Checa	SPA	Tech 3 Yamaha	1m 47.905s	2.181s	0.079s
18	Tamada	JPN	Konica Minolta Honda	1m 48.426s	2.702s	0.521s
19	Ellison	GBR	Tech 3 Yamaha	1m 48.716s	2.992s	0.290s
20	Hofmann	GER	Pramac d'Antin MotoGP	1m 48.748s	3.024s	0.032s
21	Cardoso	SPA	Pramac d'Antin MotoGP	1m 50.359s	4.635s	1.611s

FINISHERS

1 LORIS CAPIROSSI A repeat of last year's domination – only 17 seconds faster! Loris was super-quick from the first practice session and had a gap of five seconds over the opposition by the end, with some very swift laps towards the finish. A significant home win for Bridgestone, and for Ducati in an important export market.

2 VALENTINO ROSSI Never got to grips with Capirossi, but very happy to take more points out of Hayden's championship lead. Took a while to get past Melandri, then pushed to catch Loris, setting the fastest time on lap 16 out of 24, but soon realised the Ducati rider was controlling him.

3 MARCO MELANDRI His third place guaranteed Honda the Constructors' Championship. Marco's race was dictated by his decision to go with softer tyres than he used in warm-up: he was fast and comfortable at the start but, once he started to lose grip, it was a case of hanging on to third.

4 SETE GIBERNAU Lost too much time in the first quarter of the race to challenge for a rostrum position, but showed good pace and resisted Nakano's challenge towards the flag. Lucky not to be taken down when the Kawasaki crashed.

5 NICKY HAYDEN Another bad weekend, with more clutch woes at the start. Rode the first two corners like a demon but got stuck behind Elias for the first five laps. Without the Stoner and Nakano crashes it would have been even worse. At least he had a new two-year contract with HRC as consolation.

6 TONI ELIAS His best result since Turkey, the third race of the year, albeit on a track he has always liked. A slight lack of rear tyre traction stopped him from hanging on to the leaders but he outran fellow Honda man Pedrosa for the first time.

7 DANI PEDROSA His race was effectively over after a coming-together with Edwards at the second corner put him off the track. Nevertheless, won Rookie of the Year, just as he had done in the 125 and 250cc classes, and helped secure the Team Championship for Repsol Honda.

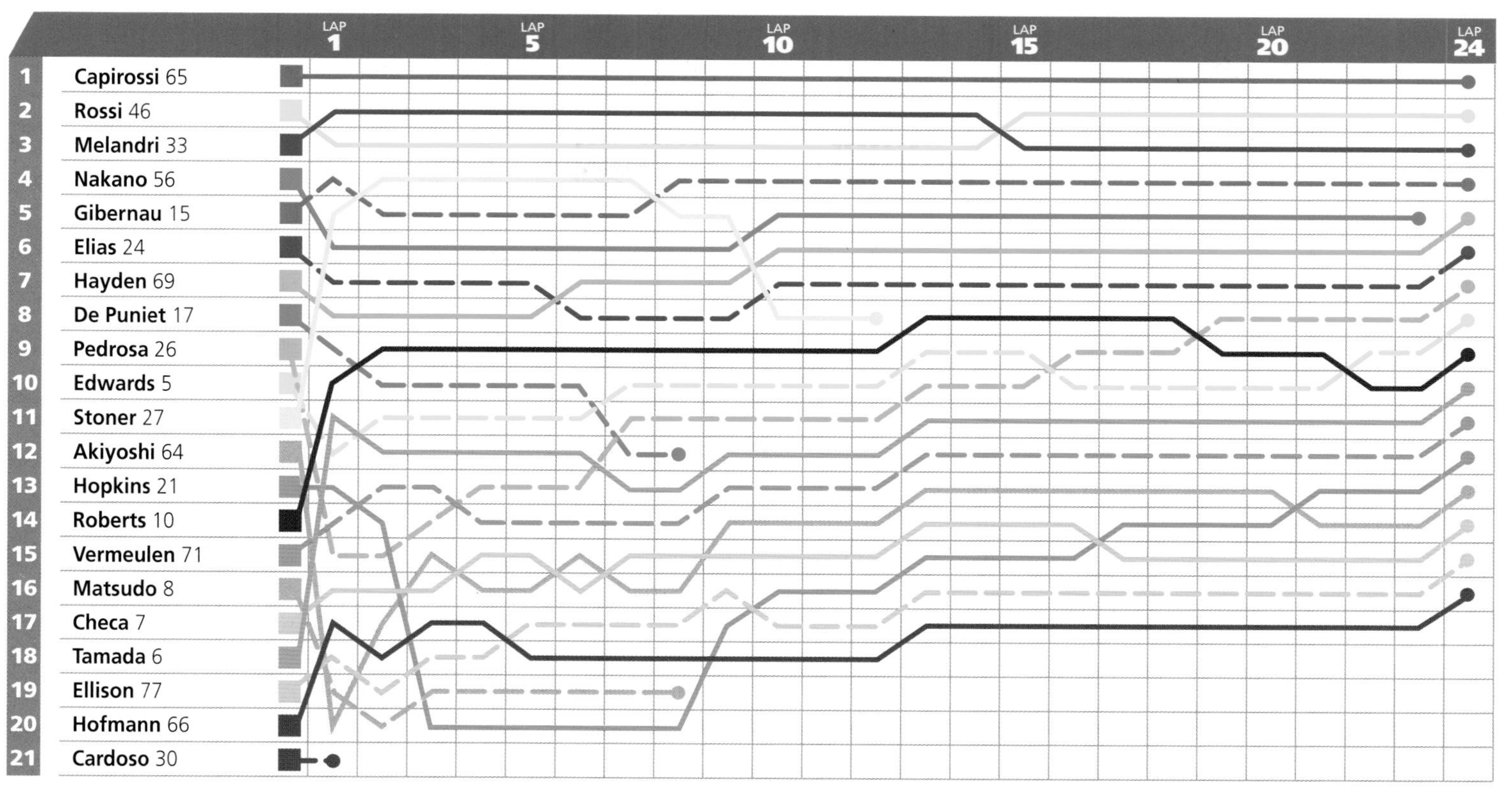

RACE

	Rider	Motorcycle	Race Time	Time +	Fastest Lap	Average Speed
1	Capirossi	Ducati	43m 13.585s		1m 47.381	99.320mph
2	Rossi	Yamaha	43m 18.673s	5.088s	1m 47.288	99.125mph
3	Melandri	Honda	43m 21.963s	8.378s	1m 47.375	99.000mph
4	Gibernau	Ducati	43m 23.297s	9.712s	1m 47.755	98.949mph
5	Hayden	Honda	43m 25.529s	11.944s	1m 47.795	98.864mph
6	Elias	Honda	43m 31.693s	18.108s	1m 47.996	98.631mph
7	Pedrosa	Honda	43m 33.522s	19.937s	1m 47.814	98.562mph
8	Edwards	Yamaha	43m 36.077s	22.492s	1m 47.884	98.466mph
9	Roberts	KR211V	43m 40.409s	26.824s	1m 47.962	98.303mph
10	Tamada	Honda	43m 44.555s	30.970s	1m 48.263	98.148mph
11	Vermeulen	Suzuki	43m 52.848s	39.263s	1m 48.917	97.838mph
12	Hopkins	Suzuki	43m 53.025s	39.440s	1m 48.446	97.832mph
13	Akiyoshi	Suzuki	43m 59.180s	45.595s	1m 48.511	97.604mph
14	Checa	Yamaha	44m 03.156s	49.571s	1m 48.922	97.457mph
15	Ellison	Yamaha	44m 22.670s	1m 09.085s	1m 49.616	96.742mph
16	Hofmann	Ducati	44m 25.333s	1m 11.748s	1m 50.077	96.646mph
	Nakano	Kawasaki	41m 34.655s	1 lap	1m 47.826	98.956mph
	Stoner	Honda	21m 48.380s	12 laps	1m 47.888	98.440mph
	De Puniet	Kawasaki	14m 38.163s	16 laps	1m 48.369	97.778mph
	Matsudo	Kawasaki	14m 51.515s	16 laps	1m 49.511	96.313mph
	Cardoso	Ducati	2m 01.020s	23 laps	2m 01.020	88.689mph

CHAMPIONSHIP

	Rider	Team	Points
1	Hayden	Repsol Honda Team	236
2	Rossi	Camel Yamaha Team	224
3	Melandri	Fortuna Honda	209
4	Capirossi	Ducati Marlboro Team	205
5	Pedrosa	Repsol Honda Team	202
6	Stoner	Honda LCR	119
7	Roberts	Team Roberts	110
8	Edwards	Camel Yamaha Team	104
9	Hopkins	Rizla Suzuki MotoGP	101
10	Gibernau	Ducati Marlboro Team	95
11	Vermeulen	Rizla Suzuki MotoGP	91
12	Nakano	Kawasaki Racing Team	83
13	Elias	Fortuna Honda	81
14	Tamada	Konica Minolta Honda	81
15	Checa	Tech 3 Yamaha	60
16	De Puniet	Kawasaki Racing Team	31
17	Hofmann	Pramac d'Antin MotoGP	25
18	Ellison	Tech 3 Yamaha	21
19	Cardoso	Pramac d'Antin MotoGP	8
20	Akiyoshi	Team Suzuki MotoGP	3

8 COLIN EDWARDS Happy with his bike and his race pace but not with qualifying. Tenth on the grid followed by a tangle with Pedrosa which put him back to 12th after the first lap meant he could never help his team-mate, as planned.

9 KENNY ROBERTS The new Team Roberts chassis proved difficult to set up. Kenny had to deal with chatter in qualifying and a lack of grip during the race. Said afterwards it felt like he was trying to carry too much corner speed, so was only really happy riding on his own rather than in a group.

10 MAKOTO TAMADA Amazingly, the first Japanese rider to finish. Depressed about his continuing inability to come to terms with the bike, specifically the lack of feedback from the front tyre. Flattered to deceive with a good opening to his race before fading.

11 CHRIS VERMEULEN Never found a good rhythm all weekend on his first visit to the Twin Rings and had to be content with being the first Suzuki home.

12 JOHN HOPKINS An unhappy weekend at a track where he has always previously been fast. Got a bad start from 13th on the grid and was riding hard to make up ground when he and Pedrosa touched at the downhill right-hander. Ran off track, losing any chance of a decent result.

13 KOUSUKE AKIYOSHI Suzuki's test rider and All-Japan Championship star qualified as fastest Suzuki and scored points in his first-ever Grand Prix – an impressive showing.

14 CARLOS CHECA Satisfied he'd done the best possible with his compromise tyre choice – after testing a boat load of rubber! Spent a lot of the race dicing with what he called 'the Suzuki team' but had to ease his pace later when the tyres went off.

15 JAMES ELLISON His result doesn't look any better than usual, but this was a much-improved performance, with James actually enjoying a race for the first time in a while. Still frustrated, though, by chatter and the knowledge he can go a lot faster.

16 ALEX HOFMANN His Dunlops didn't suit the high-grip Motegi surface too well, but Alex reported the bike was stable, the front tyre feedback was 'good' and braking stability 'all right'. The problem was lack of rear grip coming out of corners.

NON-FINISHERS

SHINYA NAKANO A last-lap charge to try and take fourth place off Gibernau resulted in a crash at the right-hander at the end of the back straight. Shinya was frighteningly near to taking the Ducati down with him.

CASEY STONER Very strong at the start before crashing out when he lost the front at the first left-hander on lap 13. Frustrated that his set-up had been changed despite being 'perfect' earlier in the weekend. It worked with a full tank but he lost front-end feeling after a few laps.

RANDY DE PUNIET Changed motors after warm-up, then got a good start. Suffered from a lack of rear grip, either due to the increased track temperature or the aggressive characteristics of his bike, so tried to make up time going into corners. Crashed just after Roberts came past, trying to keep up.

NAOKI MATSUDO The 250cc class veteran got his reward for wearing a groove in Japanese tracks as Kawasaki's test rider. It was his only outing of the year and a short one: he retired on lap nine, with the motor losing power from the start of the race.

JOSE LUIS CARDOSO Qualified last and crashed out on the second lap.

PORTUGUESE GP
ESTORIL
ROUND 16

FRIENDLY FIRE

Pedrosa committed the cardinal sin of skittling his championship-leading team-mate Nicky Hayden, but Toni Elias came to Honda's rescue with a spectacular maiden victory

Before this weekend the Estoril track was not noted for producing entertaining racing, but the 2006 Portuguese Grand Prix not only made up for any previous shortcomings but also provided at least three moments that will talked about as long as anybody maintains an interest in motorcycle sport. First, the factory Repsol Hondas knocked one another off within range of the World Championship title. Then there was the breathtaking sight of Toni Elias giving Honda renewed hope by depriving Valentino Rossi of not just the win, but a vital five points – by two-thousandths of a second. And finally there was the debut of a brand-

Fortuna
valsir
domino
BLACK PRINCE
MICHELIN
SAN CARLO
Castrol
alpinestars
RACING AHEAD
X-lite
bwin

new motorcycle from a manufacturer fresh to the sport, Ilmor, which promptly became the first 800cc bike to score a point in MotoGP. As if that wasn't enough, Kenny Roberts thought he might have won if he hadn't miscounted the number of laps, Colin Edwards re-signed for Yamaha and then rode the perfect race to back up his team-mate, and Sete Gibernau's foul luck saw him land on his oft-injured shoulder after he was taken down by Stoner's sliding Honda. The implications of the damage are serious enough to cast doubt over Gibernau's future – and, to add insult to injury, Ducati announced that Casey Stoner will replace Sete in their factory team for 2007.

However, all other issues paled into total insignificance beside the coming-together of the Repsol Hondas. The drama happened on the fifth lap, at Turn 6, the left-hander at the end of the back straight where, on the previous lap, Hayden had put a strong pass on his team-mate. The two Hondas were following the Camel Yamahas, which had qualified first and second. Rossi was in front by a second, with Edwards protecting his team leader. It may be that Edwards was slightly earlier on the brakes than usual as he waited for Rossi to open up a significant lead, but Pedrosa found himself carrying too much speed into the corner, tried to find room on the inside, ran on to the painted kerbs, locked the front wheel and fell, his RCV knocking the American's bike out from under him. Dani said afterwards that he wasn't trying to overtake, which may well be true, but he undoubtedly got in way too hot. It looked like a repeat of the moment early on at Donington where he made a mistake on the brakes at the Melbourne Loop and only missed Melandri by a millimetre or two. The Nicky Hayden who got up from the gravel trap was a totally different animal from the one the paddock is used to. You didn't need to be a lip reader to get the gist of what he was yelling at Pedrosa, and this from a guy who's never been heard to use any language stronger than 'dang'!

HRC had said before the race that they didn't give team orders, and Hayden's own view was that 'I don't write these guys no cheques so I can't tell them what to do.' According to Colin Edwards, Yamaha don't issue any formal team orders either, but as he put it, with a certain lack of political correctness, 'I ain't a f****** retard.' Colin's plan was to allow Valentino to build up a

Above Pedrosa skittles his team-mate Hayden, and turns a 12-point lead into an eight-point deficit

Opposite Unbridled joy on the rostrum from winner Toni Elias and his race engineer Fabrizio Cecchini

Below Randy de Puniet scored hs first top-ten finish in MotoGP, and Alex Hofmann was first Ducati home

lead of several seconds before he pushed hard to close the gap and hopefully break the challenge of what he assumed would be the Repsol Hondas behind him. In effect he rode as if Rossi was made of glass. Yamaha must have approved. There are plenty of instances of team managers in similar situations not issuing team orders but simply telling their riders to keep away from each other whatever the circumstances. The Camel team signalled Rossi that Hayden was out, but they didn't tell Edwards.

As pit lane fell silent with the shock of what they'd just seen, and the Repsol garage emptied instantly, the Yamaha men found they hadn't quite got rid of all the Hondas. All through practice and qualifying Rossi and Edwards had looked comfortable whatever the pace. However, the track temperature dropped by 10°C for race day and the M1s lost their edge. That enabled Toni Elias and Kenny Roberts, who had both qualified way down the grid in 11th and 13th, to close up. The two provided a complete contrast in styles. The pugnacious Spaniard was going in so deep on the brakes at Turn 6 that he looked like a dirt-tracker riding the cushion of dirt on the outside of a corner. When Elias led Rossi into that corner for the first time on lap 22 out of 28 the champion got a hell of a shock. Roberts, on the other hand, was content to sit in fourth place for much of the time, riding effortlessly and looking like the most likely winner.

There was a strange interlude next time round when Elias signalled Rossi to come past at Turn 3. Toni had 'made three mistakes at once' and, remembering his torpedoing of Valentino at Jerez and fearing the consequences of another incident, he decided to regroup. Roberts made his move at Turn 1 on the penultimate lap and led over the line, but he'd miscounted the number of laps left and, although he didn't shut off, he later said he didn't ride a good defensive line there. Not that it would have been easy to defend against Elias as the Honda rider outbraked both men in front of him, sliding across to the outside of the track and almost touching Roberts as he took the lead. Rossi immediately responded, taking second at the next corner and retaking the lead at the chicane. Toni tailed him through the never-ending right-hander that ends the lap, popped out of Valentino's draught, and won the race by the tiniest of margins.

It wasn't just Elias's first win – the result took a vital five points away from Rossi. It was also a job-saving victory for Elias, because it had been common knowledge for weeks that he wasn't going to be retained by Fortuna Honda. Come Monday morning, however, Toni had a new contract.

Rossi took his defeat very well and, like the rest of the paddock, seemed genuinely happy for Elias. He said he hadn't seen the Repsol crash but he did talk at some length about how perfect team spirit was in his own garage. For the first time this year Valentino was at the top of the championship table, turning a 12-point deficit into an 8-point lead.

Over at Repsol Honda, behind closed doors, Nicky Hayden was telling Dani Pedrosa that he had one chance to make things right, and that was by following Nicky over the line in second place at Valencia in two weeks' time. If that were to happen, and Rossi were to finish third, Hayden would become World Champion by a single point.

Opposite Garry McCoy on his way to a points-scoring debut on the Ilmor X3

Below Elias in front of a charging Rossi as they enter the final corner, and (inset) half-a-wheel in front over the line

NEW BLOOD

Garry McCoy made a welcome return to MotoGP for the first of two wild-card rides on the new Ilmor X3. The team will join MotoGP full-time in 2007 and the two races were being described as tests for their all-new 800cc V4.

They started impressively, reliably putting in the laps in practice, but the bike hit chatter when they fitted a qualifying tyre for the first time. Until then, the bike had not been last in any session and was only 3mph slower through the speed trap than the slowest of the 990s.

Garry approached the race cautiously and kept out of trouble, overtaking Cardoso before hitting electrical problems that forced him into the pits. He was sent out again while the team traced the problem to a faulty wheel speed sensor, which was disabled when he came back in. He went out again, and although he finished four laps down in 15th he had completed 75 per cent of the race distance and so was classified and scored a championship point. Who would have thought that the first 800 to score in MotoGP would be an Ilmor?

The X3 attracted plenty of interest and several luminaries were given a guided tour of it. All of them emerged impressed. Unlike other F1 engineers, who have come to motorcycles with an attitude than can best be described as condescending, Mario Ilien and his team didn't assume that motorcycle manufacturers' designers know nothing. The clever trick is that they have some technology on the bike that has obviously come from F1: the lack of fuel lines (as we usually understand them) and the way the intake air is managed look particularly clever. The X3 may already be the most technically advanced bike in the paddock.

PORTUGUESE GP

ESTORIL

ROUND 16

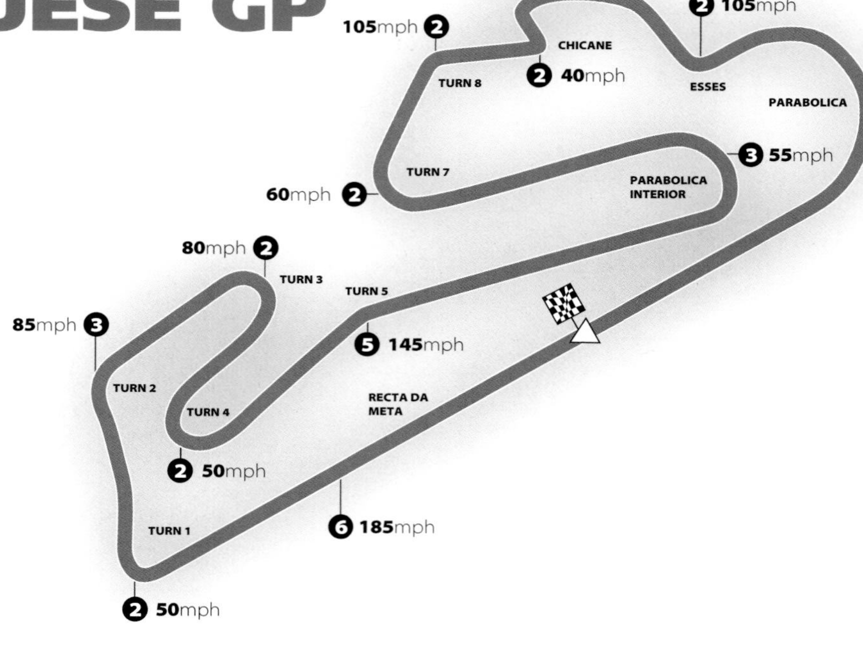

RACE RESULTS

RACE DATE October 15th
CIRCUIT LENGTH 2.599 miles
NO. OF LAPS 28
RACE DISTANCE 72.772 miles
WEATHER Dry, 20°C
TRACK TEMPERATURE 26°C
WINNER Toni Elias
FASTEST LAP 1m 37.914s, 95.484mph, Kenny Roberts Jr (record)
PREVIOUS LAP RECORD 1m 38.423s, 95.052mph, Loris Capirossi, 2004

QUALIFYING

	Rider	Nationality	Team	Qualifying	Pole +	Gap
1	Rossi	ITA	Camel Yamaha Team	1m 36.200s		
2	Edwards	USA	Camel Yamaha Team	1m 36.478s	0.278s	0.278s
3	Hayden	USA	Repsol Honda Team	1m 36.549s	0.349s	0.071s
4	Pedrosa	SPA	Repsol Honda Team	1m 36.569s	0.369s	0.020s
5	Stoner	AUS	Honda LCR	1m 36.702s	0.502s	0.133s
6	Hopkins	USA	Rizla Suzuki MotoGP	1m 36.790s	0.590s	0.088s
7	Nakano	JPN	Kawasaki Racing Team	1m 36.790s	0.590s	
8	Gibernau	SPA	Ducati Marlboro Team	1m 36.940s	0.740s	0.150s
9	Checa	SPA	Tech 3 Yamaha	1m 37.107s	0.907s	0.167s
10	Capirossi	ITA	Ducati Marlboro Team	1m 37.182s	0.982s	0.075s
11	Elias	SPA	Fortuna Honda	1m 37.245s	1.045s	0.063s
12	Vermeulen	AUS	Rizla Suzuki MotoGP	1m 37.371s	1.171s	0.126s
13	Roberts	USA	Team Roberts	1m 37.433s	1.233s	0.062s
14	Tamada	JPN	Konica Minolta Honda	1m 37.517s	1.317s	0.084s
15	Melandri	ITA	Fortuna Honda	1m 37.582s	1.382s	0.065s
16	De Puniet	FRA	Kawasaki Racing Team	1m 37.592s	1.392s	0.010s
17	Ellison	GBR	Tech 3 Yamaha	1m 38.810s	2.610s	1.218s
18	Hofmann	GER	Pramac d'Antin MotoGP	1m 39.647s	3.447s	0.837s
19	Cardoso	SPA	Pramac d'Antin MotoGP	1m 40.451s	4.251s	0.804s
20	McCoy	AUS	Ilmor SRT	1m 41.260s	5.060s	0.809s

FINISHERS

1 TONI ELIAS Led a MotoGP race for the first time, won for the first time and beat Rossi in a fair fight. More importantly, he took five points away from Valentino and kept Honda in with a genuine chance of the title. Rossi described him as 'riding like a devil', which was not a bad description, but this devil had a massive smile on his face.

2 VALENTINO ROSSI Happy, as he pointedly remarked, with his whole team, but disappointed to lose the race by such a small margin. Now led the championship for the first time, needing only to finish second in Valencia to retain the title.

3 KENNY ROBERTS Ever so slightly embarrassed to have miscounted the laps but delighted to have finished within two-tenths of the leader and set the new lap record. When he finished third at Barcelona he was nearly ten seconds behind; attributes the improvement to work done on the Monday after Motegi.

4 COLIN EDWARDS Did everything right but disappointed to finish off the rostrum. Protected Rossi in the early laps and had a good dice with Elias and Roberts. No doubt he could have run a faster pace early on but instead thought only of his team.

5 MAKOTO TAMADA His best result of the season so far. Indifferent qualifying, but overtook five riders in the race and was closing on the leaders when he suddenly experienced understeer and nearly crashed three times in the final corner. Too little pressure in the front tyre was probably to blame.

6 JOHN HOPKINS Top Bridgestone rider in both qualifying and the race – the Japanese tyre manufacturer had trouble coping with the partial resurfacing of the track. Got a bad start and tangled with Nakano on the first lap, then rode his usual combative race.

7 CARLOS CHECA Was dicing with Tamada when the pair closed in on the leaders, then lost both stability and grip from his rear tyre. Still set the seventh

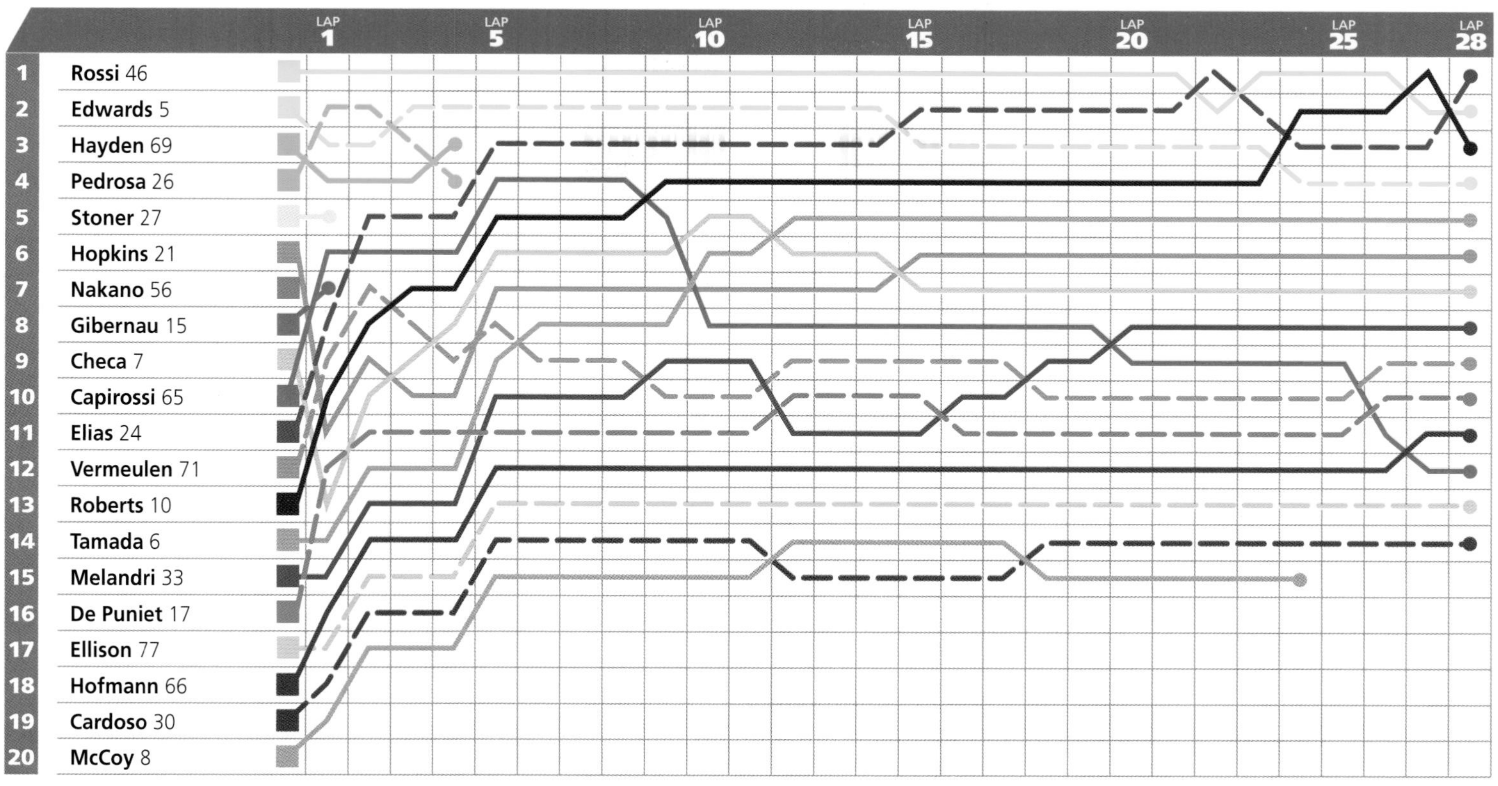

RACE

	Rider	Motorcycle	Race Time	Time +	Fastest Lap	Average Speed
1	Elias	Honda	46m 08.739s		1m 38.063s	94.548mph
2	Rossi	Yamaha	46m 08.741s	0.002s	1m 38.256s	94.548mph
3	Roberts	KR211V	46m 08.915s	0.176s	1m 37.914s	94.542mph
4	Edwards	Yamaha	46m 09.603s	0.864s	1m 38.193s	94.519mph
5	Tamada	Honda	46m 27.158s	18.419s	1m 38.063s	93.923mph
6	Hopkins	Suzuki	46m 33.920s	25.181s	1m 38.096s	93.696mph
7	Checa	Yamaha	46m 38.087s	29.348s	1m 38.306s	93.556mph
8	Melandri	Honda	46m 40.552s	31.813s	1m 38.565s	93.474mph
9	Vermeulen	Suzuki	46m 48.856s	40.117s	1m 38.810s	93.198mph
10	De Puniet	Kawasaki	46m 50.235s	41.496s	1m 39.022s	93.152mph
11	Hofmann	Ducati	46m 50.272s	41.533s	1m 39.534s	93.151mph
12	Capirossi	Ducati	46m 53.515s	44.776s	1m 38.420s	93.043mph
13	Ellison	Yamaha	47m 27.852s	1m 19.113s	1m 39.887s	91.922mph
14	Cardoso	Ducati	47m 49.455s	1m 40.716s	1m 41.288s	91.229mph
15	McCoy	Ilmor X3	47m 35.294s	4 laps	1m 41.140s	78.584mph
	Hayden	Honda	6m 42.244s	24 laps	1m 38.396s	92.971mph
	Pedrosa	Honda	6m 42.331s	24 laps	1m 38.704s	92.951mph
	Stoner	Honda	1m 45.744s	27 laps	1m 45.744s	88.414mph
	Gibernau	Ducati	1m 46.055s	27 laps	1m 46.055s	88.155mph
	Nakano	Kawasaki				

CHAMPIONSHIP

	Rider	Team	Points
1	Rossi	Camel Yamaha Team	244
2	Hayden	Repsol Honda Team	236
3	Melandri	Fortuna Honda	217
4	Capirossi	Ducati Marlboro Team	209
5	Pedrosa	Repsol Honda Team	202
6	Roberts	Team Roberts	126
7	Stoner	Honda LCR	119
8	Edwards	Camel Yamaha Team	117
9	Hopkins	Rizla Suzuki MotoGP	111
10	Elias	Fortuna Honda	106
11	Vermeulen	Rizla Suzuki MotoGP	98
12	Gibernau	Ducati Marlboro Team	95
13	Tamada	Konica Minolta Honda	92
14	Nakano	Kawasaki Racing Team	83
15	Checa	Tech 3 Yamaha	69
16	De Puniet	Kawasaki Racing Team	37
17	Hofmann	Pramac d'Antin MotoGP	30
18	Ellison	Tech 3 Yamaha	24
19	Cardoso	Pramac d'Antin MotoGP	10
20	Akiyoshi	Team Suzuki MotoGP	3

fastest lap of the race, just 0.05s slower than Rossi's best time. Not a bad way to celebrate his 34th birthday.

8 MARCO MELANDRI Crashed on Friday and twisted his left knee badly – and if Marco says it hurts then it must be bad. Lost set-up time and complained of a lack of grip. Nevertheless, retained third in the championship standings.

9 CHRIS VERMEULEN Had to use a harder tyre than he wanted, for durability. Got a good start and shoved past Checa at Turn 1. Ran off the track while passing Capirossi at mid-race distance, possibly distracted by a misting visor. A reasonable first visit to Estoril.

10 RANDY DE PUNIET His rear tyre went off after just five laps, forcing Randy to adjust his riding style and lines. Passed Capirossi late on, but a similar move on Vermeulen didn't stick. His first top-ten finish of the year.

11 ALEX HOFMANN First Ducati home in what was, after Catalunya, Alex's best ride of the season. Took a few laps to find his rhythm, then latched on to the Capirossi/Vermeulen/de Puniet group, passing the Italian three laps from the flag.

12 LORIS CAPIROSSI In serious difficulty all weekend, and raced with a tyre that Bridgestone only brought to the track on Saturday night and he tried in warm-up. Started well but was slipping backwards at one-third distance. Described it as the worst moment of his season.

13 JAMES ELLISON Lost grip early on after trying to find a way past Hofmann. Spent the bulk of the race 'sliding about' and again felt disappointed at the flag.

14 JOSE LUIS CARDOSO Lost rear grip very early on but happy to grab two more championship points.

15 GARRY MCCOY An historic first point for the Ilmor 800 on its debut. Started cautiously, overtaking Cardoso on lap 12 before a problem with a wheel speed sensor sent him into the pits twice. Achieved the team's pre-race ambition of qualifying and finishing the race.

NON-FINISHERS

NICKY HAYDEN Brought down by his team-mate on the fifth lap. Had put in superb passes on Edwards – round the outside at the first corner – and Pedrosa, and was looking good to retake Colin and, as he said, 'see what Valentino brought to the party'. Instead, his championship lead disappeared in a cloud of dust.

DANI PEDROSA Outbraked himself with disastrous consequences, crashing and bringing down team-mate and championship leader Hayden. Broke a little finger – but also looked to have ended Honda's chances of the title.

CASEY STONER Started well and was fifth when he slid off and brought down Gibernau. Suffered some bad bruising to his right leg, possibly from Sete's Ducati.

SETE GIBERNAU Launched himself into the air when he was unable to avoid Stoner's fallen Honda. Broke his hand but, much more worryingly, bent the plate fixing his much operated-on collarbone. Out of the final race of the year, and out of the Ducati team – to be replaced, ironically, by Stoner.

SHINYA NAKANO Said he thought he'd been hit from behind, but TV pictures showed he tangled with Hopkins when the Suzuki rider lent on him in Turn 4 on the first lap. Landed heavily, but thankfully not badly hurt.

VALENCIAN GP

RICARDO TORMO

ROUND **17**

TUMBLING DICE

Nicky Hayden ended the run of Rossi world titles by following the Ducatis home, and Troy Bayliss reminded everyone how fast he can be by winning – the first time a replacement or wild-card rider has ever won a MotoGP race

The new logo on the back of Nicky Hayden's leathers summed up the situation nicely. It showed a hand of cards and a big pile of poker chips; the last card was a question mark with the words 'All In', the gambler's slang for betting everything on the turn of one card. Nicky won his gamble, but not before a few side bets and old scores had been settled. Before the off it looked as if the favourite would romp home. Seven-times World Champion Valentino Rossi, starting from pole position with an eight-point advantage, just had to follow Nicky home to become the only man to win a world title under the 990cc formula. The American started from the middle of the second row – not the ideal place to be on a track where it's difficult to overtake or make up time.

Left The crash that ended Valentino Rossi's championship hopes

Opposite Come and have a go if you think you're hard enough: Bayliss on the grid

On the plus side, he had got over the clutch worries and had the support of his family at the track. As well as dad Earl and mum Rose, one of Nicky's sisters and racing brothers Tommy and Roger-Lee were in Spain. Younger sister Kathleen was at home studying.

In the red corner, another family man was looking relaxed. World Superbike Champion Troy Bayliss was replacing Sete Gibernau on the Marlboro Ducati. It was a cheerful, smiling Bayliss who told the press on Thursday that he was pleased to be topping and tailing the 990 Desmoseidici project – he'd ridden the bike on its first public outing after the 2002 Valencia GP and here he was riding it again in its last race. He was happy to be here but also content to be staying in Superbike because that way he could spend more time with his family. Tests have shown that a laid-back, no-worries Bayliss is a very fast Bayliss. The Troy that hides away in his motorhome brooding over problems tends to over-ride the bike and make mistakes. The first version turned up at Valencia keen to remind the MotoGP paddock – and some people in the Ducati hierarchy – what they'd been missing.

Valencia is a track that delivers tension rather than frantic passing action, so a good start is vital. For once Hayden got one while Rossi's bike looked like it had been equipped with a reject clutch from Hayden's Honda. The M1 tried to snap into a wheelie rather than move forward from pole and Valentino had to reorganise. That slowed him enough for most of the second row to pile past him into the first corner; Hayden appeared to sideswipe Rossi but both men reported afterwards that they didn't feel a thing. That put Rossi in seventh and that's where he stayed for the next four laps.

In a repeat of the problem he suffered at Laguna Seca, his engine temperature started to climb towards 120°C, resulting in a loss of peak power. That meant he was stuck behind Casey Stoner, unable to generate enough speed on the straights to set up a pass. That, in turn, meant he was having to ride harder in the corners than he'd planned, and on lap 5 he lost the front at the second left-hander, Valencia's favourite corner for crashing. All was still not lost, at least in Valentino's mind. He got going again, 20 seconds behind the field. It took him five laps to catch McCoy on the Ilmor. Three laps later accidents at the back of the field put him in a points-scoring position. Nicky, meanwhile, was running third behind the Ducatis. The Repsol Honda crew had shown Nicky a pit board with 'Rossi P20' writ large. At this point he'd thought 'Oh boy!' and contemplated pushing hard to try and catch Bayliss, but then Capirossi came past and the message from the Repsol pit read '3rd OK'. Nicky took the hint.

It should have said '3rd OK unless he gets up to 8th'. Finishing third and eighth respectively would have put the two equal on points and given Rossi the title on the basis of number of wins. By half-distance it was clear that Valentino wasn't going to repeat the miracle of Phillip Island. He was riding with a bent footrest and gear pedal, a broken clutch lever and a left handlebar that was twisted towards him and cramping his arm, preventing him from both pushing on the bar and supporting himself under braking.

After the disaster of Portugal, Nicky had told his errant team-mate Dani Pedrosa that he could make things right at Valencia. Dani did. On Saturday night he told Nicky that he wouldn't race him and before the sighting lap made a point of crossing the pit to shake hands and wish him good luck. As soon as Dani's pitboard told him Nicky was behind him, he left the door wide open for the pass and then slowed his pace to make sure he didn't interfere.

Up front Troy Bayliss was putting on a demonstration run. His team-mate wasn't sure if he could catch him and when he got '2nd OK' on his pitboard Loris knew that third place in the championship would be his. So Ducati got their first ever one-two finish in the top class of Grand Prix racing and Loris his best ever championship position. Troy declared it his last MotoGP race: 'It's best to leave it to the young guys.'

A tearful Nicky Hayden received fulsome congratulations from the outgoing champ on the slow-down lap before letting off some steam in the parc fermé and facing some very crowded press conferences. He was typically generous to his competitors and to his team-mate. 'I told him he had one chance: he took it. I'm a man of my word: we're cool.' As he hadn't come up through the smaller classes Nicky had often felt an outsider in the paddock – 'It's me and Squirrel [his dad] against the world' – and the support after Portugal had, he admitted, taken him by surprise. As did the lengthy round of applause from the media.

Rossi joined in the praise: 'Nicky is my personal favourite (if I don't win!), he's a great guy as well as a great rider. This is not easy in this paddock, I like him and I like his family. His father came to congratulate me at Estoril even after what happened to Nicky. He deserves the championship.'

Below Nicky Hayden arrives back in parc fermé as World Champion

Opposite It was an historic day for Ducati as well – their first MotoGP one-two finish

THE 990 YEARS

The 990cc formula lasted just five years, during which time lap and race records set by the old 500cc two-strokes have been blown away. At tracks were the layout and race distances have remained unaltered, and where there have been dry races, race time has been reduced by an average of 1min 28sec. Lap records have come down by an average of 3.4sec, pole times by 3.7sec.

The biggest reduction in lap record, 3.9sec, came at Donington Park, the final section of which was very tricky for the strokers. The smallest reduction, 2.4sec, came at Phillip Island, where the 500s were well-suited.

In percentage terms the improvements in lap records and race times are almost identical at 3.19% and 3.24% respectively, which means that on average a MotoGP bike would take 31 laps to gain a full lap on the best of the 500s.

The increase in speeds is best illustrated by the fact that the past five years have seen only four dry races where the existing lap record wasn't broken.

VALENCIAN GP

RICARDO TORMO

ROUND 17

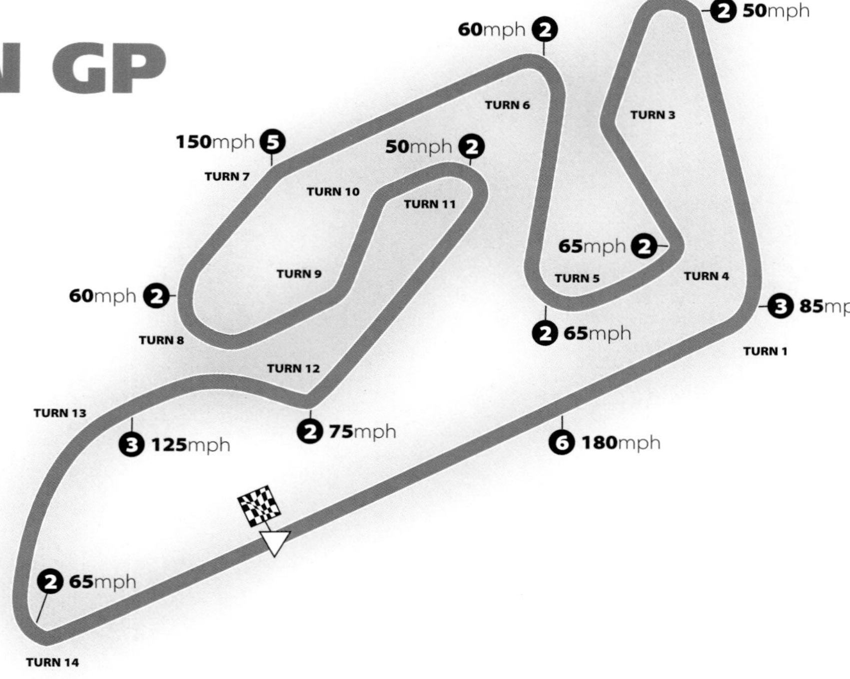

RACE RESULTS

RACE DATE October 29th
CIRCUIT LENGTH 2.483 miles
NO. OF LAPS 30
RACE DISTANCE 74.493 miles
WEATHER Dry, 32°C
TRACK TEMPERATURE 43°C
WINNER Troy Bayliss
FASTEST LAP 1m 32.924s, 96.353mph, Loris Capirossi (record)
PREVIOUS LAP RECORD 1m 33.043s, 96.793mph, Marco Melandri, 2005

QUALIFYING

	Rider	Nationality	Team	Qualifying	Pole +	Gap
1	Rossi	ITA	Camel Yamaha Team	1m 31.002s		
2	Bayliss	AUS	Ducati Marlboro Team	1m 31.210s	0.208s	0.208s
3	Capirossi	ITA	Ducati Marlboro Team	1m 31.307s	0.305s	0.097s
4	Nakano	JPN	Kawasaki Racing Team	1m 31.341s	0.339s	0.034s
5	Hayden	USA	Repsol Honda Team	1m 31.378s	0.376s	0.037s
6	Pedrosa	SPA	Repsol Honda Team	1m 31.385s	0.383s	0.007s
7	Stoner	AUS	Honda LCR	1m 31.470s	0.468s	0.085s
8	Vermeulen	AUS	Rizla Suzuki MotoGP	1m 31.606s	0.604s	0.136s
9	Hopkins	USA	Rizla Suzuki MotoGP	1m 31.663s	0.661s	0.057s
10	Edwards	USA	Camel Yamaha Team	1m 31.711s	0.709s	0.048s
11	De Puniet	FRA	Kawasaki Racing Team	1m 31.892s	0.890s	0.181s
12	Melandri	ITA	Fortuna Honda	1m 32.062s	1.060s	0.170s
13	Elias	SPA	Fortuna Honda	1m 32.144s	1.142s	0.082s
14	Roberts	USA	Team Roberts	1m 32.358s	1.356s	0.214s
15	Tamada	JPN	Konica Minolta Honda	1m 32.467s	1.465s	0.109s
16	Checa	SPA	Tech 3 Yamaha	1m 32.747s	1.745s	0.280s
17	Hofmann	GER	Pramac d'Antin MotoGP	1m 33.289s	2.287s	0.542s
18	Cardoso	SPA	Pramac d'Antin MotoGP	1m 33.755s	2.753s	0.466s
19	Ellison	GBR	Tech 3 Yamaha	1m 33.953s	2.951s	0.198s
20	McCoy	AUS	Ilmor SRT	1m 34.811s	3.809	0.858s

FINISHERS

1 BAYLISS Led every lap to become then first man to win a World Superbike and MotoGP race in one season, first replacement (Troy replaced Sete Gibernau) or wild-card rider to win a MotoGP race, oldest rider to win a MotoGP race, and the oldest premier-class winner since Jack Findlay at the boycotted Austrian GP in 1977. Brought many of his World Superbike crew with him, looked totally relaxed all weekend and took revenge on those who he considered didn't deal honestly with him last time he rode the Desmosedici.

2 CAPIROSSI Set a new lap record chasing his team-mate to Ducati's first one-two finish, and was happy to finish second after his pit signalled him it would be good enough for third in the championship. Gracious enough to say he wasn't at all sure he could have caught Troy if he'd wanted to.

3 HAYDEN Knew Rossi was down when he saw yellow marks on the track, then watched his pit board and saw that Rossi was making up places but put his trust in the 'P3 OK' message. Didn't take too many risks and brought it home to become the only man other than Rossi to be World Champion under the 990cc MotoGP formula.

4 PEDROSA Redeemed himself completely by playing the perfect team-mate to Hayden. Dani started well, let Nicky through and dropped back to give him some space. Only pushed again when he was told Rossi had fallen and wasn't behind him.

5 MELANDRI Not happy after qualifying and complained about tyre degradation (especially on the left side) after the first few laps of the race. He then dropped away from the leading group and lost out on third in the championship by just one point.

6 ELIAS An amazing result seeing as he started from 13th on the grid. He was up to seventh on lap 20, when he made a big mistake and lost two places and had to repass Nakano and Roberts. Didn't attack his team-mate who was still in the fight for third in the championship.

7 NAKANO Not the result he would have wanted in his last ride for Kawasaki but equalled the team's best finish at Valencia. Happy to see the flag for only the second time in the last five races.

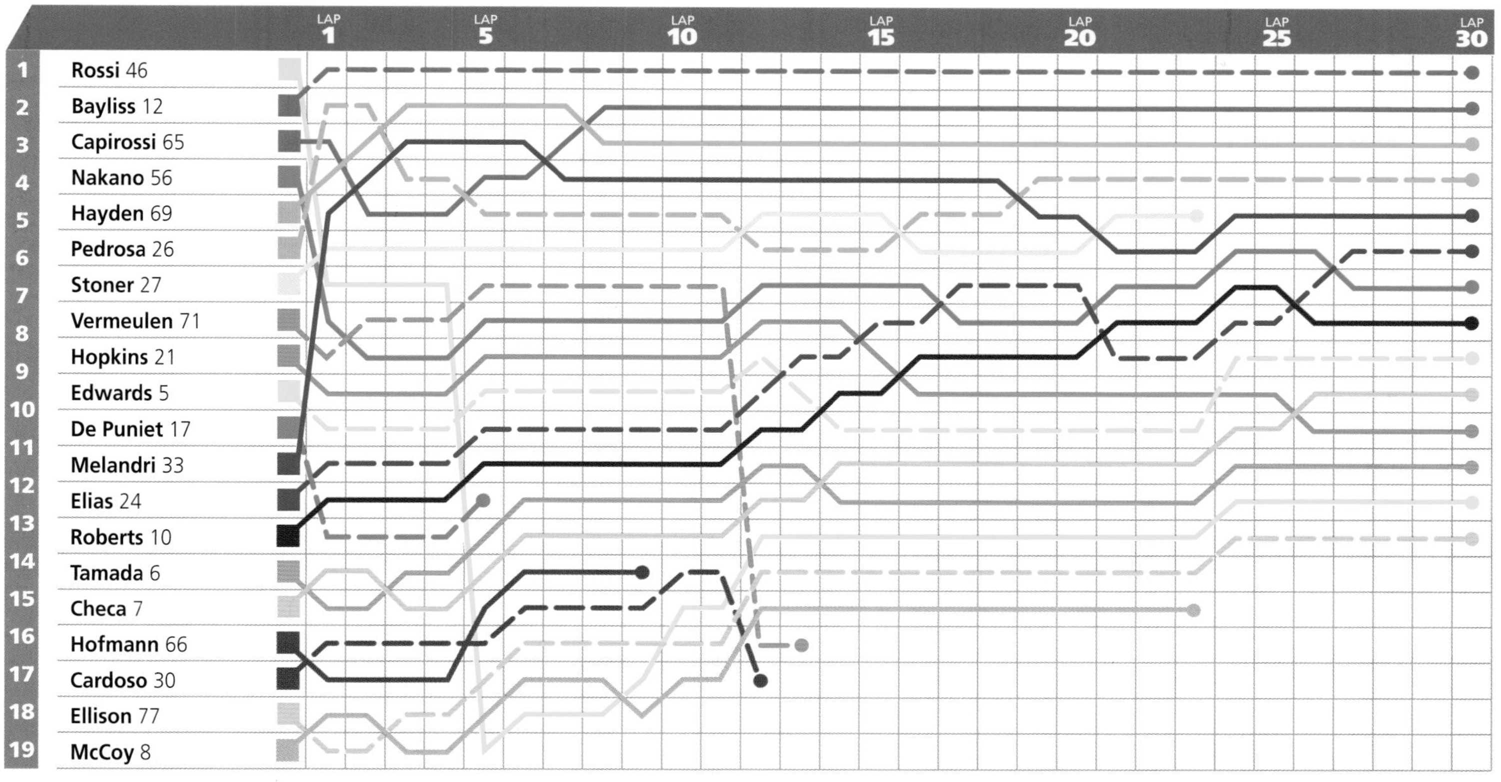

RACE

	Rider	Motorcycle	Race Time	Time +	Fastest Lap	Average Speed
1	Bayliss	Ducati	46m 55.415s		1m 33.019s	95.405mph
2	Capirossi	Ducati	46m 56.734s	1.319s	1m 32.924s	95.361mph
3	Hayden	Honda	47m 04.645s	9.230s	1m 32.976s	95.094mph
4	Pedrosa	Honda	47m 07.480s	12.065s	1m 33.320s	94.998mph
5	Melandri	Honda	47m 11.721s	16.306s	1m 33.212s	94.856mph
6	Elias	Honda	47m 12.805s	17.390s	1m 33.638s	94.819mph
7	Nakano	Kawasaki	47m 14.744s	19.329s	1m 33.409s	94.755mph
8	Roberts	KR211V	47m 18.589s	23.174s	1m 33.855s	94.627mph
9	Edwards	Yamaha	47m 21.487s	26.072s	1m 33.576s	94.530mph
10	Checa	Yamaha	47m 23.609s	28.194s	1m 33.944s	94.460mph
11	Hopkins	Suzuki	47m 24.779s	29.364s	1m 33.601s	94.420mph
12	Tamada	Honda	47m 25.122s	29.707s	1m 33.944s	94.409mph
13	Rossi	Yamaha	47m 33.961s	38.546s	1m 33.394s	94.117mph
14	Ellison	Yamaha	48m 15.428s	1m 20.013s	1m 35.311s	92.769mph
15	McCoy	Ilmor X3	47m 10.246s	7 laps	1m 34.814s	72.761mph
	Stoner	Honda	36m 05.789s	7 laps	1m 33.328s	95.087mph
	Vermeulen	Suzuki	34m 53.343s	17 laps	1m 33.465s	55.603mph
	Cardoso	Ducati	27m 32.925s	18 laps	1m 35.099s	65.001mph
	Hofmann	Ducati	14m 26.546s	21 laps	1m 35.014s	92.992mph
	De Puniet	Kawasaki	7m 58.767s	25 laps	1m 33.923s	93.506mph

CHAMPIONSHIP

	Rider	Team	Points
1	Hayden	Repsol Honda Team	252
2	Rossi	Camel Yamaha Team	247
3	Capirossi	Ducati Marlboro Team	229
4	Melandri	Fortuna Honda	228
5	Pedrosa	Repsol Honda Team	215
6	Roberts	Team Roberts	134
7	Edwards	Camel Yamaha Team	124
8	Stoner	Honda LCR	119
9	Elias	Fortuna Honda	116
10	Hopkins	Rizla Suzuki MotoGP	116
11	Vermeulen	Rizla Suzuki MotoGP	98
12	Tamada	Konica Minolta Honda	96
13	Gibernau	Ducati Marlboro Team	95
14	Nakano	Kawasaki Racing Team	92
15	Checa	Tech 3 Yamaha	75
16	De Puniet	Kawasaki Racing Team	37
17	Hofmann	Pramac d'Antin MotoGP	30
18	Ellison	Tech 3 Yamaha	26
19	Bayliss	Ducati Marlboro Team	25
20	Cardoso	Pramac d'Antin MotoGP	10

8 ROBERTS Never in tune with the bike – 'I performed below average all weekend' – but did enough to ensure his sixth place in the championship. As Kenny Senior said, 'It's pretty good that we should be disappointed with a result like this.'

9 EDWARDS Started losing the front after just two or three laps despite using the same tyre as in Portugal. Followed Hopkins for most of the race but unable to generate enough corner speed to make a pass. A difficult end to a difficult season.

10 CHECA A superb final ride for Tech 3 and Dunlop to be only just over a second behind the first Yamaha home. Very happy with the race tyre but not the qualifier. Able to pass Tamada at mid-distance and Hopkins six laps from the flag. Impressive.

11 HOPKINS Much as in Assen, the serious rise in track temperature between qualifying and race day caught out the Suzukis. The team went for a softer compound for the conditions and suffered serious grip problems in the closing stages.

12 TAMADA Another disappointing race and an anticlimactic end to his involvement with the Konica-Minolta team that was set up for him. A bad qualifying was followed by a bad start and, according to Makoto, a lack of grip both front and rear.

13 ROSSI Just like the first race of the year, he fell early (although this time it was no-one else's fault), picked the bike up and chased what looked like a hopeless cause. The long hold on the red lights at the start caught him out and then his engine over-heated, robbing him of top-end power. He fell while trying to make up time in the corners. As after Portugal, not too happy with Michelin as he said he'd tested out how far he could push the front at Turn 2 'about 400 times' over the weekend.

14 ELLISON Another struggle with chatter and another frustrating weekend of underachievement on the unmodified chassis. James knows he's faster than he has looked all year but this was his last ride in MotoGP. He hopes to work his way back via the AMA Championship.

15 McCOY A repeat of the Estoril debut of the Ilmor. Safely qualified, running with Ellison until two cylinders stopped firing when an ignition coil failed. It took nine minutes to replace and get out on track again to take the chequered flag. With 75% of race distance completed, the wild-card 800cc Ilmor again qualified as a finisher and scored its second championship point.

NON-FINISHERS

STONER Another crash, his third in succession, and again after Casey thought they had the perfect set-up and perfect tyre on Saturday. He was in a strong fifth place and only seven laps from the flag when he lost the front at Turn 2, the same corner that claimed Rossi.

VERMEULEN Ran straight on at the last corner after getting what felt like a false neutral. Toppled over in the gravel and couldn't restart. The team later found the fault that caused the problem.

CARDOSO Was running more competitively than he had all season when the bike tried to highside him and he ran off track.

HOFMANN Another victim of Turn 2. He was pressing to catch Tamada and Checa when he lost the front early on.

DE PUNIET Made a dreadful start and was 16th into the first corner. Got past a couple of riders and was closing on Roberts when he tucked the front going into – where else? – Turn 2.

NON-STARTERS

GIBERNAU Therapy on the collarbone that was re-injured in Portugal prevented him from taking his last ride on the factory Ducati.

WORLD CHAMPIONSHIP CLASSIFICATIONS

MOTOGP

	Rider	Nation	Motorcycle	SPA	QAT	TUR	CHN	FRA	ITA	CAT	NED	GBR	GER	USA	CZE	MAL	AUS	JPN	POR	VAL	Points
1	Hayden	USA	Honda	16	20	16	20	11	16	20	25	9	16	25	7	13	11	11	-	16	252
2	Rossi	ITA	Yamaha	2	25	13	-	-	25	25	8	20	25	-	20	25	16	20	20	3	247
3	Capirossi	ITA	Ducati	25	16	10	8	20	20	-	1	7	11	8	25	20	9	25	4	20	229
4	Melandri	ITA	Honda	11	9	25	9	25	10	-	9	16	20	16	11	7	25	16	8	11	228
5	Pedrosa	SPA	Honda	20	10	2	25	16	13	-	16	25	13	20	16	16	1	9	-	13	215
6	Roberts	USA	KR211V	8	6	3	3	-	8	16	11	11	-	13	13	9	2	7	16	8	134
7	Edwards	USA	Yamaha	5	7	7	16	10	4	11	3	10	4	7	6	6	-	8	13	7	124
8	Stoner	AUS	Honda	10	11	20	11	13	-	-	13	13	-	-	10	8	10	-	-	-	119
9	Elias	SPA	Honda	13	8	11	5	7	9	-	-	-	5	1	5	-	7	10	25	10	116
10	Hopkins	USA	Suzuki	7	-	-	13	1	6	13	10	8	6	10	9	10	4	4	10	5	116
11	Vermeulen	AUS	Honda	4	-	9	-	6	2	10	6	-	9	11	4	5	20	5	7	-	98
12	Tamada	JPN	Honda	6	2	6	10	9	7	9	5	5	-	5	3	2	6	6	11	4	96
13	Gibernau	SPA	Ducati	-	13	5	7	8	11	-	-	-	8	6	-	11	13	13	-	-	95
14	Nakano	JPN	Kawasaki	9	5	8	6	4	5	-	20	-	10	-	8	-	8	-	-	9	92
15	Checa	SPA	Yamaha	3	4	1	2	5	1	8	7	6	7	9	1	4	-	2	9	6	75
16	De Puniet	FRA	Kawasaki	-	-	4	4	-	3	-	2	4	-	4	2	3	5	-	6	-	37
17	Hofmann	GER	Ducati	1	1	-	1	3	-	6	4	3	-	2	-	1	3	-	5	-	30
18	Ellison	GBR	Yamaha	-	3	-	-	2	-	7	-	2	3	3	-	-	-	1	3	2	26
19	Bayliss	AUS	Ducati	-	-	-	-	-	-	-	-	-	-	-	-	-	-	-	-	25	25
20	Cardoso	SPA	Ducati	-	-	-	-	-	-	5	-	1	2	-	-	-	-	-	2	-	10
21	Akiyoshi	JPN	Suzuki	-	-	-	-	-	-	-	-	-	-	-	-	-	-	3	-	-	3
22	McCoy	ITA	Ilmor X3	-		-	-	-	-	-	-	-	-	-	-	-	-	-	1	1	2

CONSTRUCTOR

	Motorcycle	SPA	QAT	TUR	CHN	FRA	ITA	CAT	NED	GBR	GER	USA	CZE	MAL	AUS	JPN	POR	VAL	Points
1	Honda	20	20	25	25	25	16	20	25	25	20	25	16	16	25	16	25	16	360
2	Yamaha	5	25	13	16	10	25	25	8	20	25	9	20	25	16	20	20	7	289
3	Ducati	25	16	10	8	20	20	6	4	7	11	8	25	20	13	25	5	25	248
4	Suzuki	7	-	9	13	6	6	13	10	8	9	11	9	10	20	5	10	5	151
5	KR211V	8	6	3	3	-	8	16	11	11	-	13	13	9	2	7	16	8	134
6	Kawasaki	9	5	8	6	4	5	-	20	4	10	4	8	3	8	-	6	9	109
7	Ilmor X3	-	-	-	-	-	-	-	-	-	-	-	-	-	-	-	1	1	2

TEAM

	Team	SPA	QAT	TUR	CHN	FRA	ITA	CAT	NED	GBR	GER	USA	CZE	MAL	AUS	JPN	POR	VAL	Points
1	Repsol Honda Team	36	30	18	45	27	29	20	41	34	29	45	23	29	12	20	-	29	467
2	Camel Yamaha Team	7	32	20	16	10	29	36	11	30	29	7	26	31	16	28	33	10	371
3	Ducati Marlboro Team	25	29	15	15	28	31	-	5	10	19	14	25	31	22	38	4	45	370
4	Fortuna Honda	24	17	36	14	32	19	-	9	16	25	17	16	7	32	26	33	21	344
5	Rizla Suzuki MotoGP	11	-	9	13	7	8	23	16	8	15	21	13	15	24	9	17	5	214
6	Team Roberts	8	6	3	3	-	8	16	11	11	-	13	13	9	2	7	16	8	134
7	Kawasaki Racing Team	9	5	12	10	4	8	-	22	4	10	4	10	3	13	-	6	9	129
8	Honda LCR	10	11	20	11	13	-	-	13	13	-	-	10	8	10	-	-	-	119
9	Tech 3 Yamaha	3	7	1	2	7	1	15	7	8	10	12	1	4	-	3	12	8	101
10	Konica Minolta Honda	6	2	6	10	9	7	9	5	5	-	5	3	2	6	6	11	4	96
11	Pramac D'Antin MotoGP	1	1	-	1	3	-	11	-	1	2	2	-	1	3	-	7	-	33

125cc

	Rider	Nation	Points
1	Alvaro Bautista	SPA	338
2	Mike Kallio	FIN	262
3	Hector Faubel	SPA	197
4	Mattia Pasini	ITA	192
5	Sergio Gadea	SPA	160
6	Lukas Pesek	CZE	154
7	Gabor Talmacsi	HUN	119
8	Thomas Luthi	SWI	113
9	Julian Simon	SPA	97
10	Joan Olive	SPA	85
11	Fabrizio Lai	ITA	83
12	Simone Corsi	ITA	79
13	Pablo Nieto	SPA	66
14	Nicolas Terol	SPA	53
15	Tomoyoshi Koyama	JPN	49

250cc

	Rider	Nation	Points
1	Jorge Lorenzo	SPA	289
2	Andrea Dovizioso	ITA	272
3	Alex De Angelis	RSM	228
4	Hiroshi Aoyama	JPN	193
5	Roberto Locatelli	ITA	191
6	Yuki Takahashi	JPN	156
7	Hector Barbera	SPA	152
8	Shuhei Aoyama	JPN	99
9	Sylvain Guintoli	FRA	96
10	Marco Simoncelli	ITA	92
11	Anthony West	AUS	78
12	Jakub Smrz	CZE	58
13	Alex Debon	SPA	50
14	Manuel Poggiali	RSM	50
15	Martin Cardenas	COL	37

VIP Village

Best Location and Exclusive Privileges

Situated at the heart of the action, either directly above the Pit Lane or in a smart village area, VIP Village puts you as close as you can get to the world's top motorcycle racers.

Privileged Parking, excellent views, race coverage on closed-circuit TV, Pit Lane Walk, Paddock Tour, Service Road Tour and complimentary Official Programme on Sunday.

The VIP Village Game will offer all guests the chance to win the possibility to view races from the pit wall, a service road tour and one of the many licensed MotoGP products.

Best Service and Excellent Cuisine

Hospitality is of the highest quality, from the buffet breakfast in the morning to gourmet lunch and afternoon petit fours, with a complimentary bar all day.

riders
riders
helmet park
motorcycles save
WDW2002
WORLDDUCATIWEEK
riders
Stena Line

RIDERS FOR HEALTH 2005–6

by Barry Coleman

Co-founder & joint CEO, Operations – Riders for Health

You remember Jimmy Carter. Nice guy, probably too nice for the particular job he did for a while, namely President of the United States. When he left that job he went on to do something that we at Riders for Health believe is even more important, namely to set up the Carter Center, which is 'committed to advancing human rights and alleviating unnecessary human suffering'.

Now you really can't say fairer than that. And as a matter of fact the Carter Center does a very good job. Towards the end of the season (around about Motegi) they called Riders for Health and asked if we could assess the transport aspect of their programme to eradicate guinea worm in Southern Sudan. The answer was yes. And if, after our assessment, we're asked to work more closely with them, we'll do all we can. Because we, as representatives of the motorcycle racing community, are also committed to alleviating human suffering, and our contribution – using motorcycles to reach the seriously isolated poor – is vital.

You wouldn't want guinea worm, by the way. It's really nasty. It gets into your system in infected drinking water, reaches maturity in your intestine and then heads for the 'surface'. Your surface, that is. It reaches the skin, causing painful lesions, and then you have to catch it and wind it out very slowly, taking care not to break it and cause even more serious infection. I bet you'd

AT A GLANCE

Riders in 2006

How many people work for Riders in Africa?
230

How many motorcycles are managed by Riders?
1,274

How many people are Riders reaching?
10.8 million

Countries in which Riders operates (Zimbabwe, the Gambia, Nigeria and Kenya)
4

want us to help the Carter Center get rid of it now, wouldn't you?

The Carter Center story is very far from told. There is a long road ahead in any such proposed partnership and there is no way to predict the outcome. But the fact that they even called shows that Riders, the not-for-profit humanitarian organisation that began in, and has never left, the sport of motorcycle racing has made a quite definite impact on the world. Gradually, slowly but surely, what Riders has to offer is being recognised in all the right places.

Now we have started, let's do a little more name-dropping. One of the things that has happened since our last 'annual report' is that Riders has been invited to join the prestigious Skoll Foundation for Social Entrepreneurship. This foundation was set up by another prominent North American (a Canadian, in fact) who had an interesting job and then moved on. Jeff Skoll set up an auction business on the completely ludicrous basis that people who were interested in buying something would bid for it in some electronic manner and that once the bidding was over, the buyer would trust the seller to send the item and the seller would trust the buyer to send the money. Ridiculous idea. Obviously in this terrible day and age it could never work. Thus was eBay born and Jeff Skoll was the unrealistic visionary who has made it work. Maybe it takes one unrealistic visionary to know one; anyway, we were invited to join. Being members admits Riders to a somewhat prestigious group of social entrepreneurs – those people who use the everyday procedures of business to bring about humanitarian ends. We were inducted around about Mugello time and were welcomed aboard by Robert Redford, who once made a motorcycle racing film called *Big Fauss and Little Halsy* (1970). Apparently he didn't like it very much, but some people do.

Where Riders goes, motorcycle racing goes. People know where we come from and where all this started (17 years ago, by the way) and they welcome us very warmly.

Going right back to the end of last season, after our report had gone to press, round about Valencia time, Riders took another interesting turn. We were identified by *Time* magazine as 'heroes of global health' (how about that, for mere motorcycle folk?) and featured in a six-hour (two hours at a time) documentary about global health which was broadcast on American public television. I'm not going to go on about it, but the bit about us showed a lot of MotoGP as well as the work in Africa and it was narrated by – ready for this? – none other than Brad Pitt. And then the series won an Emmy!

This name-dropping is actually quite good fun, once you get started. Jimmy Carter, Jeff Skoll, Robert Redford, Brad – where will it all end?

At the time of the Laguna race your very own Riders was featured in an hour-long documentary presented by CNN's chief international correspondent, Christiane Amanpour. And then just before Estoril it was announced, in a very glitzy manner, that Riders for Health had won the Ernst & Young award for the Social Entrepreneur of the Year. The charity that began somewhere between the motorhomes of Randy Mamola, Kenny Roberts, Wayne Rainey, Eddy Lawson and the rest (that's how long ago it was) has now graduated to the point at which it wins loud public acclaim for the efficiency of its management from one of the world's 'big four' consultancy and auditing companies.

All right – enough of the name-dropping and back-patting. What does it mean?

It means that the sport of motorcycle racing has done something that no other sport has done – ever. It has created a world-class humanitarian organisation that is recognised at the highest levels as achieving its objectives and doing so in a manner that meets the highest standards of accountability and transparency. Now that's not bad for a sport that doesn't always get the headlines it deserves. We could go on to gloat about all the other sports and what kind of humanitarian organisations they have built up, but first that wouldn't be nice and second we can't because they haven't built any. So let us just say that we hope that one day golf and tennis and croquet will come through in the way that we know they could.

These days Riders for Health is reporting to some demanding partners, and we are happy to do that, given the seriousness of the work we do. But there is one report that matters above all to us, and that's this one – our report to the community that gave birth to Riders and to whom, therefore, Riders is ultimately responsible. That's you, folks! And we will continue, we hope, to do you proud and we will continue to show the world just what our great sport is capable of in unparalleled sporting achievement, fantastic entertainment and playing its part in terms of social responsibility.

Guinea worm – say goodnight.

Opposite HRH The Princess Royal cuts Riders' tenth birthday cake with Andrea Coleman

Below Barry and Andrea receiving the Skoll award with, left to right, Sally Osberg, President and CEO of the Skoll Foundation, Sir Ben Kingsley, Robert Redford and Jeff Skoll

Below right Hamish Jamieson, formerly Garry McCoy's race engineer at Red Bull Yamaha, instructing at Riders' project in The Gambia

HOW DID RIDERS FOR HEALTH BEGIN?

In 1986 Randy Mamola and Andrea Coleman began to raise money in the Grand Prix paddock to help children in Africa. In 1989 Randy and Barry Coleman made a visit to Somalia to see the situation in Africa for themselves. They were horrified to find that children were dying of easily preventable diseases and women were dying in childbirth, simply because there were very few vehicles at work in remote areas. They saw graveyards of motorcycles – motorcycles that had died after covering very few miles.

Andrea, Barry and Randy believed this was an unacceptable situation in the 20th century. So, with the help of the motorcycle community, they set about creating a solution for running vehicles successfully in Africa as well as raising funds and creating an organisation to support the work.

Riders now works in four African countries: Zimbabwe, the Gambia, Nigeria and Kenya.

THE STORY OF MANYO GIBBA

In the Gambia, a pair of wheels has become an essential tool for community health nurse Manyo Gibba. Manyo is responsible for the health of 20,000 people, whose homes are spread across 5,000 square miles of harsh terrain. She cares for pregnant women and infants in over a dozen villages, and her visits are crucial: in sub-Saharan Africa, one in 16 mothers dies in childbirth.

Manyo says: 'For the first two years of my job, I did not have a motorcycle. There was no mobility. I used to walk to go and supervise my traditional birth attendants. But now, since I've had the motorcycle, I have never failed an appointment with them.'

Thanks to Riders' training, Manyo has become an excellent rider and can also carry out basic maintenance on her bike. In the Gambia, these are rare skills – for a woman. As Manyo says, 'Some people, they find it funny to see a female riding a motorcycle. Even my mom, she was complaining that I shouldn't ride a motorcycle. I told her, well, it's part of my job. I have to do it.'

MOTOGP & RIDERS FOR HEALTH IN 2006

The Day of Champions at Donington Park is the cornerstone of Riders' funding each year. Everyone in the MotoGP paddock contributes to this extraordinary day, showing that motorcycles really do save lives. The open paddock and pit lane are unique in MotoGP and sport in general, and the auction has become a highlight of the year. This year the 125 and 250 riders joined the 'big guys' to make it the most successful Day of Champions so far.

Of course, MotoGP's support for Riders in no way begins and ends with the Day of Champions.

Even before the first laps at Jerez, a familiar face from the MotoGP paddock was making a real, hands-on difference to the Riders programme in the Gambia. In January this year Cathal Kelly (a former electrician who now works for IRTA) brought together a group of ten people to rewire all three of Riders' Gambian workshops in just two weeks. The team, known as the Bright Sparks, not only raised over £10,000 to cover the costs of their trip but also secured a donation of £15,000 worth of electrical equipment. Their Herculean efforts gave a huge boost to the Riders for Health Gambia team and caught the attention of, among others, the Gambian Minister of Health.

At the Catalunya tests, Kawasaki's Shinya Nakano presented a cheque for €5,000, raised in collaboration with sponsor Arlen Ness, which has helped to train more outreach technicians. And at Donington, team boss Lucio Cecchinello also made a €5,000 donation to help provide fuel for the Zimbabwe programme.

Then the organisers of the German MotoGP round at Sachsenring once again held a football match and a pit-lane walk to support the work in Africa. The Assen circuit organisers came up with a very inventive way of raising money, by selling pieces of asphalt from the old Assen track. In Spain the circuit of Valencia also hosts a Day of Champions and a new kind of event, Dream Days, which is growing in popularity. On this day a hundred bikers enjoy an exclusive visit to the paddock, with lunch and three laps of the track.

Two-seat Ducati rides with Randy Mamola are made uniquely available to members of the public at Donington, and this year ten people bought the opportunity to ride at race speeds with him in front of spectators. One passenger described his ride as the best thing he had ever done, and he can't wait for next year.

The Riders for Health volunteers in the UK, Holland, Germany and Spain also need a special mention. They give up so much of their time to run helmet parks, Day of Champions and our Dream Days in Spain.

The US MotoGP at Laguna Seca will join in our fundraising in 2007.

How your support helps

£15
could provide 40 families with a year of healthcare visits

£25
helps to train a health worker in essential bike maintenance

£50
helps provide replacement parts and servicing for a year

£200
supplies a full set of protective clothing for a health worker

£500
supplies a specialist toolkit for one of Riders for Health's outreach technicians

£1,200
could supply a health worker with a motorcycle that will help her reach 20,000 people with regular health care

WIN A FANTASTIC MotoGP RIDE WITH RANDY MAMOLA

IN ASSOCIATION WITH **RIDERS FOR HEALTH**

SPOT THE DIFFERENCE for your chance to ride behind the great Randy Mamola at Donington Park on the weekend of the British GP (date to be confirmed). After a full briefing, the lucky winner will enjoy two thrill-of-a-lifetime laps on the back of the two-seat MotoGP Ducati at close to race speeds.

1. There are ten differences between the two pictures right. Identify the differences on a photocopy or describe them briefly on a sheet of paper.

2. Correctly answer this multiple-choice question:

In what year did Andrea and Barry Coleman register Riders for Health as an independent charity in the UK?

1992 1994 1996

3. Add your name and address, and stick on the coupon from the back flap of this book's dust jacket.

4. We have made available 25 official MotoGP books as runner-up prizes. Indicate your preference:

MotoGP Technology or **Performance Riding Techniques**

Send to Haynes Competitions Department, FREEPOST BA730, Yeovil, Somerset BA22 7BF

Completed entries must be received by Haynes no later than 30 April 2007.

To find out more about Riders for Health and what is being achieved with motorcycles for healthcare delivery in Africa, read the article by CEO Barry Coleman (page 205) and visit

www.riders.org

TERMS AND CONDITIONS OF ENTRY

1 Only one entry per person. **2** Entries must be made as described and must be accompanied by a coupon from the back jacket of this book as confirmation of purchase. **3** This competition is open to everyone except the employees (and their families or agents) of the promoters, J H Haynes & Co Ltd. **4** Correct entries received on or before 30/04/07 will be entered into a draw which will take place on 04/05/07. **5** The prize winner will be the first correct entry drawn by an independent judge. The runners-up will be the next 25 correct entries drawn by the independent judge. **6** The judge's decision is final and no correspondence will be entered into. **7** The prize winner will be notified by post to the address on his entry no later than 07/05/07. **8** The names of the the prize winner and the runners-up will be available until 31/08/07 and can be obtained by sending a stamped, self-addressed envelope to the promoter. **9** Entrants must be over 18, weigh less than 90 kilograms and be no less than 1.5 metres and no more than 2 metres in height. **10** The ride will take place over the weekend of the British GP, the date of which is subject to confirmation. **11** The prize will include entrance tickets for the GP weekend (provided by Haynes Publishing). **12** The prize will include two paddock passes for the day, one for the prize winner and one for a guest. **13** The prize includes the use of leathers, helmet, boots and gloves provided by Ducati Marlboro. **14** The prize includes a mandatory full safety briefing with Randy Mamola prior to the ride itself. **15** The prize consists of two laps of the Donington race circuit on the back of a two-seat Ducati with Randy Mamola at close to race speeds. **16** The prize is dependent on the winner signing a release, indemnification and insurance waiver and passing a fitness test prior to the ride. **17** The prize will be provided by Riders for Health, acting in association with Ducati Corse, the Ducati Marlboro Team, and Charles Stewart & Company (Kirkaldy) Limited. **18** The ride will take place at the discretion of Ducati Motor Holdings and Marlboro. **19** If the ride cannot or does not take place for any reason whatsoever (eg, because of unsuitable weather or the unavailability of the two-seat motorcycle) there will be no alternative prize or compensation and the incidental expenses of the prize winner will not be refunded. **20** The prize winner must at all times comply with the requirements of Riders for Health and Ducati Corse, both prior to and during the day of the ride, especially those relating to information, attendance, fitness and safety. **21** J H Haynes & Co Ltd accept no liability for any loss, damage or personal injury to either the prize winner or their guest save to the extent that any liability cannot be excluded by law. **22** Should the prize winner fail to respond or decline the prize when contacted, or fail to confirm their acceptance by an agreed date, the promoter reserves the right to appoint another winner. **23** Entries from UK mainland addresses only. There is no cash or other alternative to the prizes. **24** Any entry which is damaged, defaced, incomplete or illegible or which otherwise does not comply with these rules may be deemed to be invalid at the sole discretion of J H Haynes & Co Ltd. **25** Responsibility is not accepted for entries lost or delayed in the post. Proof of posting will not be accepted as proof of delivery. Entry implies acceptance of these terms and conditions.